MAINSTREAMS OF *MUSIC*

by David Ewen

Opera

Orchestral Music

Solo Instrumental and Chamber Music

Vocal Music

MAINSTREAMS OF

MUSIC

Volume Two

⋖§ *1973*

Orchestral Music

Its Story Told Through the Lives

and Works of its Foremost Composers

by David Ewen

Franklin Watts, Inc.   *845 Third Avenue · New York, New York 10022*

Illustration Credits

The Mansell Collection: pages vi, 1, 34, 35A, 67B, 68A, 69A, 110A & B, 111A, 137, 139A, 165, 182A, 196A, 227A, 229B
The Philadelphia Orchestra Association: page 6
Albright-Knox Art Gallery, Buffalo, New York, Room of Contemporary Art Fund: page 8
The Bettmann Archive: pages 35B, 182B, 195, 196B, 197A & B, 225, 226B, 228, 229A, 254A, 255A, 285B, 288B, 290
Culver Pictures, Inc.: pages 36, 111B, 112, 167A & B, 168, 183A, 303
Staatsbibliothek, Berlin: pages 67A, 68B
The Pierpont Morgan Library, Mary Flagler Cary Music Collection: page 138
Royal Norwegian Embassy: page 139B
American Ballet Theatre: pages 166, 254B, 286A
United Press International: pages 183B, 185B, 256
Columbia Records: page 184A
Don Hunstein, courtesy Columbia Records: pages 184B, 185A
Camera Press-Pix: page 226A
Photoworld: pages 255B, 285A, 287
Magnum Photos, Inc.: page 286B
Peter Moore, New York: pages 288A, 289

Jacket photo by Don Hunstein, courtesy of The New York Philharmonic

Photo research by Wesley Day

Copyright © 1973 by David Ewen
Printed in the United States of America

Typography and binding design by Diana Hrisinko

Library of Congress Cataloging in Publication Data
Ewen, David, 1907–
    Orchestral music.

    (His Mainstreams of music, v. 2)
    SUMMARY: Traces the history of the orchestra discussing important composers and their works from the early sixteenth century to the present day. Includes a glossary of terms.
    1. Orchestral music—History and criticism.
2. Orchestra. 3. Composers. [1. Orchestral music—History and criticism. 2. Orchestra. 3. Composers]
I. Title.
ML1200.E94   785'.09   72-10839
ISBN 0-531-02619-1

Contents

Introduction

The Modern Symphony Orchestra

For the modern symphony orchestra the "magic number" is four. The orchestra is divided into four sections: strings, woodwinds, brass, and percussion. Each section, in turn, is subdivided to approximate the four compasses or ranges of the human voice (soprano, alto, tenor, and bass). Major symphony orchestras today are made up of between 104 and 108 musicians, although not all may be needed to play a particular piece of music.

In number, the string section is the largest, representing three quarters of the orchestra. The composer usually assigns to this section his most salient passages, the strings being the most lyrical, expressive, and versatile group, with the widest gamut of emotion, color, and effects. Strings can be majestic or funereal in their low ranges, songful and spiritual in the upper ones; they are capable of playing sprightly, graceful, or electrifying passages.

The basic string section comprises four instruments: the violin, viola, cello (violoncello), and bass (also called double bass or contrabass). The violin is the soprano voice of this group. The violins are subdivided into two sections, the "first" and "second" violins, although there is no difference in the instruments themselves. In major symphony orchestras today there are around twenty each of first and second violins. Each of these two sections has its own music to play, though there may be times when the first and second violins both play the same notes. Generally, however, the seconds serve in a supporting role to the firsts.

The leader of the first violin section is the concertmaster, who occupies the first chair at the left of the conductor as you face the stage. (This gives him the name of first-desk man.) His duty as first violinist is to instruct the violins when difficult problems of bowing and other techniques are posed by the music. He is also required to play solo in compositions requiring it (as in Rimsky-Korsakov's *Scheherazade,* for example). As concertmaster his responsibilities include some conducting at rehearsals and bringing the orchestra into tune before it begins to play. The violinist in a secondary position to the concertmaster is the second-desk man, who sits to the left of the concertmaster.

Next in range to the violin is the viola, the instrumental equivalent of the vocal alto. There are about twelve such instruments in a major orchestra. The viola is somewhat larger in size than the violin; otherwise it has the same appearance. Like the violin, it is held up by the player under his chin and played with a bow or occasionally plucked with the finger. Since it is tuned one fifth below the violin, the viola possesses a deeper, richer, more mellow voice.

One octave below the viola is the cello, or violoncello (an instrumental tenor). There are also about a dozen of these. Being a larger instrument than either the violin or viola, the cello is held between the knees, its end tip resting on the floor. Darker, richer, deeper colors are produced by the cellos than by the violas; the cello, then, is particularly useful for deeply solemn, emotional, or majestic music. Both the viola and cello sections have first-desk players with similar responsibilities to those of the first violinist.

The lowest range among the strings as in the voice is called the bass. There are about ten basses in a large orchestra. Even greater in size than the cello, the bass is also played in a vertical position, but the instrument is placed in front of the player, who is perched on a high stool or chair, rather than between his knees. Its deep resonant voice helps to emphasize rhythm. The cello and bass are also played with a bow or the fingers.

One additional instrument can be mentioned here, although it is sometimes grouped with the percussion instruments. That is the harp. The harp is found mainly in Romantic and modern compositions and is

dispensed with in a great segment of symphonic literature. When it is employed, the composer rarely assigns to it important passages. Its delicate,
shimmering tones and sensitive arpeggios and glissandi can serve as delightful background decoration. Major orchestras use two harps. This instrument differs radically from all other strings not only because it is
always plucked but also in its structure. All other orchestral stringed instruments have four strings. The harp has forty-six. An unusual feature
of the harp is that some of the strings are colored for visual recognition.
Seven pedals can raise the harp's pitch by either a half or a whole tone.

As we progress to the other sections of the symphony orchestra, we
find that in virtually every instance, as in the strings, the descent in range
is similar to that of the human voice, from soprano to bass. Also, we always refer to a major symphony orchestra, with a total complement of
over one hundred players, when we indicate the number, which is approximate, of each of these instruments in the overall ensemble.

Next in importance to the strings are the woodwinds, so called because these instruments were originally constructed from wood and re-
quire the wind of a musician's breath to produce sound. Now, however,
woodwinds are mostly made of metal. There are about sixteen woodwinds in an orchestra, of four types, which again correspond to soprano,
alto, tenor, and bass. They are the flutes, oboes, clarinets, and bassoons.
Each of these sections is led by a first-desk man.

There are usually three flutes in their section, along with one piccolo, an instrument half the size of the flute and with a shrill, penetrating sound. The flute is the more important instrument, whose dulcet
tones are particularly effective for gentle, poetic, pastoral, dreamy melodies, or delicate running passages. The flute and piccolo are held hori-
zontally at the lips, rather than vertically as in the case with other woodwinds. Tones are produced by blowing across a hole and pressing down
keys covering fingerholes on the face of the instrument. The other woodwinds are fingered in the same fashion, but the player blows directly into
them.

The oboe has a sweet, plaintive sound, but rounder and fuller than
that of the flute. Its mouthpiece is a double reed that vibrates when
blown into. There are three oboes and one English horn. The latter is a
type of oboe, larger than the regular oboe and with a bulbous end. Its
range is one fifth below the oboe, and its voice has a tender, bittersweet
quality.

The clarinet, of which there are three, is a single-reed instrument
that resembles the oboe in appearance. Two types of clarinets are in gen-

eral use. The one heard most often is the B-flat clarinet. The A clarinet is more functional for music in keys with sharps. Another member of the clarinet family is the bass clarinet (there is one in the orchestra), its range one octave lower than the B-flat clarinet.

The bassoon is a double-reed instrument two octaves lower than the oboe. There are three bassoons in the orchestra. In size it is the largest of the woodwinds, so much so that its tube has to be doubled up. The double bassoon (or contrabassoon) is one octave lower than the bassoon. It has a sixteen-foot-long tube that is doubled up four times. There is one of these instruments in the orchestra.

The third orchestral body is the brass, all of whose instruments are constructed from that metal. Like the woodwinds, they are blown into by the player. There are four trumpets, eight French horns, four trombones, and one tuba in the brass section of a major orchestra. Again, they correspond to the descending ranks of the voice. As a unit, the brass creates loud, sonorous, ringing music of brilliance and nobility.

The trumpet has the highest pitch, its tone so piercing that it readily penetrates through the mazes of orchestral sound. It is pitched in B-flat, which can be lowered to A by manipulating a special valve. More than an octave lower is the French horn, whose sound is produced with the help of three valves. Tones can be muffled by the performer placing his hand in the lower opening, where the sound emerges. The French horn can be romantic or evocative; its richly vibrant tones blend well with the sounds of other instruments.

The trombone uses a slide to manipulate pitch, a lower pitch being realized when the slide is pulled out. Trombones are now pitched in B-flat, with a valve that lowers the tone to F. The tuba is a large, rather cumbersome-looking instrument with ponderous tones. It is nevertheless capable of creating heroic or majestic sounds, with the aid of four valves.

The only section with louder dynamics than the brass is the percussion family, useful in projecting rhythm and in building up forceful climaxes. This is the only orchestral group where our magic number of "four" must be dispensed with, and which cannot be conveniently divided into the four ranges of the human voice.

The kettledrums, or tympani, are the principal instrument of the percussion section. The three large round drums produce rolling sounds of varying pitches when the performer beats with two felt-covered, flexible drumsticks on the skins of the drums. Tympani are useful for fortissimo passages, but they can also be played quietly to create an atmosphere of mystery. T-shaped thumbscrews on the rim of each of the drums allow the percussionist to adjust the tension of the drumhead and thus to change the pitch. He often has to do this while the orchestra is playing full; this is the reason why from time to time you will notice the tympanist placing his ear close to the rims of his drums. The percussionist is able to reduce lingering reverberations of the drum by placing his hand on the drumhead.

The side drum (or snare drum) produces soft rumbles of percussion sound. The bass drum, a large drum, produces either a boom or a throb depending upon how the percussionist manipulates the padded knob of his drumstick on the two heads of parchment on either side of the drum.

Cymbals create ringing tones when the edges of their two metal plates are struck against each other in a sliding way. They can also be sounded by striking one of the metal plates with a kettledrum stick.

The percussion family is a prolific brood with a houseful of relatives. The celesta and the glockenspiel (the latter also known as the bells) contribute exotic tinkling tones. The celesta has a keyboard like a piano's, while the glockenspiel consists of a horizontal series of tuned metal bars struck by hammers. Exquisite sounds emanate from the triangle, which is a triangular steel rod upon which a piece of metal is tapped lightly. More resonant and more exotic sound qualities can be realized by the tambourine, xylophone, chimes, and gong (the last of which can deliver only a single note). The piano (when a score calls for one) is considered a percussion instrument. Three percussion players are ordinarily required—one for the tympani, and two for the other percussions as needed. Occasionally a second tympanist is added. A staff pianist is also a member of the modern symphony orchestra.

There are several variations in the way the sections of the orchestra are placed on the stage. One of the most popular for many years, and still used by some orchestras, is to group the first violins at the left of the conductor, as the audience faces the stage, and the second violins at his right. Violas and cellos are directly in front of the conductor's dais. The woodwinds are grouped behind the violas and cellos, and after them come the brass and percussion. Double basses are lined up in a row in the rear.

But another kind of grouping has come into considerable favor in recent years, as used by the Philadelphia Orchestra, for example. All the violins (the second as well as the first) are grouped to the left of the conductor; the violas, cellos, and harp are at his right. Facing directly frontward in the center are flutes and oboes in one row, the clarinets and bas-

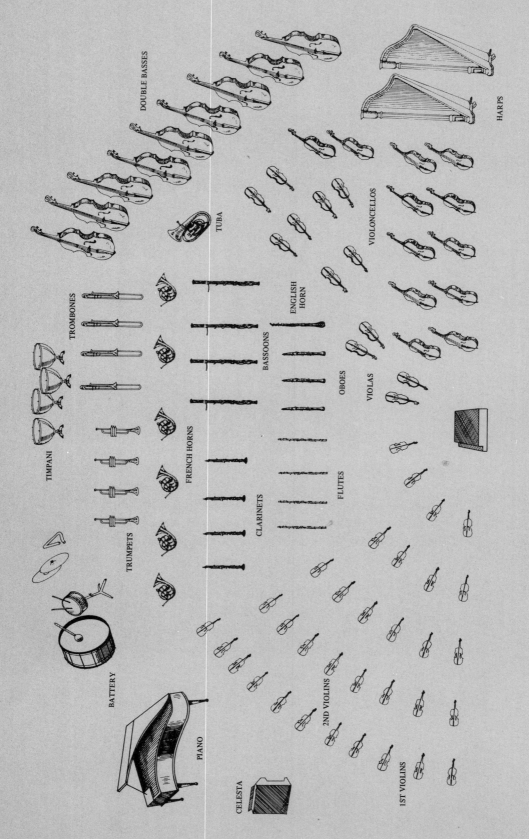

The seating arrangement of the Philadelphia Orchestra.

soons in a second row, the French horns and tuba in a third row, trumpets and trombones in a fourth row. Fringing this ensemble from left to right are the celesta, piano, various other percussions, and the basses.

And, finally, the conductor faces the orchestra from his podium, on which rests the score. With his baton he gets the orchestra started, indicates the time, the volume, and the quality of tone, and generally directs the ensemble to play according to his interpretation of the composer's work.

I

The Beginnings of Orchestral Music

The modern symphony orchestra was not created in a day. It was the result of a long evolutionary process, and its present form is of comparatively recent development. Before 1600, an orchestra could be a group made up of lutes, a treble viol (predecessor of the present-day violin) and a bass viol (ancestor of the present-day cello), a primitive kind of flute, and a harpsichord (predecessor of the piano). Take, for example, the orchestra used by Jacopo Peri (1561–1633) for the first two operas in history: *Dafne* (1597) and *Euridice* (1600). It was made up of some lutes, old-time flutes, a bass viol, and a harpsichord. But this was by no means a standard orchestra for this period, since no single standard was then in existence.

Whatever instruments were available at the time were gathered together without too much regard for homogeneity, balance, or contrast. A most curious combination could be found at the Berlin court in 1582: sixty wind instruments and just twelve string or plucked instruments. An orchestra found at the English court of Henry VIII (first half of the sixteenth century) was made up of fourteen old-time trumpets, ten old-time trombones, four drums, two treble viols, three old-time flutes, a bagpipe, and a tambourine. Another sixteenth-century orchestral combination was made up exclusively of viols of different pitches, referred to as a "consort," or "chest of viols." A good deal of music was written for this gathering of string instruments in Italy, England, and Spain. When these viols were combined with other instruments, the group was called a "broken consort." Such haphazard groupings of random instruments into orchestral bodies prevailed until the eighteenth century.

At this point, it is important to remember that the first great era in "modern" musical history placed significance not on instrumental music but on choral music, that is, music produced by groups of voices. This was the golden age of polyphony ("many voices"), which began in the thirteenth century and flourished in the fifteenth and sixteenth centuries. In polyphonic choral music several different melodies (from two to seven or eight) are sung simultaneously and independently by small or large groups of voices made up of sopranos, altos, tenors, and basses. This type of music developed in the thirteenth century in church services, and as the great composers of the polyphonic era appeared, they concentrated their efforts on this choral music rather than on music for a single voice and accompaniment, or on music for instruments or orchestral ensembles.

One reason for the lack of orchestral music was that the instruments existing at that time had a most limited range of color, dynamics, and technical possibilities. The creativity of a composer was stunted by these limitations. Choral music, however, offered far greater opportunities for rich, varied artistic expression. Not until the older, less expressive, and less versatile instruments were replaced by newer ones with greater musical potentialities did composers become interested in writing compositions for them.

The first such significant development came about with the construction of the violin and viola, both of which were the sophisticated offspring of old-time viols, the violin of the treble viol, the viola of the tenor viol, or the viola da braccio. In the shape by which they are now recognized, violins and violas came into existence in the sixteenth century. Perfection in the construction and improvement in the tone quality of the violin came about in the Italian city of Cremona, at the hands of a group of master instrument makers, the best known of whom was Antonio Stradivari (1644–1737). Cellos, as we know them today, were first fashioned between 1560 and 1570, while the double bass during this period was just the viol with a few physical changes.

Living in an age when choral music was at the height of its importance, the makers of the first violins, violas, cellos, and basses fashioned these instruments so that each could simulate—as we have seen that they do—a different compass of the human voice. Since the violin, viola, and cello had the singing quality of the voice, composers could now write for these instruments as freely and as imaginatively as they did for a chorus of human voices. But, still incapable of understanding the individuality of each of these instruments, or of relating their sounds to each other, composers wrote for them as if they were human voices —contrapuntally (that is, with separate musical lines) and with no attempt to introduce harmony (that is, a combination of sounds).

It took a major revolution in music to advance the techniques of writing for instruments, to bring into being new instruments and instrumental forms, to develop a new type of music more grateful to instruments than polyphony, and, finally, to help develop the modern orchestra. This revolution came about when homophony began to replace polyphony in the closing years of the sixteenth century and in the beginning ones of the seventeenth. Homophony was a style emphasizing a single melody with harmonic accompaniment, instead of several different melodies sung or played simultaneously. This changeover came about in a musical era now identified as "Baroque." *Baroque* is a word taken from architecture, signifying large, ambitious designs embellished by ornamental details. One reason why the music of the seventeenth and the first half of the eighteenth centuries is referred to as Baroque is because of the tonal cathedrals then being constructed by Johann Sebastian Bach (1685–1750) and George Frideric Handel (1685–1759) in their choral masterpieces. But even while Bach, Handel, and their contemporaries were producing magnificent choral musical edifices, homophony was slowly beginning to attract the interest of composers—composers of the first operas ever written, for example.

It was in early opera composition that the beginnings of modern orchestral writing developed, most significantly in the works of Claudio Monteverdi (1567–1643) whose first opera was *La Favola d'Orfeo* (1607) and his last *L'Incoronazione di Poppea* (1642). Monteverdi expanded the size of his orchestra to forty instruments: twelve violins, five viola da gambas (or bass viols, predecessors of the present-day cello), two basses, three muted trumpets, a piccolo, a high trumpet, two trombones, two small organs, and two harpsichords, among others—a group without precedent at that time. Without precedent, too, was the way in which Monteverdi used this orchestra, not just as a chordal or strumming accompaniment for the singers on the stage (as Jacopo Peri had done before him), but as a significant means of arousing emotional or dramatic interest. Monteverdi was a true pioneer in evolving an "instrumental" concept: that is, writing for instruments differently from the way composers wrote for voices. He enhanced the importance of the orchestra by introducing all kinds of orchestral episodes into his operas: short introductions before the rise of the first-act curtain; dance numbers; brief instrumental sections preceding or following a vocal number; interludes between two vocal numbers. As he continued writing operas, he became more and more concerned with making the orchestra expressive. He experimented with tone colors by using different groupings of instruments. He invented such devices as tremolo and pizzicato for the strings. He evolved an "agitated" style for use in projecting powerful emotions or building up tensions.

To the development of opera, in fact, we owe some of the important changes taking place in orchestral music in the seventeenth and early eighteenth centuries. Alessandro Scarlatti (1660–1725), a Neapolitan, was the first to divide strings into the four divisions of violins, violas, cellos, and basses. The "father" of French opera, Jean-Baptiste Lully (1632–1687), was the earliest to give the strings the prominence in the orchestral scheme they would henceforth enjoy; he also assembled a far better balanced combination of instruments for his orchestral ensemble by combining the strings with flutes, oboes, bassoons, trumpet, and harpsichord.

Practically the same kind of ensemble was used by Jean-Philippe Rameau (1683–1764). Since Rameau, besides being a remarkable opera composer, was also one of music's first great theorists, he brought a scientific approach to orchestral writing. His was a subtle hand in creating sensitive balances among the sections of the orchestra; his, a knowing ear for producing contrasts in color, dynamics, and harmonic combinations; his, an uncommon gift for writing solo passages for individual instruments, pointing up the capabilities of each instrument. The orchestra, in Rameau's operas, received increasing attention, which was even more the case with Christoph Willibald Gluck (1714–1787), another opera composer. Gluck further enriched orchestration by finding a permanent place in his ensemble for instruments formerly ignored by his predecessors (for example, the trombone, the harp, the piccolo, the English horn, bass drums, cymbals, the triangle, the side drums). Where earlier composers had been prone to assign a negligible role to the viola, cello, and percussion, Gluck took full advantage of these instruments to contribute color and sound values.

By the mid-eighteenth century, the orchestra had begun to assume a more or less standardized form, made up of strings, woodwinds, brass, and percussion. For this kind of ensemble, four basic forms had begun to crystallize: the suite, the concerto grosso, the concerto, and the symphony.

The suite is a composition made up of several movements in the style of old dances (minuet, gavotte, gigue, sarabande, and so forth). Sometimes, for variety, a composer might interpolate a movement not in dance form, such as a prelude or overture to open the suite, or a lyrical section between two movements, or some other kind of piece somewhere in the suite. The suite developed during the early Baroque period in compositions for keyboard instruments or for solo instrument and keyboard accompaniment. As a work for orchestra, the suite was brought into significance by Johann Sebastian Bach, who wrote four works in the form between 1717 and 1750, of which the most celebrated are the second, in B minor (written sometime between 1717 and 1723), and the third, in D major (which came about ten years later). The Suite No. 2 is scored for flute and strings, opens with an overture, and includes such old dance forms as the rondeau, sarabande, bourrée, polonaise, and minuet. Stately music (the overture and the sarabande) is mated to music that is light and pleasant (the polonaise). This suite digresses from the norm by ending with a "badinerie," which means a "trifle," and which has a playful spirit.

In the Suite No. 3 (scored for two oboes, three trumpets, drums, and strings), the most celebrated movement is not a dance but an "Air." This "Air" has become known mainly through a transcription for violin and piano by August Wilhelmj, *Air on the G String.* In the Bach suite, the "Air" is music of the kind of spiritual radiance that was Bach's hallmark as a church composer; it provides a radical digression in character and mood from the other movements, the opening being an overture, and the others being a gavotte, a bourrée, and a gigue.

The suite, as a collection of dances, passed from general usage after the Baroque era. In later years, the suite acquired a new meaning: a composition on some unifying subject made up of several movements that interpret varied aspects of that subject.

The concerto grosso (immediate precursor of the concerto for a solo instrument, or solo instruments, and orchestra) is a Baroque form of music. This is a work in several movements for two or more instruments and orchestra. Though some composers had written such works early in the seventeenth century, it took Arcangelo Corelli (1653–1713) to finalize the style and structure by which this form would be identified. Corelli did this in a set of concerti grossi, op. 6 (1714). (*Op.* stands for opus, meaning "work," the term mainly used in numbering a composer's works.)

The concerto grosso is characterized structurally by having one, two, or more instruments (called the *concertino*) combined with, or set against, the orchestra (called the *ripieno*), in a kind of dialogue. With Corelli, the *concertino* consisted of two violins and cello, while the *ripieno* was a string orchestra supplemented by a harpsichord. The concerto grosso was a kind of democratic musical establishment in which the solo instruments and the orchestra are not competitors but equal partners in presenting, elaborating upon, and embellishing the basic thematic material. Collaboration became the basic creative principle. Most of the stylistic characteristics of the concerto grosso can be found in Corelli: the alternation of light and shade (loud and soft); tossing a thematic idea back and forth from the solo instrument or instruments to orchestra; concentration on a single major thematic idea per movement.

One of the finest of Corelli's concerti grossi is the *Christmas Concerto* (no. 8 in G minor). It bears a descriptive title because Corelli is believed to have written it for the night of the Nativity. This contention gained support with early Corelli biographers because the last movement is a "pastorale"—religious music of great serenity describing Christ's cradle in Bethlehem. The concerto has six movements alternating between lively and stately music, some of the latter full of feeling and melodic beauty. It is unusual, however, to find a concerto grosso ending with a reverent pastorale as this one does.

The concerto grosso became a form greatly favored by Baroque composers for orchestras, who produced hundreds of such works. Antonio Vivaldi (1675–1741) is believed to have written over four hundred concertos. His masterpiece in this structure is the Concerto Grosso in D minor, op. 3 no. 11. The opening movement has a sense of drama, and the closing movement is marked by exciting contrasts of harmonies and dynamics. But it is in the second movement that Vivaldi is at his greatest. This is a largo, with a melody of exalted beauty that anticipates the eloquence and poetry of the slow movements in concertos by such later composers as Haydn and Mozart.

Vivaldi also produced a most unusual set of four concerti grossi collectively entitled *Le Quattro stagioni* (*The Four Seasons*). Here the *concertino* is a solo violin. These four compositions pictorially describe the four seasons of the year, beginning with spring. While faithfully pursuing the methods of concerto-grosso writing, Vivaldi here opens a path all his own by printing a sonnet at the head of each concerto (the poem probably the work of the composer himself) to indicate the program for his music. To make sure that the reader-listener correlates text to music correctly, Vivaldi sprinkles throughout his sonnet identifying letters that are then printed over the music describing those lines. Within this music Vivaldi indulges in vivid programmatic writing: translating into music extramusical sounds. We can hear the splash of playing fountains, the thunder of a storm, the chirping of birds, the weeping of a shepherd, the buzz of insects, the chattering of teeth during winter's cold.

The last great composers of the Baroque era were George Frideric Handel and Johann Sebastian Bach. It is they who brought the concerto grosso to such an advanced stage of artistic and structural evolution that the composers who followed them, feeling there was nothing further to be developed, abandoned the form. (Many years later, several composers resurrected the concerto grosso; even some prominent twentieth-century composers used it.)

Handel wrote six concerti grossi, op. 3 (c. 1720), in which he used the works of Corelli and Vivaldi as his model, though with greater richness of orchestration and greater individuality in the employment of the *concertino*. About two decades later Handel produced another dozen concerti grossi, op. 6. The final point of development of the concerto grosso, beyond which it could progress no further, was reached with this op. 6 set of Handel's, and with Johann Sebastian Bach's six *Brandenburg Concertos* (1721). The Bach concertos were written first; they are probably the greatest works produced in this form. The extraordinary originality of method and the vigor, grandeur, and nobility of musical thought that are encountered so frequently in many other Bach compositions characterize these six concertos as well.

The Concerto no. 2 in F major boasts unusual instrumental colors through the use of a high-pitched trumpet. The Concerto no. 3 in G major is novel in that it is scored for three string groups of three instruments apiece, and that it comprises just two movements. The expected slow movement between the two fast ones is supplanted by two chords. (Often a slow movement from another work of Bach's is inserted here in performance.) The Concerto no. 5 in D major has an extended section for solo harpsichord that endows this instrument with an importance it had never before enjoyed in an orchestral composition. And the Concerto no. 6 in B-flat major has a dark, haunting character through its emphasis on the violas and cellos. In view of the fact that these six concerti grossi survived as worthy representatives of Bach's genius, it is amazing to remember that while Bach was still alive, in 1734, the manuscripts of these concertos were disposed of at the price of about ten cents apiece.

Twenty years after Bach's *Brandenburg Concertos* came Handel's Concerti Grossi, op. 6, which we have mentioned, the most important and original of his orchestral compositions. Handel completed all the twelve works in this set in one month; sometimes he managed to write a whole concerto grosso in a day. Where Bach was partial to a three-movement structure, Handel used between four and six movements. These twelve works are a veritable cornucopia of musical riches: dances, tone pictures, infectious moods, somber thoughts, skillful counterpoint, enchanting melodies, and such innovations as utilizing variations or fantasialike sections to enlarge or change basic melodies.

It is such a short step from the concerto grosso to the concerto for a solo instrument (or solo instruments) and orchestra that frequently Baroque composers identified certain compositions as concertos when they were actually concerti grossi. This proved particularly true of Vivaldi and Handel, and to a lesser degree of Bach. Bach wrote concertos for one or more pianos; * for one or two violins; and for violin and oboe. All are in three movements: fast, slow and lyrical, and fast and vigorous. A single theme is used in each movement, altered through changes of key and transferred back and forth from solo instrument or instruments to orchestra very much as in a concerto grosso.

Bach was one of the first important composers to write concertos for one, two, or three pianos and orchestra. The negligible regard Bach held for the individuality of the instrument for which he was writing, when he combined it with orchestra, is proved by the fact that some of his piano concertos are transcriptions of his violin concertos; that his Concerto for Violin, Oboe, and Orchestra is a transcription of his Concerto for Two Pianos and Orchestra; and that his Concerto for Four Pianos and Or-

---

* Bach did not actually write for the piano, since the piano was not in use in his time. Bach's concertos were written for the keyboard instruments that preceded the piano, such as the clavichord and the harpsichord. Bach preferred to write for the clavichord because it was the more responsive of the two instruments. The strings of these instruments were struck or plucked, but the piano we know with its felt-covered hammers and its sustained tone did not make its appearance until about 1710, and did not come into common use until the 1760's. Henceforth in this book, when we speak about compositions written for the antecedents of the piano we shall, for the sake of simplicity, use the term *piano*.

16

chestra is a transcription of Vivaldi's Concerto for Four Violins and Orchestra. Not until we come to Mozart does the individuality and virtuosity of the solo instrument become emphasized; and not until Mozart does the concerto assume something of the structure and style by which we know it today.

Nevertheless, there is enough invigorating motor energy and eloquence in Bach's greatest concertos to have assured their survival. Bach looks backward in his concertos by adopting concerto grosso methods and writing polyphonically. But sometimes the lyricism of his slow movements looks forward to the new age of homophony. Between 1717 and 1723 Bach wrote the first violin concertos still played, those in A minor and E major. This is also the period that brought us perhaps Bach's greatest concerto of all, possibly the greatest concerto of the era before Mozart, that in D minor, for two violins and orchestra. Polyphonic writing abounds in the outer movements, as the main subject is presented in imitation. ("In imitation" is a method in counterpoint in which a theme is stated by an instrument or voice that continues on with it as another instrument or voice enters, repeating the theme. Both proceed with their theme as a third instrument or voice makes its entry with the same theme—and so on. This type of music in an extended form and with amplifications is called a fugue. A song like "Three Blind Mice" is written in imitation.) But it is in the slow movement that Bach touches heights of inspiration, as the two violins, once again in imitation, offer a melody whose radiance and spiritual beauty have few rivals in Baroque orchestral music.

In or about 1730, Bach produced music history's first important piano concertos. Bach wrote seven such concertos. Still given are the Concerto no. 1 in D minor, the Concerto no. 4 in A major, and the Concerto no. 5 in F minor. Between 1730 and 1733, Bach completed concertos for two pianos and orchestra, three pianos and orchestra, four pianos and orchestra, and for violin and oboe and orchestra.

If the concerto of the Baroque era suggests rather than realizes the concerto of a later generation, the same truth holds for the Baroque symphony.

The word *symphony* comes from *sinfonia,* a term used in the seventeenth century for any piece of instrumental music, including overtures to operas. The operatic overtures, or sinfonias, Alessandro Scarlatti developed in Naples (designated as "Italian overtures") have a three-part form in which a middle lyrical section, its melody resembling that of an

17

opera aria, is flanked by two fast movements, the last usually in a dance form. This type of overture or sinfonia is the direct ancestor of the earliest symphonies. Nevertheless, even after some composers began using the word *symphony* for three-movement orchestral compositions, modeled after the Italian overture, there were still other composers who prefered adhering to the term *sinfonia.* As late as 1773 (by which time the classic symphony had become established) Carl Philipp Emanuel Bach, son of the great Johann Sebastian, wrote the Sinfonia no. 3 in C major for string orchestra and piano. This is actually an Italian overture rather than a symphony.

The word *symphony* comes into general use in the early eighteenth century with Francesco Geminiani (1687–1762), who also wrote a good many concerti grossi. But both the symphony as a musical form and the orchestra are really outgrowths of those developed in the German city of Mannheim by Johann Stamitz (1717–1757). Stamitz's ensemble consisted of forty to fifty men whose core was the string section (twenty violins, four each of violas and cellos, and two basses), and which also included two each of flutes, oboes, horns, and bassoons, and one trumpet and two tympani. It is important to notice that this organization did not include a piano, which in earlier sinfonias or symphonies was continually used to provide the so-called continuo or "thorough bass"—a background of chords improvised in the right hand to bass notes under or above which were marked in the score figures suggesting what chords should be played in the left hand ("figured bass"). The elimination of both the piano and the technique of continuo transferred the harmonic background to the wind instruments. This, in turn, introduced new sounds and colors to the harmonies while assigning an increased importance to the winds in the orchestral makeup.

Stamitz's orchestra was a well-balanced ensemble, wearing a coat of many colors and possessing a voice capable of a wide gamut of expression. Through his meticulous leadership, Stamitz made this orchestra into a truly virtuoso ensemble, capable of producing soft and loud passages, beauty of tone, precision in the opening and closing of a movement, and an agility and clarity in the production of fast passages no other orchestral ensemble could rival. The venerable English music historian Charles Burney noted in the eighteenth century: "No orchestra in the world has ever surpassed the Mannheim orchestra in execution. Its forte is thunder, its crescendo is a cataract, its diminuendo is a crystal stream babbling along in the distance, its piano is a breath of spring."

Because of Stamitz's work with his orchestra, by Haydn's time there were pliable, well-organized ensembles for which he could write his own symphonies. Haydn's orchestra was only about half the size of that Stamitz had assembled, but of the same makeup. Besides bringing the first modern symphony orchestra into existence, Stamitz also wrote the first "modern" symphonies very much in a style and format Haydn would adopt and extend. Stamitz produced some sixty symphonies, in which much of the "classic" structure and procedure was crystallized.

It was Stamitz who established the enlargement of the overall symphonic structure from three to four movements; who used two contrasting themes, instead of a single one, in his first movement (in later symphonies known as "binary form"); who used a two-part or three-part melody for his second movement, and a minuet for the third; whose finale represented an energetic buildup of a single theme.

With Stamitz we leave the Baroque era and enter the age of Classicism. The Classical period in music began in the mid-eighteenth century and lasted into the early nineteenth century. Classicism glorified music that was graceful, clearly written, and elegant. It is music that conforms to established forms and rules. Symmetry and balance are emphasized; emotion becomes subservient to controlled precision of design and style. Homophony becomes the principal technique, instruments, rather than the voice, the major medium. The Classical era expanded those forms of instrumental music in which the distinguished composer could produce masterworks that have still not lost their appeal for audiences: the sonata, the concerto, the string quartet, the symphony.

Where polyphonic skill had been the pride of the Baroque composer, the ability to carve out beautifully shaped melodies (instrumental rather than vocal in style) was the aspiration of the Classical composer. Haydn said, "It is the air which is the charm of music, and it is that which is most difficult to produce. The invention of a fine melody is the work of genius." And Mozart told a friend, "Melody is the essence of music. I should liken one who invents melodies to a noble race horse, and a mere contrapuntist to a hired post-hack."

Century-old traditions, however, do not die overnight. It should, therefore, cause no surprise to find in the Classical era carry-overs from the age of the Baroque. Even in Classicism we find composers like Haydn, Mozart, and Beethoven producing monumental, ornamented, detailed polyphonic works for chorus, such as had been the pride and glory of the Baroque period; even in Classicism we encounter such polyphonic forms as the fugue or such polyphonic techniques as imitation. *19*

But in opposition to polyphony we find homophony, in opposition to
elaborate designs and structures we get an underlying simplicity. Classical melodies are sometimes decorated with trimmings (trills, grace notes,
mordents), but there is a discernible structure beneath the decoration.

We should also mention here a style of musical composition that appeared at the end of the Baroque period, the *style galant,* characterized
by profuse ornamentation of suave melodies, but in works of much
smaller scale and intent than those of the Baroque age. The *style galant*
is best typified by the works of Carl Philipp Emanuel Bach (1714–1788).
This kind of music is also known as rococo (from the French *rocaille,* a
shell, referring to decorative ornamentation, often in shell form, as in
wood carving). The basic development, however, was from the many
voices of polyphonic music to the single-voice emphasis of the classical
period.

During the Classical period, even more than in the time of Baroque,
the making of music and the support of composers depended almost
solely on the patronage of royalty and nobility. Concerts for the general
public were few and far between. There was hardly a court in Europe
that did not have its own orchestra, and some even had their own opera
houses. These musical forces were led by the more important composers
of that age (men referred to in Germany and Austria as Kapellmeisters).
They had at hand a musical organization, or organizations, ready to perform whatever they wrote. The development of orchestral music owes a
great debt to this system of patronage. But he who pays the piper calls
the tune. A good deal of the orchestral music of the Classical era is for-
mulistic and stereotyped because it was written to meet the favor of the
patron. Royalty and nobility owed their exalted power and positions to
law and order, and to the unquestioning subservience of the masses to
the rule of their superiors. Those in high station brooked no deviations
from the status quo. This probably explains why the Classical age was
characterized by such disciplined writing within accepted frameworks.
This proved true even in many of Haydn's compositions. But when he
was at his greatest we continually confront innovation and experimentation that opened new horizons for music and coincidentally for the symphony. The creativity of true genius can never be permanently hemmed
in by restricted boundaries.

Joseph Haydn has often been called "the father of the symphony." We
have already noticed that this is not so: there were symphonies before
Haydn wrote any of consequence. But while the symphonies of the late
20 Baroque and early Classical eras are sometimes heard at concerts and

have been recorded, and while they provide pleasurable listening, music lovers tend to regard Haydn as the first major composer of symphonic music. With Haydn's predecessors and contemporaries the symphony had been a newborn infant without much distinction. With Haydn the symphony passed into adolescence and after that to maturity. Its mind and muscles were so greatly developed by him that it had both the form and the mentality to achieve full manhood with Mozart and Beethoven.

All that had happened to the symphony before Haydn came on the scene had just set the stage for the emergence of an unqualified genius. That genius was Haydn. And it is with him that our story of orchestral music begins.

2

Rococo Elegance

Joseph Haydn

Thirty miles from Vienna, near the Hungarian border, lay the little market town of Rohrau. At the end of the marketplace stood a small thatched cottage occupied by Mathias Haydn and his family. The man earned a humble living by fixing the wheels of carriages and wagons and by serving as the sexton of the parish church. His wife, Maria, had worked as a cook. During their marriage she bore her husband twelve children, the second of whom was Franz Josef Haydn (more popularly known as Joseph Haydn), who came into the world on March 31, 1732.

Poverty might easily have cast its dark shadows across the Haydn household but for the fact that the family found so much joy in music. Though he had never studied, Mathias Haydn played the harp by ear and sang well. The mother also had a pleasing voice. On many an evening or holiday the Haydn home was brightened with the making of music in which some of the townspeople participated.

Joseph was just a child when his father turned him over to the village schoolmaster for violin lessons, at which Joseph made such progress that he attracted the interest of a relative, Johann Mathias Franck, a schoolmaster and trained musician who lived in the nearby town of

Hainburg. When Joseph was five, Franck took the boy into his own household to give him intensive music instruction. The boy spent three unhappy years with the Francks. They resented his presence and were so hostile that Joseph had to keep pretty much to himself, germinating that feeling of loneliness and aloofness that haunted him all his life. To make matters still worse, Franck was a schoolmaster who firmly believed in the proverb that to spare the rod was to spoil the child. He used the rod unsparingly during the long hours he taught Haydn the violin, the piano, and singing. Later in life Haydn recalled that he received from Franck more blows than food. But as far as the boy's musical development was concerned, this treatment was as fruitful as it was cruel. Franck made the boy into a thorough young musician—something for which, incidentally, Haydn expressed gratitude as long as he lived.

When Haydn was about eight, he was selected for the choir and the choir school of St. Stephen's Cathedral in Vienna. This was hardly a change for the better. Life at St. Stephen's was even more insufferable than it had been in Hainburg. The living conditions were execrable. The cubicle serving as Haydn's room was always freezing cold. The food was barely enough to keep him from starvation. Haydn was thoroughly miserable, particularly since the musical director disliked and maltreated him (probably because, being a chronic mischief-maker, young Haydn was always getting into trouble). The teachers neglected him to a point where Haydn received practically no instruction. But, as Haydn subsequently recalled, "by dint of hard work I managed to get on." Without the help of teachers, he labored at the keyboard, practiced his singing lessons, and acquired a command of theory by memorizing textbooks. "I was industrious when my companions went to play," Haydn later said. He made rapid headway because "the talent was in me." He even tried his hand at writing a Mass, a musical setting for the Catholic service. His ambitious effort inspired only contempt from the music director.

A practical joke led to his dismissal from the school and the choir when he was seventeen. One day in class he cut off the pigtail from the wig worn by the student in front of him. This offense, for which he was soundly thrashed, combined with the fact that Haydn was losing his voice anyway, convinced the music director he had had enough of the boy. In November of 1749 Haydn was unceremoniously ejected from St. Stephen's—penniless, without a home, his only possessions being the clothes he wore. He found shelter in the attic home of an acquaintance for a while, during which time he earned some money singing in choirs, playing the violin at balls and other festivities, teaching, and sometimes playing in orchestras that, in those days, used to perform serenades in the streets.

He made some friends, one of whom lent him the money to rent his own room: an attic in the Michaelerhaus in the Kohlmarkt district (where the house still stands). It was not much of a home, but it was his own—a place to keep his piano and to practice on it for hours on end, a place to study texts, a place to compose. He wrote a new Mass in or about 1750 and two years later did the music for a farce that, though it had only three performances in Vienna, was also heard in several German cities and in Prague.

His neighbors at the Michaelerhaus included a cook, a footman, a printer, and one of the most celebrated opera librettists of the age as well as court poet, Pietro Metastasio. Through Metastasio, Haydn met Niccolò Porpora, a distinguished singer and composer in Vienna. In return for singing lessons, Haydn performed for Porpora the menial duties of a houseservant and, when needed, was his accompanist at the piano. Being a musician of renown, Porpora continually came into contact with the powerful figures in Vienna. It was through Porpora's influence that Haydn was able to do so too. Among those Haydn met and impressed was Baron Karl von Fürnberg. The baron often presented concerts in his summer residence at Weinzierl. He soon asked Haydn to write music for these performances.

And so in 1755 Haydn wrote a good deal of music in forms then much in vogue: cassations, nocturnes, divertimenti, serenades. These types of compositions—sometimes for string quartet, sometimes for small wind ensembles, and sometimes for orchestra—were so much alike in structure and content that it is difficult to differentiate one from the other. Actually, during the Classical era, the designations of serenade, cassation, and divertimento were used interchangeably. All were in several short movements (usually four); all were light and entertaining; all were intended for court entertainments or for outdoor performances by wandering musicians. Actually, the most accurate term that might be applied to each of these forms is that of *suite*.

For his performances at Weinzierl, Haydn wrote some divertimenti and cassations for sundry combinations of instruments. Those for strings represented his earliest attempts at writing for orchestra. This was slight music at best, but it pleased the nobility, many of whom came to the baron's palace expressly to hear it. One such highborn visitor was Count Maximilian von Morzin, a Bohemian nobleman who maintained an active and important music establishment at his palace near Pilsen. By offering Haydn a position of music director with a salary equivalent to about $65 a year with board and lodging, Count von Morzin was able to lure Haydn to Pilsen. Haydn stayed there two years. In 1759 he wrote his first symphony (D major), scored for two oboes, two horns, and strings—though in reality this is structurally and stylistically a divertimento or a serenade rather than a symphony. It took Haydn almost a decade (and about thirty compositions all called symphonies) to understand that the symphony was—or could be—something quite different from the more trivial forms he had been using.

On November 26, 1760, Haydn was married. Sad to say, this was more of a convenient arrangement than a romance, since he did not marry the girl he really loved. His beloved was one of his pupils— Therese Keller, a gentle, soft-spoken, sympathetic, affectionate, and highly religious person. Therese, however, chose to enter a convent. Overwhelmed by disappointment, and spurred on by Therese's father, Haydn decided to accept her sister, Maria Anna, as a substitute.

Maria Anna was a dynamic and strong-willed woman. She knew nothing about music and looked upon professional musicians as beggars. Haydn did not appeal to her for other reasons, too. He was not attractive physically (indeed, he always regarded himself as ugly). His short legs made him seem misshapen. His face was disfigured by pockmarks, and his long nose was swelled by nasal polyps. Pressure by her parents and her own fears of spinsterhood now that she was thirty-one (and decidedly unattractive) led her to enter upon what at best was just a marriage of convenience. Bearing nothing but contempt for her husband, Maria Anna became a sullen, ill-tempered, high-strung shrew. She had such little respect for Haydn's genius that she used some of his manuscripts sometimes as scrap paper, at other times to line her pans. After several years of misunderstandings and quarrels, Maria Anna and Haydn decided to separate permanently. The kindly Haydn had tried his best to make the marriage work. Having failed, he bore no grudges against his wife, providing for her financially as long as he lived, and never speaking an unkind word against her.

But if his personal life had worsened in 1760, his professional one would soon suddenly take a turn for the better. In 1761 Count von Morzin disbanded his orchestra. Haydn was immediately pressed into service as assistant Kapellmeister for one of Austria's most powerful and renowned noblemen, Prince Paul Anton Esterházy. The prince, being an avid music lover and generous patron, had combed all Europe for the best musicians he could hire for his palace at Eisenstadt, where concerts and opera were given regularly. In Haydn, he knew he had a remarkable musician well able to assist the Kapellmeister in maintaining the highest possible standards.

Haydn was given a comfortable three-room apartment in the palace, board, and a salary of about $100 a year. But more important to Haydn than this improvement in living conditions was the excellent orchestra with which he had to work, some of whose members were exceptional virtuosos. With such an outstanding ensemble at his disposal he could, as he put it, "make experiments, observe what produced an effect and what weakened it, and was thus in a position to improve, alter, make additions and omissions and to be as bold as I pleased." It was because he now had such favorable conditions in which to develop his genius that in the ensuing years he produced his first important symphonies with the recognizable marks of Haydn's hand on them.

Haydn had been employed at Eisenstadt a little more than a year when Prince Paul died and was succeeded by Nicolaus Joseph "the Magnificent"—so called because of the splendor with which he always surrounded himself. With true princely opulence, the new head of the Esterházy had a palace built for himself at Esterháza costing about five million dollars. It had two theaters, one for opera, the other for marionette shows. It had a wonderful orchestra that gave numerous concerts in the grand ballroom. When Esterházy's first Kapellmeister died in the year that this new palace opened, Haydn took over the post. He was now the director of as outstanding a musical establishment as could be found in Europe.

Distant as it was from Vienna, the appointment at Esterháza meant a life of confinement, removed from the activities of the outside world. Though he was kept continually busy by his many duties as Kapellmeister, and though he worked indefatigably on his compositions, Haydn was terribly lonely. "Here I sit in my desert," he wrote in a letter, "forsaken, a poor orphan, almost without human companionship." But this withdrawal from friends and relatives and a social life had profound advantages for his musical growth. At Esterháza he found the peace and the opportunities to produce a vast and varied library of music in virtually every form. Though his output was prolific, he was a painstaking workman, always revising and polishing what he had written, always seeking out fresh methods. As he progressed from one work to the next —and specifically from one symphony to another—he grew increasingly bold in his innovations, more independent in his thinking, freer in abandoning pat methods that had formerly tied him to tradition. He knew

he was carving a path of his own, and he also knew why. "Cut off as I
was from the world," he explained, "there was no one to confuse and
torment me, and I was forced to become original." Besides, the prince
"was always satisfied with my work" and he had "the encouragement of
constant approval."

Haydn completed almost ninety symphonies during the more than
quarter of a century he was the Esterházy's Kapellmeister. Three written in 1761 already had symphonic character and employed symphonic
procedures, so that they can no longer be considered as divertimenti or
serenades. This trio of symphonies attempts to describe the three periods
of the day; they are therefore named *Le Matin,* or *Morning* (D major),
Le Midi, or *Afternoon* (C major) and *Le Soir,* or *Evening* (G major).

Upon the foundation stones laid by Johann Stamitz, Haydn began
building a permanent structure, one that would, of course, change with
later composers who would enlarge it, develop it, alter it in details, and
transform a comparatively modest abode into a grandiose edifice. But the
basic structure was Haydn's work. All later improvements and moderni-
zations notwithstanding, the essence of the symphonic form was Haydn's
contribution.

The four-movement structure of Stamitz was retained. Haydn liked
to preface the first movement, an allegro, with a brief, stately introduction. (Such introductions, while not basic to the definitive symphonic
structure, were sometimes used by many later composers, including
Schubert and Brahms.) The "sonata form" (so called because it carried
over into the symphony a format first realized in sonatas for solo piano,
or a solo instrument and piano) became the mold of Haydn's first movement. The sonata form has three sections. The first (exposition) presents
two contrasting themes—the first virile, and the second more lyrical, in
a complementary key. Once these ideas are presented they are allowed
to change, expand, and be varied in the second section (development).
After that the two subjects are restored to normalcy (recapitulation).
The first movement frequently ends with the recapitulation, but some
composers, of whom Haydn was the first, preferred to add a brief appen-
dage (a coda) to bring the movement to a satisfying or dramatic conclusion.

Other structural innovations made by Haydn should be singled out.
For the songlike second movement Haydn occasionally deserted the
three-part form for a theme and its variations: a melody followed by a
series of alterations in which the basic tune is readily recognizable. For
the third, minuet, movement he used unusual tempos. In his last move-

ment, Haydn at times leaned toward the sonata form, instead of building up an energetic finale from one or two robust subjects. In all four movements, Haydn extended the possibility of theme development, introduced changes of key for special effects, experimented with rhythmic patterns, and expanded the technical demands made on the different instruments of the orchestra.

What may very well have been Haydn's greatest achievement in symphonic music was to substitute subjective feelings for the kind of objective writing found in the work of his predecessors and early contemporaries. There were two facets to Haydn's personality. On the one hand he was a man with wit, a man capable of levity, a man retaining from childhood a love for perpetrating pranks. On the other hand, he was obsessed with melancholy. Both facets are continually reflected in his symphonies. From the formal graceful dance it had been with Stamitz, the third-movement minuet was transformed by Haydn into sparkling, playful, good-humored music. Even elsewhere in his symphonies we find him, from time to time, doing the unexpected—in a spirit of jest rather than experimentation. This lightness, these excursions into musical pranks, personalized his writing.

But his symphonies also contain a sense of the dramatic, or a gentle melancholy, or a sense of tragedy, or feverish and passionate moods never encountered in a Stamitz symphony. The Germans have a phrase *Sturm und Drang,* meaning "storm and stress," in the emotional sense. This phrase has been applied to many of Haydn's symphonies beginning in 1768. One of these, for example, is entitled *Tragic* (or *Mourning*) (no. 44 in E minor, 1772), another *Passion* (no. 49 in F minor, 1768). *Sturm und Drang* also applies to the deeply felt feelings expressed in the slow movement of the Symphony no. 45 in F-sharp minor, known as the *Farewell* (1772). This is the first of Haydn's symphonies with which the average music lover is familiar.

The title *Farewell* deserves an explanation. In the finale, the orchestra begins to dispense now with one instrument, now with another, until just two solo violins are left to end the movement. There was a reason for this happening. Some historians maintain that when this movement was first performed, each musician who came to the end of his own part blew out the candle that in those days lit up the music stand and quietly slipped off the stage. This was intended (so goes a familiar story) to hint to the prince that the musicians were entitled to a vacation. Another story suggests that Haydn used this strange procedure to dissuade the prince from disbanding his orchestra, which rumors had hinted he was

going to do. Whatever the intent of the symphony, the orchestration of
the finale is a highly original concept, with Haydn the prankster coming
to the foreground.

Haydn the prankster emerges again in two of six symphonies completed in 1786 on a commission from Paris. In the Symphony no. 82 in C major Haydn playfully simulates in the finale the roar of a bear in the bass notes; this is why this work is now known as *The Bear*. Symphony no. 83 in G minor is named *The Hen* because in the first movement repeated notes from the oboe (used as a background to the second theme) sound like cackling.

But in his last two symphonies before his long tenure as Kapellmeister at Esterháza ended, Haydn is reflective, sad-hearted, religious. This side of Haydn's personality speaks softly but gloriously in the slow movements of each of the two symphonies. In the Symphony no. 88 in G major (1787)—one of the most popular symphonies Haydn wrote—a soulful song rises from oboe and cellos and then is subjected to a few variations. In the middle of such reflective music there is a sudden outburst of Haydn's one-time *Sturm und Drang* style through powerful chords and a vigorous, muscular section for orchestra; but the gentle serenity and loveliness is only momentarily disturbed.

In the Symphony no. 92 in G major, the *Oxford* (1788), we come upon Haydn's deeply religious nature through the reverent main melody of the slow movement. This symphony is called *Oxford* because Haydn chose to play it in London in 1791 when he received an honorary degree from Oxford University. Actually, Haydn had written a special new symphony for so august an occasion, but the orchestral parts had arrived from Vienna too late to allow for adequate rehearsals. Haydn selected a symphony he had written three years earlier and whose music was then readily available in London.

A new creative period in Haydn's life—and his greatest—began after he had freed himself of his obligations and duties as Kapellmeister at Esterháza. When, in 1790, Prince Nicolaus died, his successor economized by reducing the size of the musical establishment; at the same time he dismissed some of its finest musicians. Without too much regret (since it meant that, for the first time in twenty-five years, he now had full freedom both as man and artist) Haydn left Esterháza for good, made financially secure through a handsome pension for life.

He made his home in Vienna, in the apartment of one of his friends. But he was not long allowed the luxury of enjoying freedom from pressing commitments. Offers came from many places. One was made by Johann Peter Salomon, an English impresario, who offered Haydn an enormous fee to write six new symphonies and direct their premiere in London. Haydn accepted. It was true that the journey from Vienna was long and arduous, including the crossing of the English Channel, then regarded as both difficult and hazardous. It was also true that Haydn, at fifty-eight, was no longer a young man. But England for him meant a new world to explore and conquer, a new adventure for one who had had so few of them.

Haydn left Vienna on December 15, 1790. He crossed Europe by coach, weathered a fearfully stormy Channel crossing, and finally reached London on January 1, 1791. He found comfortable quarters in Golden Square, which forthwith attracted the most distinguished members of London's social and musical life, as well as ambassadors from Austria and Naples, come to honor him. His privacy was further shattered by the necessity of having to attend innumerable parties given almost nightly for him. He had to attend the court ball, picnics, excursions, and public banquets. All this taxed his physical resources. "My mind is weak," he wrote, "and it is only the help of God that will supply what is wanting in my power."

He found that power when the time came for him to rehearse and perform his six new symphonies. His first public appearance in London took place on March 11, 1791. This and Haydn's subsequent concerts became the most talked-about events in London. They attracted the socially prominent, including the Prince of Wales. The response to both Haydn and his new symphonies was rapturous. So taken was London that one newspaper expressed the hope that "the first musical genius of the age may be induced, by our liberal welcome, to take up his residence in England."

Haydn, of course, did not remain permanently in London, as the quoted newspaper hoped he would. But he did pay London a second visit in 1794. History repeated itself, and once again all of London was at his feet. The adulatory reception of his London concerts and his second group of symphonies is partially indicated in the following lines by a London correspondent for a journal in Weimar, Germany:

But what would you now say to his new symphonies composed expressly for these concerts? . . . It is truly wonderful what sublime and august thoughts this master weaves into his works. Passages occur that render it
impossible to listen to them without becoming excited. We are altogether

carried away by admiration. . . . In every symphony of Haydn, the
Adagio or Andante is sure to be repeated each time, after the most vehe-
ment encores. The worthy Haydn . . . conducts himself on these occa-
sions in the most modest manner. He is indeed a goodhearted, candid,
honest man, esteemed and beloved by all.

Such enthusiasm was well deserved. The twelve symphonies Haydn
wrote for London (six in 1791, six in 1794), collectively referred to as
the *London* Symphonies, belong with the best that the eighteenth century produced. Each work is a shining jewel. In each Haydn's technical
and inventive powers are at their peak. Whether his hand is light or
whether his heart is heavy, his genius showing in these works helped to
establish permanently the symphony as the most significant and popular
of all instrumental forms.

Some of these symphonies bear titles provided by Haydn's publisher.
For example, the second of the first London set—Symphony no. 94 in
G major—is called *Surprise*. In the second movement, a simple tune for
strings is interrupted unexpectedly with a thunderous chord for full orchestra. Legend (not fact) explains that Haydn introduced this chord because he was convinced audiences habitually fell asleep during a slow
movement and he wanted to wake them up.

The Symphony no. 100 in G major is entitled *Military* because bugle
calls are sounded and the percussion group includes such instruments as
the side drums and cymbals, then associated with military music. The
slow movement of the Symphony no. 101 in D major has a stately melody accompanied by staccato figures that sound just like the ticking of a
clock—hence the name *Clock* Symphony. The Symphony no. 103 in E-
flat major has an unconventional opening, a roll of the tympani. Later in
the movement a unique effect is achieved by repeating the roll in the
drums. This symphony thus acquired the nickname *Drum Roll*. And the
last of the dozen symphonies—no. 104 in D major—bears the same
name as the whole group (*London*), although why this is so has never
been discovered.

Haydn came back to Vienna in the summer of 1795, a man who had
gathered more accolades, wealth, and honors than any orchestral composer of his generation. There was nobody too exalted to sing his
praises. But if any single event touched him to the depths of his heart, it
happened not in London, Vienna, or any other European capital but in
his little native town of Rohrau. Soon after his return from his first trip *31*

to London, Rohrau invited him to attend festivities for the unveiling of a Haydn bust. This represented Haydn's first visit to the house where he was born since he had left as a child. When he arrived there, he went down on his knees to kiss the threshold. Then, entering the humble abode, he wept like a child, as a rush of memories brought images of the family that had so loved him and that he had known so briefly.

Haydn spent his last years in a house in the Viennese suburb of Gumpendorf. His career as composer was by no means over. The Austrian emperor asked him to write a new national anthem, which was officially introduced on the emperor's birthday on February 12, 1797, in all of Austria's theaters: "Gott erhalte Franz den Kaiser" ("May God protect Franz the emperor"). The emperor told Haydn, "You have expressed what is in every loyal heart." It remained Austria's anthem until 1918. Germany, too, adopted the melody in "Deutschland, Deutschland über alles," which was formerly that country's anthem.

Haydn wrote other music too—though no more symphonies: his last string quartets, into one of which he interpolated the melody of his national anthem; also the only oratorios he ever wrote *Die Schöpfung* (*The Creation*) in 1798 and *Die Jahreszeiten* (*The Seasons*) in 1801. He was driven to write these, his last two masterworks, because of his great admiration for Handel and his ambition to create an oratorio of the Handel type before he died.

After 1803 Haydn deteriorated physically and mentally. Sometimes he did not recognize friends. For this reason he devised a couplet that he had printed on a card for distribution to those visiting him. It read:

> *Gone forever is my strength,*
> *Old and weak am I.*

The last time he was seen in public was on March 27, 1808, at a performance of *The Creation* given to celebrate his seventy-sixth birthday. Now totally feeble, Haydn had to be carried into the auditorium in an armchair. When the audience saw Haydn, it swept to its feet in homage. And, early in the oratorio, at the words "And then there was light" (accompanied by an outburst of orchestral sonority), the audience could not contain its enthusiasm. The cheers made it impossible for the music to continue for a while. Haydn's reaction was, "Not I, but a Power above me created this music."

His days were now numbered; they were not happy. He was wasting
away, and he was aware that his beloved Vienna was being shelled by

the French, who soon occupied the city. After the troops invaded Vienna, a French officer paid Haydn a call, not as a conqueror but as a humble admirer. The officer asked and received permission to sing for Haydn a part of *The Creation*. Deeply moved, Haydn rose and embraced his enemy. "God bless you my son!" Haydn said softly. "You have made me very happy today."

He knew he was dying. He drew up his will, carefully remembering anybody who had ever done him a service or who had once been kind to him. Then he gathered his servants to bless them. "Do not weep for me," he told them. "I have lived well, served God and music, and have no regrets. It is not too hard to go. I am tired—tired." He then asked to be carried to his piano, where he played his Austrian anthem three times. He died peacefully in his sleep a few days later, on May 31, 1809.

Though he was originally buried in the cemetery of a church near his house, his remains are now to be found in a church in Eisenstadt to which they were removed in 1820.

Musicians entertaining at a court festival in sixteenth-century England.

Joseph Haydn.

Alessandro Scarlatti.

A nineteenth-century performance of Haydn's Toy Symphony by children of the Royal Asylum of St. Anne in England.

Classicism in Excelsis

Wolfgang Amadeus Mozart

In 1781 a fateful meeting took place in Vienna—fateful both for the two composers involved and for the destiny of music. It was then and there that Joseph Haydn and Wolfgang Amadeus Mozart met for the first time face to face. Haydn was almost fifty years old, a composer of great renown. Mozart was twenty-five; most of his already written masterworks were comparatively little known.

Mozart venerated Haydn. He had studied Haydn's works and had learned from them much about classical style and structure, and how they can be worked with imaginatively. "If they melted us both together," Mozart once told a fellow musician, "there would still not be stuff enough to make a Haydn." On another occasion, when a highly unorthodox effect in one of Haydn's compositions led this same musician to remark to Mozart, *"I* would never have written *that,"* Mozart replied swiftly and incisively, "Nor would I! And do you know why? Because neither you nor I would have had so excellent an idea."

In thus glorifying Haydn (as Haydn so well deserved) Mozart was undervaluing himself. By 1781 he had already written some three hundred works in all forms. He had already proved that he was capable of a creative invention, daring, and inspiration greater even than those of Haydn. And nobody realized this more forcefully than Haydn himself.

In the years following 1781, as Haydn listened with wonder, awe, and at times bewilderment to the kind of music Mozart was writing, and the way in which he was writing it, his enthusiasm knew no limits. To Mozart's father, Haydn said in 1785, "Before God and as an honest man I tell you that your son is the greatest composer known to me either in person or by name." Later Haydn added, "Mozart is the greatest composer that the world now possesses. . . . Oh, if only I could explain to every musical friend, and to the leading men in particular, the inimitable art of Mozart, its depth, the greatness of its emotion, and its unique musical conception, as I myself feel and understand it, nations would then vie with each other to possess so great a jewel within their frontiers."

Haydn and Mozart met only infrequently after 1781, on those rare instances when Haydn visited Vienna. When they did meet it was with an undiminished exchange of the most profound mutual respect. In personality they were opposites. Mozart was mercurial in temperament, disordered in the way he conducted his financial affairs, a man interested in frivolities and trivialities. He loved dancing, women, playing billiards, drinking punch in great quantities, and being the bon vivant. He could be as gleeful as a child over a new velvet jacket or lace cuffs. The staid, respectable, precise, orderly, withdrawn, and lonely Haydn stood in sharp contrast to Mozart. Yet though their personalities were dissimilar, their awe for each other's genius made them one. They tolerated each other's idiosyncrasies and way of life, just as they respected each other's achievements.

Wolfgang Amadeus Mozart was born in the Austrian city of Salzburg on January 27, 1756. The narrow street (Getreidegasse) and the five-story cream-colored plaster house (now no. 9), in whose third-floor four-room apartment with kitchen Mozart lived until the 1770s, look today very much as they did in the eighteenth century. The street, the house, and the apartment have become central points of tourist interest for those who stream into Salzburg each summer to attend its world-famous festival, which features Mozart's music extensively.

Mozart's father, Herr Leopold, was second Kapellmeister at the palace of the archbishop. In 1747 he had married Anna Maria Pertl. They had seven children, of whom only two survived. One, Maria Anna (affectionately nicknamed Nannerl) was born in 1751, five years before Wolfgang Amadeus.

Herr Leopold was promoted to court composer a year before Wolfgang was born. Leopold was a solid musician, a good composer, a fine violinist, and the author of one of the earliest methods of violin instruction. He was a musician well able to cope with prodigies and give them both the background and the training they need to thrive.

Nannerl began studying the piano when her little brother was two. Leopold at once realized how inherently musical she was, became her teacher, and developed her within two years into a skilled performer. Then the father began to notice how the child Wolfgang was responding to music. Nannerl had proved herself to have a talent—true; but Wolfgang, Herr Leopold realized immediately, was something far rarer: a genius.

One of the characteristics of genius according to the Funk & Wagnalls dictionary is a "phenomenal capacity regarded as relatively independent of instruction or training." The child Mozart possessed a capacity for music that seemingly required little or no guidance. How could one fail to notice an infant of three when he clambers toward the piano keyboard and tries to reproduce the intervals and chords his sister has just played? Herr Leopold playfully began teaching Wolfgang the elements of piano playing when the child was four, only to discover that the boy learned with a facility to stagger the imagination. Little Mozart had to hear Leopold play a lesson just once in order to play it through perfectly as if he had practiced it for hours. Within a year or so of his first piano lesson, Wolfgang was not only able to play the piano well but was already inventing little minuets, which his father faithfully wrote down for him.

One day the child was found scratching notes on paper in an effort to write a concerto (this without having received a lesson in composition). At the age of six, without any instruction, he learned to play a small violin. He developed an uncommon gift for improvising on any given melody for hours at a stretch, never at a loss for new ideas. And what dedication and intensity the child brought to music! His father later revealed to him, "As a child and a boy you were too serious even to be childish; and when sitting at the piano, or doing anything in the shape of music, you would not stand a joke from anyone. Indeed, from the precocity of your talent, and the extremely thoughtful expression of your countenance, many people feared you would not live to grow up."

Europe would take notice of such a musical miracle. Of this Herr Leopold was thoroughly convinced. And so he decided to put both Wolfgang and Nannerl on exhibit in the great courts of Europe. First Munich, then Vienna were overwhelmed by Wolfgang's incredible gifts. The emperor of Austria called him "a little magician." Starting in 1763, Wolfgang performed in Frankfort (Germany), Paris, and London. In Paris, after an exhibition at the palace of Versailles, Mozart was described by Baron von Grimm, a German man of letters, as "so extraordinary a phenomenon that one finds it difficult to believe it unless one has seen him with one's own eyes and heard him with one's own ears." In London, Wolfgang came to the court of George III, known to us for his role in the American Revolution. There the Kapellmeister—Johann Christian Bach, son of Johann Sebastian—could contrive no musical test the child could not pass, or invent any musical feat the child could not perform.

In Paris, during this tour, Mozart emerged officially as a serious composer with the publication of four sonatas for violin and piano—his first works to get into print. He was eight years old at the time. He was still only eight when he wrote the first composition he designated as a symphony (K. 16). This happened in London. The work was really a three-movement sinfonia, rather than a symphony, calling for a limited ensemble of strings, two oboes, and two horns. The young Mozart soon wrote two more sinfonias for the same orchestral ensemble (K. 19 and K. 22). The boy conducted the premiere of both these works at public concerts at the Vauxhall Gardens in London, where some of his programs were devoted exclusively to his own works.

(This is probably as convenient a point as any to explain why a number preceded by the letter *K* is used with every Mozart composition. Although almost all the masters used opus numbers for identification, a practice still in existence, Mozart did not. For many years considerable confusion existed as to the chronological order of Mozart's works. Then, in 1862, a Viennese musicologist, Ludwig von Köchel, completed a catalogue of Mozart's compositions in the sequence they were written. Chaos was now resolved into order. By using the number in the Köchel catalogue—designated by the letter *K*—it was now possible to pinpoint when Mozart completed each of his works.)

Other musical tours followed. In Italy, in 1770, Mozart became the youngest musician ever given a membership in the renowned Accademia Philharmonica of Bologna; he also received there a commission to write an opera. He continued to perform the seemingly impossible as if it were just child's play. When required in Bologna to prepare an elaborate polyphonic setting of a given subject, he did it in half an hour, though even the most highly esteemed theoreticians would have required hours for so exacting an assignment. He wrote five new symphonies in Italy (K. 74, 79, 81, 84, and 95), each a giant step away from the sinfonia or overture structure toward a symphonic one.

Most incredible, perhaps, is what he did in Rome. Each year a complicated polyphonic work, Allegri's *Miserere,* was performed by the papal choir during Holy Week. Since performance of this composition was forbidden at any other place or time, the manuscript was always kept under lock and key, to be taken out only in time for another performance. Mozart heard just one performance of this giant work on the Wednesday of Holy Week, then returned to his hotel room and wrote it down from memory note for note, correcting one or two passages after hearing it a second time, during the repetition on Good Friday. For such flagrant disobedience of papal dictate, the child Mozart might have been excommunicated. But the pope was so amazed by this accomplishment that he not only forgave Mozart but rewarded him with the Cross of the Order of the Golden Spur.

Before the year ended, Mozart's commissioned opera, *Mitridate, Rè di Ponto,* was a triumph in Milan. And so young Mozart did not lack for recognition or rewards.

Back in Salzburg, however, it was quite another story. The young idol of musical Europe was no hero in his native city, nor did his phenomenal musical powers attract interest, let alone inspire adulation. A new archbishop had come to Salzburg: Hieronymus von Colloredo. His tastes in music were too plebian for him to comprehend Mozart's musical stature. Besides, the archbishop was contemptuous of Salzburgians and, in addition, was a miser. All this made him a most undesirable employer. He paid Mozart a mere pittance to work for him at court as composer and virtuoso and treated him in the high-handed dictatorial fashion he did all his humble employees. Rebellion seethed within Mozart—but for the time being he controlled his temper and did what was expected of him.

Temporary relief from his irritations and frustrations came through trips occasionally (but often grudgingly) allowed him by the archbishop. One such trip brought him to Mannheim, where he heard its great orchestra for the first time and was overwhelmed by the experience. In Mannheim Mozart also embarked on a love affair, with a dark-haired singer, Aloysia Weber. With her in mind he wrote a passionate aria with instrumental accompaniment ("Non so d'onde viene," K. 294). Then he was off for Paris, where he hoped to repeat the triumphs of his childhood, but he failed because the high society of Paris preferred the attractions of a child prodigy to the distinction of a grown-up genius.

Between trips, during the decade of the 1770s, Mozart had to suffer in Salzburg the mental cruelty of his tyrannical employer and even the abuse of his fellow musicians, who were jealous of his successes outside Salzburg and of his formidable musical abilities. Yet it would be a mistake to assume that Mozart's life during this time was altogether bleak. The sense of fun and love of good times that would later be so helpful in carrying him through many a dark hour now kept him from succumbing to despair. On Sundays he played quoits with his family and neighbors. Many an evening he went to the carnival hall to dance with the girls. He mingled well with friends, enjoying the exchange of jokes (for which he had a ready tongue, which was not above indulging occasionally in vulgar humor), playing cards, and participating in the Salzburgian pastime of aiming an air gun at targets. Though not particularly handsome, he attracted the interest of the female sex with his well-groomed appearance, his poise and sophistication, and his repertory of stories about his travel experiences.

Such delights as Mozart found in Salzburg to dull the edge of his resentment against the archbishop and against his own humble station at court were, however, incidental to his main drive: writing music. He wrote as never before, one work coming after another in a staggering abundance. Composing always came easily to him. The process of creation was a joy and not anguish. He produced symphonies, vocal and choral music, string quartets, piano compositions, and operas. Each work revealed some new facet to his ever-developing technique and ripening invention. It was during the decade of the 1770s that Mozart took wing as an orchestral composer, although his orchestral output up to 1771 had already included fourteen symphonies, minuets, two serenades, a cassation, and a country dance. Up to 1771 his genius revealed itself most forcefully in his operas, although none of his major operas were written up to that time.

But influenced by what he was learning from Haydn's music, Mozart began broadening his orchestral outlook by introducing highly original touches in 1772. The first symphony where we begin to confront something of Mozart's later gifts is the Symphony in F major, K. 130, in 1772. It was Mozart's eighteenth work in this form, but to Georges de Saint-Foix, a French authority on Mozart, it was really Mozart's first major symphony. What Mozart had acquired from Haydn in structure and style he had by now assimilated. The time was ripe for Mozart to think for himself, and in doing so he gave the symphonic form a new dimension, as well as new methods. Here, as in his later symphonies, adds Georges de Saint-Foix, ". . . it is Mozart alone who displays and bestows the acquired riches; *bizarrerie* and boldness in the minuets, tender delicacy in the andantes, gaiety or whirlwind force in the finales, strength and power in the design."

It is truly regrettable that some of the earlier Mozart symphonies are not better known (though they have been recorded and are sometimes performed). They are a storehouse of musical riches. There is nobility and elegance in the Symphony no. 25 in G minor, K. 183 (1773), together with a new-found freedom in trying the untried: for example, replacing the expected development sections of the first and last movements with a fantasia, a freely imaginative type of composition in which Mozart not only worked out his main themes but introduced new ones. The Symphony no. 29 in A major, K. 201 (1774) brings to the *galant* style a new grace and elegance in rococo writing. The Symphony no. 31 in D major, K. 297 (1778) (called *Paris* since it was commissioned by the director of Parisian concerts) requires the largest orchestra Mozart had ever used (two each of clarinets, flutes, oboes, bassoons, horns, and trumpets, together with strings and drums); in this symphony Mozart omits a third-movement minuet to proceed from the slow movement directly into the spacious finale, though in 1782 he added one (K. 409).

And with what daring did Mozart conceive the last symphony of this decade, the Symphony no. 34 in C major, K. 338 (1780)! Unusual procedures, concepts, interpolations are continually encountered to spring surprise and delight on the unsuspecting audience. In the first movement Mozart brings in a new somber passage for strings and wind before he progresses to the recapitulation section. The second movement enlists unusual instrumentation: strings and bassoons, with the bassoons doubling for the basses and the violas divided. To the renowned English musicologist Daniel Francis Tovey, this movement is "the richest slow movement Mozart had as yet produced, and he did not often surpass it in subtlety." Once again here, as in the *Paris* Symphony, Mozart felt the artistic necessity of omitting a minuet movement.

Besides his symphonies, Mozart's purely orchestral output during this decade (specifically, between 1776 and 1779) were two divertimenti and three serenades. Two of the serenades have particular interest. In the Serenade in D major, K. 239, entitled *Notturna,* two ensembles (one consisting of two violins, viola, and bass, the other of two violins, viola, cello, and drums) continually indulge in an enchanting dialogue. The Serenade in D major, K. 250 is called the *Haffner* (not to be confused with a later symphony also named *Haffner*). Sigmund Haffner was Salzburg's burgomaster. When Haffner's daughter was married in 1776, Mozart wrote his serenade as light entertainment for a joyous occasion; but in his hands it became a genuine work of art. To Saint-Foix this eight-movement composition represents "the climax, not to say the apotheosis of the period . . . designated as *galant.* . . . It is really in every sense of the word, a musical feast, in which Mozart gives reign to his fancy creating almost new forms."

ORCHESTRAL
MUSIC

It was probably in the field of the concerto (for one or more solo instruments and orchestra) that the history of orchestral music is most vitally affected by Mozart's genius during this decade of incredible achievements. Nobody had recognized the full artistic potential of the concerto until Mozart began in the 1770s to fashion it into what we may justifiably regard as the "modern" commodity.

Before beginning to assess Mozart's contribution to concerto literature it might be wise to describe the form as we today know it.

A concerto may be designated as a symphony for a solo instrument (or two or more instruments) and orchestra. It is a major work, usually three movements, in which the solo instrument is given a starring role with the orchestra serving primarily as an accompaniment (though this accompaniment is by no means of minor musical interest). Like the symphony, the concerto uses the sonata form in the first movement. The second movement is lyrical, sometimes in the two-part form, sometimes in three parts; sometimes it consists of a theme and variations. The closing movement, which is fast and lively, may be in the sonata form, or it may be in the form of theme and variations; most often, however, it is in the form of a rondo.

To understand the rondo form, it might help if you had in mind the image of a seven-layer cake in which different colored icings are separated by a layer of the cake. The layer of the cake in the rondo is the main melody, which recurs again and again. But a new melody (each represented by the different-colored icings in our layer cake) appears before each recurrence of the main melody. To use the letters of the alphabet as a convenience in designating the rondo form, with *A* representing the main melody, and subsequent letters standing for other melodies, the rondo form can be described as follows: "A-B-A-C-A," or "A-B-A-C-A-D-A," or "A-B-A-C-A-B-A."

One of the distinguishing features of a concerto is the use of a cadenza at or near the end of the first movement and sometimes other movements as well. The cadenza is a passage for solo intrument (or instruments) *without* accompaniment, in which the performer embellishes upon one or more of the thematic ideas of the movement with virtuosity. Originally performers improvised their own cadenzas during the actual performance, the composer having clearly designated in his score an exact place where the cadenza should appear. Mozart and Beethoven sometimes wrote their own cadenzas, and so did many later composers. But during the past century it has been the general practice for performers or other musicians to write cadenzas for the famous concertos to be used by these and other virtuosi.

We have already had occasion to speak of concertos for one or more solo instruments by Johann Sebastian Bach, and to suggest that other Baroque masters, such as Vivaldi and Handel, also wrote concertos. Joseph Haydn wrote almost fifty concertos for a great variety of solo instruments. In Haydn we find a permanent break with the concerto grosso concept held by the Baroque composers; structurally, the Haydn concertos suggest the modern concerto form even to the point of using the sonata form in the first movement. Nevertheless, Haydn's concertos are a negligible advance in the growth of this important medium. The reason for this is that Haydn wrote his concertos as display pieces for some of the better performers in his orchestra. Being no virtuoso himself such as were Mozart and Beethoven, Haydn did not think in terms of technique; he did not exploit the individuality of the instrument for which he was writing. He was far more concerned in writing entertaining music with which the performer held the spotlight and the orchestra was reduced to a subsidiary role, a discreet and not too obtrusive background for the soloist. Thus Haydn's concertos are slight. Though delightfully tuneful, they are music whose appeal is found on the surface and rarely penetrates the depths. Today, of Haydn's many concertos one is played most consistently. It is the Concerto no. 2 in D major for cello and orchestra, op. 101 (1783). The wealth of Haydnesque melody with which the composer flooded this composition has made it a staple in cello music; in fact it is one of the earliest cello concertos to have survived. Beautiful and aristocratic though it is, it nevertheless fails to fulfill completely the many technical, emotional, and aesthetic demands made by the "modern" concerto on both the solo instrument and the orchestra.

It took Mozart himself a long time to understand and meet these demands. He, too, produced concertos that were functional, written for special occasions or for specific performers. During the decade of the 1770s he fashioned several such *pièces d'occasion:* a concerto for bassoon (B-flat major, K. 191, 1774), commissioned by a baron, an amateur musician; one for flute and harp (C major, K. 299, 1778), a thoroughly delightful work to meet the needs of one of his pupils; two flute concertos (G major and D major, K. 313 and 314, 1778), at the request of an amateur Dutch flutist.

No instrumental form was closer to Mozart's heart than the concerto—especially the piano concerto, since he was a first-class virtuoso. We have already seen how as a child of five he tried to scratch out one of these   *45* pieces on paper. He completed his first concertos for the piano when he was nine. These, and the three that followed, were just transcriptions of sonatas by other composers. Not until the 1770s did he finally emerge with a piano concerto comprising his own materials (no. 5 in D major, K. 175, 1773). The year of 1776 saw the writing of two more piano concertos (and one for three pianos); one solo concerto came in 1777; a two-piano concerto in 1779–1780. It cannot be said that any of these are of the exalted caliber of Mozart's later piano concertos, but they do have historic importance. Virtuosity becomes an important element in concerto-writing for the first time; the orchestra is finally treated with the importance it deserves; the lovely thematic material is imaginatively worked out. These concertos of the 1770s bring into focus finally what a concerto really should be.

Mozart's greatest concertos in the 1770s were, however, not for the piano, but for the violin. He finished five of them in the single year of 1775. Two are such masterpieces that to this day they are treasured: the Concerto no. 4 in D major, K. 218, and the Concerto no. 5 in A major, K. 219. Here the *galant* style achieves its utmost in perfection; here the melodic material is pure gold; here the understanding of the role of the solo instrument and the orchestra and their interrelationship is fully understood; here the structures are of impressive dimensions.

In both concertos Mozart injected surprise. Usually a Mozart concerto opens with an orchestral preface in which the main themes are introduced. Then the solo instrument enters with a statement of the first theme, which it then embellishes. After some exchanges with the orchestra, the solo instrument presents the second subject. But in both the D major and the A major Violin Concertos the unexpected happens. When the violin is heard initially in the first movement it is not in any of the subjects previously stated by the orchestra but with an altogether new (and reflective) thought —a temporary digression from general practice. This tendency to bring in fresh, and invariably enchanting, new material recurs in the third movements of both concertos: in the D major, with a new dancelike tune after the two main themes have been developed; in the A major, with the inclusion of an eastern-style melody, never previously heard in the work, the reason why this concerto has come to be known as the *Turkish*. (At that time anything exotic or eastern was spoken of as Turkish.)

In this same decade Mozart completed an important composition, neither a symphony nor a concerto but a combination of both. It is the Sinfonia Concertante in E-flat major, for violin, viola, and orchestra, K. 364 (1779). The sinfonia concertante was a popular form in Baroque and Classical music, differing from the concerto in that the orchestra is used more

46

extensively and symphonically than it is in the concerto of Haydn and Mozart. The E-flat Sinfonia Concertante is one of Mozart's important works: profuse in its melodic riches (there are, for example, *two* sets of principal themes in the first movement); in the subtlety of the blending of the different shades of color characteristic of the violin and the viola; and in the noble tragedy unfolded by the two main themes of the second movement.

Neither Mozart's professional position at the archbishop's palace nor his relationship with his employer showed any sign of improvement. The archbishop continued to treat Mozart contemptuously, in spite of the fact that outside Salzburg accolades were being heaped upon him. One such came on January 29, 1781, in Munich where Mozart's new opera, *Idomeneo,* caused a furore of enthusiasm.

His success in Munich clarified for Mozart the truth that if he were to advance himself as a musician he would have to break his ties with both Salzburg and the archibishop. He did so in 1781, and this is how it came about. While still in Munich he received a summons from the archbishop to join him and his entourage in Vienna, the archbishop having gone to the Austrian capital to pay his homage to the new emperor, Empress Maria Theresa having died the year before. In Vienna Mozart and the archbishop exchanged bitter words because the employer expressed his disapproval of Mozart's giving benefit concerts. An even greater storm between them erupted when the archbishop ordered Mozart to return to Salzburg a few days earlier than Mozart had intended. When the archbishop hurled insults at Mozart and threatened to have his salary dropped at once, Mozart heatedly retorted that his written resignation would be submitted the following morning.

Thus the bonds that had enslaved Mozart to the archbishop and to Salzburg were at long last cut. Mozart found a place to live in Vienna— Vienna, which would be his residence for the rest of his life. There were some encouraging signs that Mozart would be getting full recognition in the Austrian capital. An opera that the emperor had commissioned (*Die Entführung aus dem Serail—The Abduction from the Seraglio*) enchanted the city when it was produced on July 16, 1782. Convinced that a well-paying post, probably at the court, would soon be forthcoming, Mozart embarked on matrimony. For a wife he chose Constanze, the sister of a girl he had once loved and who had rejected him, Aloysia Weber. Constanze and Mozart were married in St. Stephen's Cathedral on August 4, 1782. Since there was no money, the young couple had to spend their honeymoon in the modest little apartment they rented at what today is known as Wipplingerstrasse 25.

The job Mozart was expecting, however, did not come. Powerful Viennese musicians, in and out of court, envied his fabulous musical powers and realized that these represented a major threat to their own positions. They did what they could to obstruct Mozart's musical progress, and they succeeded. It was owing to the machinations of the court Kapellmeister Antonio Salieri that a new opera the emperor had commissioned from Mozart—*Le Nozze di Figaro* (*The Marriage of Figaro*)—quickly turned from success to failure after being produced in 1786. As for the emperor, however generous he was with praises, he was most stingy with money. He not only paid Mozart a pauper's fee for writing *The Marriage of Figaro* but also refused to find a post for him at court. Reduced to giving lessons, Mozart earned hardly enough to provide his family with life's bare necessities.

But when he sat down to write music, not frustrations, not despair, not bitterness could arrest the outpouring of masterworks. Mozart well knew that creatively his power and originality were growing in great leaps; that the music flowing so abundantly from his pen (and so easily) could not be matched by any composer, anywhere. This was balm for his wounds. Solace too (though very little money) came from the city of Prague, where *The Marriage of Figaro* was received with great enthusiasm. Prague commissioned Mozart to write a new opera for that city, *Don Giovanni,* whose success in 1787 was also one of the first magnitude.

It was after Mozart's triumphs in Prague that the emperor finally called upon him to serve at court as chamber musician and composer. But the salary was so miserly that Mozart still could not make ends meet and was reduced to the humiliation of hounding his friends continually for loans, promising to repay them "with full interest."

In such distressing circumstances Mozart gave the world his greatest orchestral music. In the year of 1784 he completed six new piano concertos, each a giant creation, and two (no. 14 in E-flat major, K. 449, and no. 17 in G major, K. 453) filled with a melancholy and a conflict we do not find in his earlier concertos. Greater still is the passionate turbulence and the intensity of emotion in what are perhaps Mozart's four greatest piano concertos of all, written between 1784 and 1788: no. 20 in D minor, K. 466; no. 21 in C major, K. 467; no. 24 in C minor, K. 491; and no. 26 in D major, K. 537. What drama stirs in the opening orchestral introduction of the D minor Concerto, before the piano enters with a gentle serenity that temporarily at least resolves conflict into peace! How exalted is the slow movement of the C major Concerto, almost as if the heavens have suddenly opened to reveal vistas of sublimity never before experienced by man! What a high sense of drama prevails in the C minor and D major Concertos, the latter identified as the *Coronation,* having been played by Mozart at the coronation ceremonies of Emperor Leopold II at Frankfort, Germany, in 1790! And how adventurous Mozart always is in handling his materials, experimenting with new techniques, and ever allowing himself the luxury of digressing into new unexpected thoughts, even though the basic structure makes no provision for them!

The originality, the variety of means and ideas, the consummate technique, the sublimity of emotion and thought now enter into his symphonic writing as well: in the Symphony no. 35 in D major, K. 385 (1782), no. 36 in C major, K. 425 (1783), and no. 38 in D major, K. 504 (1786). The first is named *Haffner,* having been a contribution to the celebration of the ennoblement of the son of the Salzburg official Haffner; the second is called *Linz,* intended for a concert in that Austrian city; and the third, prepared for an all-Mozart concert in the Bohemian capital, is entitled *Prague.*

But great as these symphonies are—and not even Haydn had at that time written anything to equal them—they were surpassed by three more, the last Mozart was destined to write. They are the crown atop his regal symphonic output, the apotheosis of his symphonic writing, the greatest such works to come until those by Beethoven. That three such masterworks should have been completed in just two months, between June 26 and August 10 of 1788, surely remains a phenomenon in orchestral history, a phenomenon of which only Mozart was capable.

The span of Mozart's expressivity is pointed up by the way in which each of these three symphonies differs from the others. Symphony no. 39 in E-flat major, K. 543, is light and gay in its fast movements, and particularly so in the minuet and finale. But there is a beatific beauty to its slow movement, just as there is in the way the Symphony no. 40 in G minor, K. 550, opens. That first theme is one of Mozart's most heavenly thoughts, whose radiance never loses its glow no matter how often we listen to it. But the G minor Symphony, as a whole, is at turns more melancholy and more agitated than the E-flat major. The melody of the second movement is lightly touched by a gentle sadness, while the finale, once it unfolds, is nervously alive.

In Symphony no. 41 in C major, K. 551, we find a continuous alternation between strength and tenderness. This becomes obvious in the very opening, where the orchestra sounds forth forcefully in the first two measures to receive a tender reply from the violins in the next two. But *49* strength overpowers tenderness as this movement progresses, particularly in one of the most expansive development sections Mozart ever conceived (stretching for one hundred measures); and strength takes over completely in the finale, where much of the excitement and stress appear in fugato (fugue-style) passages, which Mozart uses for climactic effects. This symphony is popularly known as the *Jupiter,* a name bestowed upon it not by Mozart but by someone, perhaps his publisher, who either regarded it as of Olympian proportions, or as music worthy of the ruling god of mythology.

Mozart's uncommon capacity to detach himself from whatever conditions surrounded him personally when he wrote music is something that characterizes his last years again and again. Things for Mozart the man were going from bad to worse. His poverty, the pressure of debts, the constant illness of his wife brought on periods of melancholia that sometimes collapsed into despair. Occasionally his sense of fun and his passion for some of the extramusical delights of his life helped him to overcome, at least temporarily, his dark moods—but far less often than heretofore. But whether he was in good spirits or depressed, his music was a thing apart from his personal life. We know that he wrote some of his most tragic music when he was in a happy state. And, by the same token, he could write buoyant, joyful, light-hearted music when his spirits were at their lowest ebb. The E-flat major Symphony, mentioned above, gives no hint of the inner turmoil tormenting the composer when he wrote it. Nor do some of the other orchestral pieces from his last years suggest how crushed he was by the weight of personal problems.

In 1787 he conceived two of his most infectious little works for orchestra. One was a satirical item, *Ein musikalischer Spass* (*A Musical Joke*), K. 522, where clashing discords and disjointed themes were his way of poking fun at inept composers trying to write ambitious orchestral compositions. Another of his lighter orchestral pieces of 1787 is the lovable *Eine kleine Nachtmusik* (*A Little Night Music*), K. 525. This four-movement serenade makes no pretense at being anything but what Mozart had intended: a pleasant musical entertainment, slight in structure, overflowing with enchanting little melodies that receive only the most elementary kind of development or variation.

Then in the last three years of his life, though in the depths of despondency, Mozart wrote numerous lively country and German dances with the joyfulness of a man for whom the world is a perpetual dance. These were also the years when he created two of the greatest comedy operas ever written: *Così fan tutte* and *Die Zauberflöte* (*The Magic Flute*).

Though his body was wasting away in 1791 with undernourishment, overexhaustion, and possibly nephritis, there was no weakening of his will to create, nor a decline in the loftiness of his inspiration. *The Magic Flute* came that year, and so did one of his greatest string quintets, the remarkable Piano Concerto no. 27 in B-flat major, K. 595, the sublime *Ave Verum,* and the Requiem, both of the last two for chorus and orchestra.

Mozart knew he did not have long to live when he worked on his Requiem. In spite of weakness and pain, he labored with passion, trying to finish a song of death that (though it had been commissioned by a count) Mozart was really writing for himself. He did not live to finish it; that job had to be done by one of his pupils, following Mozart's explicit instructions. The day before he died, Mozart asked a few of his friends to join him in singing one portion of the Requiem, almost as if he wanted to conduct his own memorial service. That night he bade his family farewell. A few hours later—just one hour after midnight of December 5, 1791—he died.

There were few mourners at St. Stephen's Cathedral at his funeral services, and even less to follow Mozart's body to its final resting place. His wife was too ill to attend either the church or the burial service. There had been just enough money to pay for a third-class funeral, but none for the purchase of a burial plot. Mozart's body had to be consigned to a pauper's grave with no monument or cross to identify it. When, at long last, a suitable monument for Mozart was placed in St. Mark's graveyard in 1859, a guess had to be made as to the place were Mozart's remains were interred.

4

"A Titan Wrestling with the Gods"

Ludwig van Beethoven

On April 2, 1800, a concert took place in Vienna that marked a new epoch for orchestral music. Here is how the event was announced in a newspaper:

Today . . . Herr Ludwig van Beethoven will have the honor of giving a grand concert for his own benefit in the Royal Imperial Court Theater beside the Burg. . . . The pieces which will be performed are . . . a grand concerto for the piano, played and composed by Herr Ludwig van Beethoven [and] a new grand symphony with complete orchestra composed by Herr Ludwig van Beethoven.

The "new grand symphony" was Beethoven's first. Thus a new century had arrived hand in hand with Beethoven's first symphonic effort. Little could the audience attending that concert have realized that they were present at the making of musical history. Only nine years after Mozart's death, a successor had arisen who was destined to give to the symphony both structural emancipation and artistic fulfillment of a kind to bring a true revolution.

That revolution erupts not only in Beethoven's first symphony, but even in the opening measures (almost as if Beethoven was impatient in proclaiming the birth of a new symphonic era). This symphony, though in the key of C major, does not open with a chord in that tonality, as was then the practice. It begins in the seemingly alien key of F major and passes on to the key of G major before finally settling down comfortably to C major. What Beethoven was trying to do was to create a tension that would make the appearance of his first sprightly theme much more effective. But in 1800 who had ever heard of such an outlandish harmonic practice?

There were other things about that first symphony that sounded unusual to the ears of 1800. Beethoven used the wind instruments and the tympani in a way to create deeper and richer orchestral sonorities and to give these instruments new independence, so much so that to one critic the orchestra sounded like a "brass band." And instead of the lightness of foot characterizing the minuets of Haydn and Mozart in their symphonies, there is in Beethoven's First a heavier tread—strength replacing grace. This was Beethoven's first warning that he was beginning to arrive at a totally new concept of what a symphonic third movement should sound like.

The First symphony proved a puzzle to the citics, who called Beethoven an "ignoramus" and a "poorly tutored student"; they described the music as "the confused explosions of the presumptuous effrontery of a young man." How could those critics have guessed that this was a new age speaking? In the aftermath of the French Revolution, this was an age beginning to defy tradition and to question existing social and political values.

One has merely to place the personalities of Mozart and Beethoven side by side and compare them to get a vivid picture of the great changeover in the nineteenth century. Mozart was always well groomed, in the powdered wig and the sartorial finery favored by the eighteenth century. He was a man of social refinements. Beethoven, on the other hand, was sloppy in dress; no powdered wig hid his short, unkempt hair; his manners were uncouth; his behavior tactless, at times bumptious. Mozart showed respect and subservience to royalty and nobility when seeking and getting favors; and when he rebelled against the treatment given him by his employer in Salzburg he fumed inwardly for a long time without betraying any outward signs of revolt. Beethoven, even to his benefactors, was outspoken to the point of tactlessness. Favors given him by nobility (and they were numerous and generous) were accepted not

53

with servile, knee-bending gratitude but with the pride of one who felt that all this was his due. When offended, Beethoven did not hesitate to speak his mind. Once, while performing at Prince Lichnowsky's palace, he was disturbed by the conversation of several noblemen. He slammed down the lid of the piano and shouted, "I shall not perform before such swine." At another time, when walking with the great poet Goethe, Beethoven refused to step aside to permit two noblemen to pass. "It is *they* who should make way for *us,"* he bellowed. He believed it implicitly when he exclaimed, "I, too, am king." But what he meant was that he was "king" of the soul and the spirit, not one who had the power to subjugate others. For Beethoven was the complete democrat, who greatly admired Britain's parliamentary system, who had read and absorbed the philosophy of Jean-Jacques Rousseau (which preached the right of people to be free), and who passionately believed in the equality of all men.

Sensitive and delicate in his physical makeup, Mozart was representative of a genteel era and society. Beethoven was a child of an age disturbed by revolution, fears of revolution, skepticism, rebellion, and the stirrings of discontent among the common people. Short and stocky, he had a leonine head with broad nostrils, piercing eyes with a wild look, a pockmarked face, and a square jaw that spoke of ungovernable strength and iron will. Though Mozart knew the full value of his genius, he could never express himself as openly as Beethoven did when he said, "With whom need I be afraid of measuring my strength?" or "With men who do not believe in me . . . I cannot and will not associate." Words such as these—filled with self-pride that almost borders on arrogance—spring from the lips of one who was unafraid of asserting himself both as a human being and as an artist and who was completely conscious of his destiny. It is the new age that echoes and reechoes in Beethoven's verbal outbursts.

"I *must* write," he said, "for what weighs on my heart I *must* express." He wrote. What weighed on his heart he expressed. And in doing so he changed the destiny of music.

Beethoven was born in the German city of Bonn, today the capital of West Germany, on December 16, 1770. His father was a singer in the Electoral Chapel Choir; his mother was a cook.

The father was a drunkard who was determined to make his child, Ludwig, into a profitable musical entertainer as a prodigy, just as the child Mozart had been. He subjected Ludwig to the strictest discipline, even to corporal punishment, to keep him at the piano hour after hour.

Many a night the father came home drunk and dragged the child from his sleep to practice on the piano. The child loved music and revealed exceptional ability. But neither in his appearance nor in his ability to perform wonders in music was he Mozart's equal. Father Beethoven soon had to reconcile himself to the fact that his dreams of fame and wealth, acquired through a prodigy son, would never be realized.

When Beethoven was around eleven he found a highly sympathetic teacher in Christian Gottlob Neefe. The boy now began to reveal more forcefully what he was capable of doing. He wrote three piano sonatas, which were published. When he was thirteen he filled the job of piano accompanist at the rehearsals of the court theater orchestra. And a year after that he became an assistant organist at the court of the elector of Cologne.

Through the bounty of this elector, Beethoven was able to visit Vienna in 1787. There he played the piano for Mozart, his improvisations inspiring the master to say, "This young man will leave his mark on the world." This visit to Vienna was cut short by the news that the one person who meant most to Beethoven, his mother, was dying. He rushed back to Bonn in time to be with her in her last hours.

His father, a chronic drunkard, was dismissed from his job at the Electoral Chapel. Ludwig, aged sixteen, was obliged to support his father and two younger brothers. He took on whatever musical job he could find: he played the viola in the theater orchestra; he gave piano lessons to children; he performed at court. Busy though he was, he did not neglect composition, producing some piano and choral music that greatly impressed some of Bonn's most influential families. Beethoven even attracted the notice of the great Haydn, who, passing through Bonn to London in 1790, heard a performance of a Beethoven cantata. He pronounced its composer "a man of great talent," adding, to Beethoven, "You must come to Vienna and study with me."

Beethoven got the opportunity to return to Vienna in November of 1792. This time he stayed there or in its suburbs for good. For a while he studied with Haydn, but neither one was impressed with the other; the old world continually clashed with the new. Beethoven then tried studying with other teachers. They, too, failed to appreciate what Beethoven was striving for. For them, too, Beethoven had little respect, or they for him. "He has never learned anything and he can do nothing in decent style," one of these teachers said.

If he failed to impress his teachers, he did not lack for appreciation among the powerful highborn—though more for his ability at piano playing and improvisation than for his compositions. Prince Lichnowsky, Prince Lobkowitz, and Baron van Swieten had him perform at their palaces. With his awkward behavior, crude manners, uncontrollable temper, and unattractive appearance—and with his undisciplined stormings at the piano—Beethoven was strangely out of place in those glittering, gilded surroundings. Yet, strange to say, the nobility tolerated his outlandish appearance, behavior, and music-making. Some deep instinct seemed to make them sense that Beethoven was someone special.

Beethoven gave his first public concerts in Vienna in March of 1795, when he made two appearances, at one of which (on March 29) he introduced his Piano Concerto no. 2 in B-flat major, op. 19 (1795). Actually this was Beethoven's first piano concerto, but it is designated as "second" because it was published after the Piano Concerto no. 1 in C major, op. 15 (1797). Though in both concertos the young giant is stirring restlessly—with faint rumblings of rebellion discernible from time to time—Beethoven is here still satisfied to write concertos in the structure and manner of Mozart, whom he intensely admired. In fact, there is still a good deal of Mozart even in Beethoven's Piano Concerto no. 3 in C minor, op. 37 (1800); but there is also much of Beethoven, too, in the way he increases the importance of the orchestra and uses modulations and progressions freely, and in the power and imagination of his thematic developments and variations.

By the time he came forward with his first symphony, in 1800, Beethoven had written a considerable amount of music: for piano (including ten sonatas); for various chamber music groups (including his first six string quartets); for voice (including the song "Adelaide" and the scena and aria "Ah, perfido!"—the latter for voice and orchestra). For orchestra he produced German dances, minuets, and his first two piano concertos. Many of his works were published, apparently successfully, since Beethoven found publishers at his beck and call.

By 1802, Beethoven had freed himself from the influence of Mozart and from the other ties that had bound him to the older Classical era. The loosening of those ties becomes evident in the Symphony no. 2 in D major, op. 36 (1802) in which the suave *galant* style of Mozart is replaced by a fiery spirit, a dynamic energy, and stormy moods. One of the innovations in this symphony is the replacement of the minuet by a scherzo as the third movement. Like the minuet, the scherzo is in three-part form—but it is faster in tempo and more vigorous in style, in keeping with Beethoven's temperament.

The years of apprenticeship were over. "From today I mean to take a new road," Beethoven said at the time. A period of wondrous creativity was about to begin. But across that period of fruitful musical achievements lay the immense shadow of a tragedy that had a powerful impact on the kind of music Beethoven was now to write. As early as 1800 Beethoven had begun to suspect that he was becoming deaf. By 1802 he despaired of a cure. "What a sad life I am now compelled to lead," he wrote to a friend. "I must avoid all that is near and dear to me." In Heiligenstadt, a suburb of Vienna, he put down on paper a testament in which he gave free rein to his agonized despair and in which he announced his withdrawal into solitude and loneliness. "For me there can be no recreation in the society of my good fellow creatures," he wrote, "no refined conversations, no interchange of thought. . . . I am compelled to live as an exile."

But Beethoven would not succumb to defeat. "Plutarch taught me resignation," he wrote. "I shall seize fate by the throat; it shall certainly never overcome me!" In the crucible of his terrible suffering he shaped his destiny—not as a man but as a composer who found within himself new powers of creativity. In his self-imposed solitude he acquired that full independence he had so long been seeking in his music. He became music's emancipator, the one who could make music express what it had never done before. Within larger dimensions and with larger orchestral forces than those previously used by Haydn and Mozart he produced a new musical language and a personal way of using it. He was interested in poetic ideas and human ideals, not in beautiful sounds. The storms that rage in his fast movements seem to reflect his rebellion against tyranny, injustice, the inhumanity of man to man. The sublimity of his slow movements appear to conjure up for us a new world where all men are free, and are brothers. Thus Beethoven endowed music with new extramusical implications. Each of his major orchestral works is a drama in tone, a drama without text or program, but a drama nevertheless, and one in which we become participants.

In his orchestral music, Beethoven's mighty ideas and ideals sound loud and clear for the first time in the Symphony no. 3 in E-flat major, op. 55 (1804), the *Eroica*. According to his friends and early biographers Anton Schindler and Ferdinand Ries, Beethoven had originally intended it for Napoleon, when Napoleon appeared as a champion of human rights and the common man. But when Napoleon became emperor, Beethoven angrily scratched out Napoleon's name from the title page and substituted the word *Eroica*, dedicating his symphony then "to the memory of a great man." The "great man" Beethoven had in mind was one who fought the battle for high ideals. The two staccato chords that open the symphony are hammer blows striking defiantly at an old tyrannical social and political order (and at the older order in symphonic writing as well). Then comes an elementary theme (Beethoven would henceforth often use elementary and not particularly tuneful themes—sometimes even fragments—rather than fully developed melodies in his fast movements). It becomes the main source of a Gargantuan exposition, development, and coda. The development extends for 250 measures; the coda, for 140. As this basic theme grows, changes, expands, and builds up a harrowing tension through discords, displaced accents, unorthodox modulations, and powerful sonorities, we are truly witnessing what Richard Wagner described as a "Titan wrestling with the gods."

Then comes one of the noblest funeral marches ever written (the first time a funeral march entered a symphony). The music honors the hero who has fallen in the struggle for his ideals. The music, therefore, has grandeur rather than pathos—that is, until the very end, when, in the last repetition of the opening march music, the voice breaks with grief.

The third-movement scherzo brings us temporary relief from tensions and overcharged emotions, but the finale reverts to the passionate and turbulent spirit of the first movement, ending on a note of triumph. For in the end, justice and freedom must prevail—of this Beethoven was confident. The main theme of this finale (first heard in plucked strings, and then transformed through variations) is one that must have been precious to Beethoven, since he used it in several other compositions.

The *Eroica* was first heard publicly in Vienna on April 7, 1805. Being so radically different in sound and form from any symphony ever written, it invited severe criticism and misunderstanding. One critic called it "a tremendously expanded, daring and wild fantasia"; another said that it "loses itself in lawlessness" and that "the principle of unity is almost wholly lost sight of"; a third remarked that the "inordinate length of this longest and perhaps most difficult of all symphonies wearies even the cognoscenti and is unendurable to the music lover." Beethoven brushed off these and similar opinions as if they were just so much dust on his sleeve. He knew with finality he had found himself creatively in the *Eroica*. This was the kind of music to which he would now devote himself, music glorifying the human spirit.

And so, between 1806 and 1808, driven by the demons within him, he added to his orchestral output three more symphonies, his fourth piano concerto, his only violin concerto, the *Leonore* Overture no. 3

(the third version of what was originally the overture to his opera *Fidelio*), and the *Coriolan* Overture. And with them we enter upon a new world of musical experiences.

Each Beethoven symphony has a personality of its own. It would be difficult to imagine a work so different in content and purpose from the *Eroica* than the symphony that followed it: no. 4 in B-flat major, op. 60 (1806). Robert Schumann once described it as a "slender Greek maiden between two Norse giants," referring to the *Eroica* and Fifth symphonies. The Fourth Symphony is surely slender and graceful—but it is also more than that. Two sections rank among Beethoven's greatest revelations. The first is the opening adagio of the first movement, which establishes and builds up a feeling of suspense with a subject for strings that descends over a background of a sustained B-flat in the winds. The other section is the second movement, as unforgettable an abstraction of beauty as we can encounter anywhere in the works of this period. "Such must be the song of the Archangel Michael as he contemplates the world's uprising to the threshold of the empyrean," Berlioz said of this music.

The Symphony no. 5 in C minor, op. 67 (1807) may very well be the most famous symphony ever written, and the opening theme of its first movement (which appears without any introduction) the most celebrated symphonic theme ever conceived. Whoever said that the highest art of all is that of being simple would have found indisputable evidence in this theme, the most elementary ever used as a major subject for a symphony: three eighth notes followed by a half note, G-G-G followed by E-flat. That is all. Could anything be more basic? Is it at all possible to reduce further a musical thought to essentials? Yet this four-note subject is the germinal idea out of which grows one of the mightiest dramas in orchestral music. "Thus knocks Fate at the door," Beethoven was reputed to have told his friend Anton Schindler in explaining the meaning of those four notes. Once this musical declaration is made, it creates a momentum all its own that has the force of a cyclone. Briefly, the storm is arrested with the soft breeze of a lyrical passage. But the tempest is not altogether abated: actually we are just in the eye of the hurricane. Notice, for example, how the four-note theme throbs in the cellos and double basses as a background to the lyrical second theme. Then the storm gathers its strength and rushes toward the coda, where it reaches the peak of its fury.

The second movement is the calm after the storm: a series of variations on two majestic themes. The third movement establishes a feeling 59 of mystery and awe as an ominous subject is heard in the lowest strings, to which the violins reply. Then the horns come forth with a triumphant subject that once again consists of just four notes. The tympani beat out a four-note figure (again four notes!) as background to the long sustained C in the violins. The throbbing in the tympani continues during the extended crescendo, at the peak of which emerges the triumphant first theme of the finale in full orchestra. Apparently once again there was no doubt in Beethoven's mind that the struggle described in the first movement (be it with fate or some other inexorable force) must end in victory.

The poetic emotion governing the Symphony no. 6 in F major, op. 68 (1808), the *Pastoral,* is Beethoven's love of nature. This is a lovable and melodious hymn to the beauties of woods, brooks, birds, and even a summer storm. The programmatic title to each of the five movements reveals what the music is describing: the buoyant and exuberant "Awakening of Joyful Feelings upon Arriving in the Country"; "The Brook," in which we hear the chirps and calls of cuckoos, nightingales, and quails; "The Village Festival," jolly music where, at one point, Beethoven pokes fun at the bungling performance of a village band; "The Storm" and "The Shepherd's Hymn," where nature, after having been bathed by the lashing rains, glows more beautiful than ever, and a song of thanksgiving is sounded that the storm has finally ended.

The Symphony no. 7 in A major, op. 92, belongs with Beethoven's epics, and the Symphony no. 8 in F major, op. 93, with his lyric poems. Both were written in 1812. The Seventh is in a large design. It opens with an extended slow introduction, none of whose material is later used in the rest of the movement. What characterizes this movement after the introduction, and two other movements as well, is the way in which a rhythmic figure is built up powerfully (particularly in the last two movements, where gigantic rhythmic forces are released). It is because of its rhythmic vigor and vitality that this symphony was dubbed by Wagner as "the apotheosis of the dance." But there is very little in the music to suggest dances. Liszt was far more accurate in describing the work as "the apotheosis of rhythm." The second movement is a graceful allegretto whose main melody passes from cellos and basses to the second violins until a fugato passage leads into the only vigorous part of the movement.

Wagner said of the Eighth Symphony that it mingles "Herculean vigor with the games and caprices of a child." The games and caprices predominate over Herculean vigor. There is a good deal of joviality throughout the symphony. In the second movement Beethoven abandons the lyricism of a slow movement for a scherzando in which he is suspected of making fun of his friend Maelzel, who had invented the metronome. Brightness of face and levity of spirit continue into the third movement, where Beethoven reverts to the old classic practice of using a minuet rather than a scherzo. The finale is an outburst of exuberant feelings.

But the levities of the Eighth Symphony were merely a breathing spell for Beethoven before he plunged into the writing of one of the mightiest and noblest symphonies ever conceived: the Symphony no. 9 in D minor, op. 125 (1823). For years Beethoven had aspired to provide a musical setting to one of his favorite poems, Schiller's "Ode to Joy," which speaks for the brotherhood of man. Not until he was drawing toward the dusk of his life did Beethoven feel himself qualified to produce music worthy of Schiller's high-minded poetry. He made the poem the culminating point of what proved to be his last and greatest symphony, to become a climax of monumental grandeur to Beethoven's last will and testament in symphonic music.

There is no program for the first three movements of the Ninth Symphony. Nevertheless it is not too difficult to find in the first movement (as Wagner did) a Titanic struggle of the soul "against the oppression of that inimical power which places itself between us and the joys of the earth." Only the hint of a theme is suggested as the first movement opens, whispered by the violins, completed by violas and basses. This theme swells into an exultant proclamation. Later on in the movement there transpires the battle of the soul as fragments of other themes, together with fully developed melodies, provide a panorama of human attitudes from pride to defiance, from defeat to resignation.

The accepted procedure of placing a slow movement after the first, and a scherzo movement after the second, is here reversed, and with good reason. The other-worldly inspiration of the third slow movement could be followed only by the torrent of the finale's opening and the ensuing "Ode to Joy." The second-movement scherzo was interpreted by Wagner as a search for life's joys, while the exaltation of the third represented to him the peace and serenity that follow resignation and a spiritual awakening. The sublimity of the third movement is then shattered by the crashing opening discords of the finale. The cellos and basses give stern warning that this confusion must end, but once again disruptive forces find release. At long last chaos is resolved into order. The time has come to sing in praise of joy, of man's brotherhood. In search for a melody worthy of Schiller's poem, Beethoven brings back one by one *61* main themes from each of the preceding three movements, only to deal each a decisive rejection from the low strings. Suddenly a new melody is heard in cellos and basses; the violas join; the violins take over. Here, indeed, is music worthy of an ode to joy. Human voices (a quartet of solo voices supplemented by chorus) now join the orchestra in this paean. This is the heart of the finale. This is the climactic point toward which the earlier three movements had been reaching. Man becomes ennobled through love and tolerance.

The world premiere of the Ninth Symphony was possibly one of the most poignant concerts ever to take place. The place, of course, was Vienna, the date, May 7, 1824. Beethoven was sitting with the orchestra players, near the conductor, but with his back to the audience. When the symphony ended, the audience erupted into an uproar of approbation. Poor Beethoven, totally deaf, did not hear what was happening. One of the singers had to conduct him to the edge of the stage to acknowledge the tumultuous ovation. When the audience realized that Beethoven could not hear its vocal acclaim, it was shocked and electrified. "A volcanic explosion of sympathy and admiration followed," recalled one of the singers at this concert, "which was repeated again and again, and seemed as if it would never end."

Poetic or dramatic ideas were Beethoven's prime interest even when he wrote orchestral compositions other than symphonies. Between the conception of the *Eroica* and the *Pastoral* symphonies, Beethoven produced three concertos that are in a class with his greatest symphonies: the Piano Concerto no. 4 in G major, op. 58 (1806); the Violin Concerto in D major, op. 61 (1806); and the Piano Concerto no. 5 in E-flat major, op. 73 (1809), the *Emperor*.

Only six years separate the third and fourth piano concertos—but what a vast gap lies between them! The Third Piano Concerto is still a child clinging to the apron strings of Classicism. The Fourth Piano Concerto is of the nineteenth century, the voice of a musical age soon to be transformed by Romanticism. No longer is the piano the hero of all the proceedings, as it had been in the Third Concerto. It must now share the stage center with the orchestra, which is used with a power and an importance as if Beethoven were writing a symphony.

In the Fourth Piano Concerto, Beethoven the emancipator is not slow in breaking with tradition. The very opening is revolutionary. The piano solo states the principal subject of the first movement before the expected orchestral introduction. Only then does the orchestra adopt the theme, to develop it dramatically. There are two more major themes after that, elaborated upon along the monumental lines we find drawn in Beethoven's symphonies. The second movement is one of the most elevated discourses in concerto literature: actually a dialogue between solo instrument and orchestra. The orchestra speaks defiantly; the piano replies in soft tones of resignation. The give and take between the comparatively stormy orchestra and the meditative piano continues until, midway in the movement, the piano is heard in an exultant monologue. In the finale, a rondo, excitement is generated by the electrifying presentation of the first theme by the strings, beginning pianissimo and growing in dynamics to a fortissimo of dynamic arpeggios.

Nobody really knows for sure why Beethoven's Fifth Piano Concerto is called the *Emperor*. One story has it that when this concerto was first heard in Vienna, an enthusiastic French army officer exclaimed from his seat in the audience: "This is an emperor among concertos!" Others maintain that "Emperor" was a descriptive noun that an unidentified music publisher used on the title page to emphasize the majesty of the music. Whatever the reason, the word *emperor* well serves the composition, whose grandeur, epic stature, and heroic style have won it a crown that it wears with dignity.

The words *grandeur, majesty, epical stature, heroic style* also describe Beethoven's only concerto for the violin. Surely this work belongs with the half dozen greatest violin concertos ever written, and there is more than one reputable music historian who would place it at the very top of this repertory. Here we once again find those qualities that place Beethoven's greatest piano concertos in a class by themselves: an expansive structure; grandiose melodic materials; limitless imagination in working out those melodies as they shift from solo instrument to orchestra and back; the way the solo instrument provides decoration to the main themes when they are stated by the orchestra.

While producing symphonies and concertos the like of which the music world had not experienced, Beethoven also worked with his incomparable inspiration with the shorter structure of the overture. An overture is primarily an orchestral introduction to an opera, play, or oratorio. Beethoven wrote only a single opera, *Fidelio* (1805), for which, at different times, he wrote no less than four different overtures. The most celebrated is the *Leonore* Overture no. 3 (the title of the opera's libretto had originally been *Leonore*), conceived for a revival of his opera in Vienna in 1806. It is a giant among overtures. In essence, it is a tonal summation of the high points of the opera's plot, containing quotations from some of the opera's music. (Mozart had been the first composer to use quotations from an opera in an overture, in *Don Giovanni*.) In trying to project the varied moods and emotions of the text before the curtain rises—the anguish, gloom, struggles, and final victory of the two principals, Florestan and Leonore—Beethoven produced a self-contained music drama within the overture form.

We can say as much for two other monumental Beethoven overtures, those to *Coriolan* and *Egmont*. The struggle for liberty that is the underlying theme of *Fidelio* and the *Leonore* Overture no. 3 is also the poetic idea in the *Egmont* Overture, op. 84 (1809–1810). *Egmont* is a drama by Goethe for which Beethoven wrote incidental music (nine numbers besides the overture). The Count of Egmont is a hero struggling for the liberation of the Netherlands from Spanish domination. He is executed, the victim of an infamous conspiracy. His heroism, strength, and nobility are expressed in the strongly accented chords with which the overture opens. We then hear music suggesting the ominous atmosphere that precedes rebellion. The overture ends exultantly with a hymn to freedom.

Coriolan was a play by Heinrich Joseph von Collin produced in Vienna in 1802, for a later performance of which Beethoven was asked to write an overture. The subject is the same as that of Shakespeare's famous tragedy, *Coriolanus*. In the music of *Coriolan* Overture, op. 62 (1807), Beethoven translates the action of the play with infallible dramatic instinct. The Roman people revolt against their tyrannical consul Coriolanus and bring about his banishment. In revenge, Coriolanus heads an army in order to attack Rome, but he is dissuaded from doing so by the pleas of his mother and wife. In the end, in Collin's play, he is driven to suicide. The dramatic opening of the overture speaks of Coriolanus's pride. The virile first theme is a portrait of Coriolanus in action, while the second theme is thought to represent the gentle pleas of his wife. The powerful unison chords ending the overture describe Coriolanus's death.

As the years passed, Beethoven grew increasingly careless about his own appearance and that of the apartments he occupied in or near Vienna. He became more and more ill-tempered, scornful, combustible, inconsiderate. A most trivial offense, even a most innocent remark by a close friend, could drive him into fury. A minor episode led him to break with lifelong friends, at least for a time.

Yet, however much he abused them, his friends tolerated his tantrums and clung to him because, with amazing insight, they realized that the creative struggles raging within him put Beethoven in a perpetual state of torment. After each misunderstanding, his friends returned to him with renewed warmth and understanding—the rich and powerful as well as the more humble. Even the Archduke Rudolph was sympathetic to Beethoven's mercurial moods, as well as to his republican views. Together with Prince Lobkowitz and Prince Kinsky, the Archduke Rudolph raised in 1809 a fund providing Beethoven with an annual income, in order to prevent him taking a position elsewhere.

Beethoven, then, did not lack for good friends. What he missed sorely were a woman's love and marriage. He loved many women through the years, but invariably they were out of his reach because they were too young, or of too high a social position. When the realization finally dawned upon him that he would never know the happiness a sympathetic, understanding, and loving wife could bring him, he wrote a passionate three-part love letter on July 6 and 7 of 1812, in Teplitz, Bohemia, which he later concealed in a hidden drawer in his desk, to be discovered only after his death. This letter was a strange emotional outburst, but stranger still is the fact that Beethoven did not identify the woman to whom he was addressing such overpowering feelings. For whom was this communication—known as the letter "to the immortal beloved"—intended? Many guesses have been made, many theories have been propounded. Some authorities maintain that this letter was not intended for any specific woman at all but for all womankind—Beethoven's lament at having been denied a relationship he hungered for.

In recent years, however, an American musicologist, Maynard Solomon, came upon a long-overlooked Beethoven manuscript which provided him with a clue as to who the "immortal beloved" might be. This discovery led him to an extended and painstaking search through documents, manuscripts, and other data. Little by little, at least to his own satisfaction, he filled in the missing parts of what resembled a jigsaw puzzle. When completed, the puzzle revealed the picture of Antonina, the wife of one of Beethoven's closest friends and benefactors, the merchant, Franz Brentano. Mr. Solomon builds up an interesting and frequently convincing case that it is she who is the "immortal beloved," which will have to be carefully analyzed and studied by musicologists before we can say that the riddle has at long last been solved.

Between the years of 1812 and 1818 Beethoven was creatively quiescent. During some of this time he was involved in ugly litigation. Having become emotionally attached to his nephew, Karl (whose guardian he had become upon the death of the boy's father), Beethoven fought long and hard in the courts to prevent the boy's mother from taking him away. Ludwig's right to retain Karl was upheld legally. But this was hardly a victory in which Beethoven could rejoice. Karl proved to be shiftless and irresponsible, a liar and a cheat, a boy who amassed debts and expressed nothing but contempt for his eccentric uncle. Beethoven must have loved the boy dearly, for he was always ready to forget and forgive Karl's indiscretions. In the end Beethoven sorrowfully had to wash his hands clean of this hopeless reprobate.

It is hardly likely, however, that this extended period of struggle and disenchantment was the reason why Beethoven wrote so little music between 1812 and 1818. He had known greater tragedies and had never allowed them to interfere with his creativity. It is more accurate to believe that this temporary silence represented a transition in Beethoven's musical development. He was about to enter a new phase—the third of his creative periods, and the most awesome of all. The emancipator was now determined to free completely both his music and his spirit. He would change structure; he would arrive at a totally new method of presenting and developing melodic themes; he would propound deeper, richer, profounder poetic concepts. Beginning with the *Hammer-klavier* Sonata for piano, in 1818–19, he arrived at a freedom of method and an incandescence of speech not to be found in his preceding masterworks. "Art demands of us that we shall not stand still," he told a friend. As he moved forward, he wrestled with new forms, reached out for unfamiliar ways of expressing ideas and feelings. Never before had his fancy been so rich. Remote new worlds were explored in tones, remote new experiences found a voice. This third period yielded just one major orchestral work—the Ninth Symphony. But in his last quartets and piano sonatas the personality of the *new* Beethoven emerges most strongly.

On May 7, 1824, Beethoven appeared in public for the last time to attend the premiere of his Ninth Symphony, an event we have already described. By 1826 he was suffering seriously from pneumonia, jaundice, and dropsy. Gifts from all of Europe came to his apartment to cheer him up. By early 1827 Beethoven knew that his end could not be far off. He revised and signed his will on March 23, submitted to the Last Sacraments the following day, and then lapsed into a coma. "His powerful frame," revealed his friend Gerhard von Breuning, "his weakened lungs, fought like giants with the approach of death."

Beethoven passed away on March 26, 1827. It has been said that he died during a thunderstorm and that his last gesture was a fist shaken at the dark skies. If this was so, it would have been typical of Beethoven. Always he was the indomitable fighter against the powers of darkness.

The boy Mozart at eight years of age, playing the clavier for French courtiers.

*Wolfgang
Amadeus Mozart.*

Ludwig van Beethoven

The music store of Haslinger—Beethoven's publisher—in Vienna in 1825.

The manuscript title page of Beethoven's Eroica Symphony, *with the dedication to Napoleon scratched out.*

Beethoven's birthplace in Bonn, Germany.

5

The Flowering of Romanticism

Franz Schubert, Robert Schumann,

Felix Mendelssohn

The old order in orchestral music ended in Beethoven's time. Discipline, self-restraint, the *galant* style, the respect for form that had characterized the music of the Classical era had in Beethoven's music given way to greater freedom, ardor, and intensity. A new epoch—the Romantic period—was now at hand. It would last virtually till the end of the nineteenth century. Imagination and emotion now took precedence over reason and the intellect; self-expression and the insistence on enhancing poetic content became more important than the architecture of musical forms. Given direction by Beethoven, the Romantics might still work within the confines of recognizable structures. But these composers used such structures flexibly, and when existing structures did not serve the artistic aims of these composers, new ones were devised. Melodies were filled with subjective feelings that at times bordered on passion. These were supported by the background of a more original and expressive harmony. Dramatic climaxes, using the resources of an enlarged orchestra for sonority, dynamics, and color were employed more opulently than in the Classical age.

New influences were brought to bear on the Romantic composer.

Romantic literature—poetry in particular—frequently provided composers with subject matter for compositions (particularly for songs, the reason why the song developed into a major art form during the Romantic era). Romanticism introduced love of landscapes and stimulated an interest in exotic settings and supernatural beings, in legends and fantasies, in superstitions and mysteries.

The Romantic composer could write as he pleased, far more so than the Classical composer was able to do. This was made possible through a change in the composer's place in society. During the Romantic era the composer was no longer the hireling of a king or nobleman, compelled to produce functional music for specific occasions or to cater to the often circumscribed tastes of his employer. Once he had established himself in Vienna in the early nineteenth century, Beethoven did not work for king, prince, or nobleman. When those in power supported him financially, the purse strings did not strangle his creativity. All this proved particularly true of the Romantics who followed him.

Public concerts, infrequent in Mozart's day, proliferated throughout Europe during the Romantic era. The concert auditorium was filled with the masses, not with just a select few of wealthy, highborn patrons. Freed from the necessity of writing to please any one man in order to retain his post, and faced with the opportunity of exhibiting his works to audiences with varied tastes, the Romantic composer could follow the dictates of his artistic conscience. This proved equally true when the Romantic composer was commissioned to write special works for performers or patrons. The only restraint placed on the composer was the type of work he was to write (a symphony, a choral work, a composition for a solo instrument). In fulfilling the assignment the composer was guided solely by his own integrity and artistic purpose.

The Romantic era in German orchestral music, initiated by Beethoven, unfolds further in the work of three masters: Schubert, Schumann, and Mendelssohn. None was an innovator; with one or two minor exceptions, the symphonic structure changed little in their hands. Each, however, had his own personal style and methods. All three possessed the gift to fill their writing with romantic ardor, hypersensitive feelings, and poetic beauty.

It is true that Schubert's genius found its most felicitous outlet in the song form. He was not only one of the greatest melodists of all time, but also the first great composer of German art songs (*Lieder*). It was in this field, which we will discuss elsewhere, that he was a pioneer, an innovator, the discoverer of a new musical world. In his other music, he was a traditionalist, though he did adapt existing traditions to his own tastes and creative personality.

Schubert wrote eight symphonies, the cream of his orchestral output. The earliest ones were influenced by Haydn and Mozart, some of the later ones by Beethoven. But Schubert, while influenced, was nobody's imitator. Though he pursued accepted procedures, the way he wrote symphonies was uniquely his own.

For many years in the twentieth century Schubert's symphonies were severely victimized by unjust appraisals. Critics insisted that Schubert had a single strong suit, melody, and that, for the rest, he led from weakness. They criticized him for his deficiencies in thematic development and variation, for the looseness of his organization, for the weakness of his structural logic. What was happening was that these critics were condemning Schubert for not being Beethoven. And it has taken quite a number of years—and the brilliant perception and analyses of several musicologists—to bring to sophisticated music lovers the concept that they must render to Schubert that which is Schubert's and not Beethoven's. Schubert's magic is his own: the way he augments one beautiful melody with another in the most incredible profusion; the way he builds up his expositions; the way he introduces surprises through ever-changing tonalities, freshly conceived harmonies, and impressive polyphony. He endowed his symphonies with sweetness and romance—three symphonies in particular that are landmarks in Romantic orchestral music: Symphony no. 5 in B-flat major (1816); Symphony no. 8 in B minor, the *Unfinished* (1822); and Symphony no. 9 (sometimes numbered 7) in C major, *The Great* (1828).

Born in Vienna on January 31, 1797, Franz Peter Schubert was the son of a schoolmaster, who owned his own school by the time Franz was four. Franz's first music lessons came from his father, his older brother, and a parish organist, the last of whom said, "He seems to know the lessons perfectly before I begin to explain them to him."

In his eleventh year Schubert entered a school called the Konvikt, which trained boys to become singers at court. Life at that school was harsh. The students lived in unheated rooms and suffered from lack of food. Time and again Franz pleaded with his family to send him money so that he might supplement his starvation diet at school with an apple or some bread. But Schubert was not unhappy. He was surrounded by music and involved in it all the time, and that was all that mattered. In

1811 came his first composition, a song. Other songs, as well as piano and choral compositions, came soon after that. His remarkable ability did not pass unnoticed. The great and influential musician Salieri told him, "You can do everything, for you are a genius."

In 1813 Schubert left the Konvikt to prepare for a career as schoolmaster. By that time he had written his first string quartet and his first symphony. Between 1814 and 1818 he earned his living teaching school. In class, instead of paying attention to his students, he would continually work at his desk scribbling music. Once freed from the classroom, he produced one work after another with unbelievable rapidity. By the end of 1816 he had written an opera, four more symphonies, several Masses, piano sonatas, short piano pieces, short works for chorus, and over one hundred and fifty songs (among the last of which are two epoch-making compositions. "Gretchen am Spinnrade" and "Erlkönig"). A Mass, performed in a small church in 1814, was Schubert's first work to have a public hearing.

The most interesting of Schubert's first four symphonies is the Symphony no. 4 in C minor (1816). The effect that Beethoven's Fifth Symphony had made on Schubert is revealed in this work not only through the use of the same tonality, but also through a four-note rhythmic phrase (not much different from the one that opens Beethoven's symphony), which reasserts itself again and again throughout the work. This symphony is named *Tragic,* but the only place where tragedy is sounded is in the somber introduction to the first movement. The rest of the symphony is thoroughly Schubertian, in its use of glorious melody (as in the second movement), in its springtime warmth and freshness, and at times in the novel way Schubert moves his themes from one key to another.

The Symphony no. 5 in B-flat major (1816) is the one of the three Schubert symphonies performed regularly. Temporarily, Schubert deserts Beethoven as a source of inspiration to return to the structure and traditions of Haydn and Mozart. But the melodies and the buoyant moods are unmistakably Schubertian. Except for the second movement (in which a melancholy mood strokes the lovely melody as lightly as a feather), the symphony is consistently vivacious, just as it is consistently lyrical.

Detesting teaching, Schubert deserted the classroom in 1818. From then on, up to the end of his life, he had to depend upon the generosity of his friends to provide him with a roof, food, and the few pleasures he enjoyed, such as drinking wine in cafés. Schubert resided now with one friend, now with another. If his friends resented anything at all, it was not that they were compelled to support him, which they did willingly, since they all loved him and were all conscious of his genius. Their grievance was leveled against the world outside their own circle that failed to recognize Schubert's greatness. For, despite his enormous output—and the extraordinarily high level of its artistic content—nothing of Schubert was published, and nothing was performed in a major auditorium, until 1820. The only income Schubert earned came from teaching the family of Count Esterházy in Hungary during two summers (1818 and again in 1824). "His situation was really oppressive," revealed one of his dearest friends, Joseph von Spaun. "There was not a publisher who would have ventured even a small sum for his wonderful creations. For years he remained the victim of money worries. This man so rich in melody could not afford a piano."

Yet Schubert was far from unhappy. The evenings he spent with his friends—called "Schubert evenings" because his music dominated all the proceedings—were an undiluted joy. Schubert and his friends drank wine, became heady, and indulged in pranks and horseplay, in which Schubert was always an enthusiastic participant. His friends saw to it that his supply of manuscript paper was never depleted: Schubert could write as much music as he wished, and since he had no job, whenever and wherever he wished. "His troubles," continues Spaun, "did not in the least lessen his diligence. He had to write, it was his life. And he was always cheerful."

For a while, in 1820, it looked as if Schubert's fortunes as a composer were taking a turn for the better. Two of his operettas were produced, each in a major Viennese theater. But both were dismal failures and had to close down after a few performances. When Schubert's first pieces of music were finally published in 1821, a number of songs including the famous "Erlkönig," it was only because his friends had raised a subscription to pay for the publication.

A small token of recognition came in 1823, when Schubert was made an honorary member of a music society in the Austrian city of Graz. The society was an insignificant one, and the membership carried with it no remuneration. The only reason this modest honor was conferred on Schubert was because one of his close friends, Anselm von Hüttenbrenner, was president of the society. But to Schubert, starved as he was for public admiration, this membership came as if from heaven. He had to show his gratitude; the only way he was able to do so was through his music. And so, for the Graz musical society he wrote his Symphony no. 8 in B minor—reciprocating a highly insignificant gesture of homage with one of the greatest symphonies ever written.

We know this symphony as the *Unfinished,* because it consists of only two movements, instead of the usual three or four. Why is this the only Schubert symphony without a third-movement scherzo and a fourth-movement finale? The question has often been asked, and the explanations vary. A conclusive answer has never been found. We do know the composer tried his hand at producing a third-movement scherzo, because he put down on paper the first nine measures. Had he actually completed two more movements and have they been lost? This is hardly likely, for if the first two movements were preserved, together with the opening measures of the third, why should the completed last two movements have been separated from the manuscript, and why have they never been located? Did Schubert fail to write the last two movements because he had run dry of musical ideas? This is even harder to believe. Thematic material came to Schubert so rapidly that he hardly put one idea down on paper when dozens of others began to hound him.

One explanation for the unfinished state of this symphony seems to make more sense. It is that Schubert realized that in the first two movements he had created one of the most exquisite symphonic works ever conceived, music so perfectly realized in every detail, so consistently inspired from the first measure to the last, that further movements were superfluous, and would have detracted from the luminous beauty of what he had produced in one of his highest flights of inspiration. The Symphony in B minor is *not* an "unfinished" work. It is a self-sufficient masterpiece, a complete art work. The romanticism alternating with agitation of the first movement—with the unfolding in the cellos of one of the most rapturous melodies in all symphonic literature—and the uninterrupted joy of the second movement, whose spell on the listener remains unbroken until the final whispers, find Schubert at the summit of his wondrous creative powers.

Schubert did not live to hear the symphony performed. After the society received the work, it decided not to play it—why, nobody knows. Anselm Hüttenbrenner put the manuscript on a shelf in a closet, where it collected dust. Not until thirty-seven years after Schubert's death (on December 17, 1865) was this now beloved symphony finally performed.

Was there to be no end to Schubert's frustrations, no end to the way he was hounded by destiny? In 1823 he was asked to write incidental music for *Rosamunde,* a play by Wilhelmine von Chézy. The play itself was so silly that it received only two performances, yet among the eleven pieces the composer wrote for this ridiculous text are some of pure Schubert genius. There is the deservedly popular Ballet Music in G major, the essence of Viennese charm! There is also one of Schubert's supreme melodies, the Entr'acte in B-flat major, which Schubert liked so well that he used it in one of his most famous string quartets. As for the overture known as the *Rosamunde* Overture, one of Schubert's best-known orchestral works outside his symphonies, this music was not actually written for that play, but rather for a play called *Die Zauberharfe,* one of two operettas that were produced in 1820. Today this music is always identified as *Rosamunde* Overture, a confusion arising from the two works having been published together.

Frustrations, failures, the need to depend upon his friends for financial support, his inability to get his best works performed or published, the fact that he was totally unknown to the Viennese music public: all these exacted their toll from Schubert. After 1823, he became increasingly despondent. His health was beginning to deteriorate. "Picture to yourself someone whose health is permanently injured," he wrote to a friend in 1824, "and who, in sheer despair, does everything to make it worse rather than better; picture to yourself, I say, someone whose brilliant hopes have come to naught . . . someone whose inspiration . . . for all that is beautiful threatens to fail and then ask yourself if that is not a wretched and unhappy being. . . . Every night when I go to sleep I hope never again to wake again, and each morning reopens the wounds of yesterday."

The death in 1827 of Beethoven—the one composer whom Schubert worshiped above all others—piled grief upon despair. From this moment on both his spirit and his health degenerated. And yet in what was destined to be the last year of his life he wrote one of his greatest works: the Symphony no. 9 in C major (1828). This work is sometimes programmed as no. 7 because it was published *before* the *Unfinished* Symphony (no. 8), although written after it.

In his last symphony, the lyric poet of the *Unfinished* became the writer of an epic. Bigness of size and sound led to its being named *The Great.* The delicacy, sensitivity, controlled sentiments, and transparent texture of the *Unfinished* gave way in the C major to grandiose statements, rhythmic strength, sweeping climaxes, powerful sonorities. We do not lack for Schubertian lyricism, by any means. The extended first-movement introduction has a haunting melody first for horns, then for

76 oboes, clarinets, and bassoons, while midway in the same movement

comes an otherworldly message from the trombones. The entire second movement is Schubert melody at its best, exquisite in every detail. The middle section of the third-movement scherzo has unforgettable loveliness. But in the C major there is more dash and fire than tenderness and sweetness. Dynamic forces so prominent in parts of the first and third movements are let loose without inhibitions in the finale, a mighty crescendo carrying the movement to an electrifying conclusion. If there is much in this symphony that is Schubertian, there is much more that makes us think of Beethoven.

For one brief moment (almost like a token of penance by the gods) Schubert had a taste of success. This came on March 26, 1828 (the first anniversary of Beethoven's death), when a complete concert of Schubert's music was given in Vienna. The house was sold out and most enthusiastic. A Dresden critic reported that a new shining star had just been discovered in music's firmament.

But it had come too late. Dusk was at hand. Just as Schubert's spirits were beginning to soar as a result of this long-overdue success, his body began to weaken. His brother took him into his own apartment in a suburb of Vienna and put him to bed. On November 11, 1828, Schubert wrote to a friend: "I am sick. For eleven days I have eaten nothing, drunk nothing, and wander, exhausted and tottering, from chair to bed and back." He was probably suffering from typhoid. His mind was beginning to wander. He kept asking if Beethoven were lying next to him, in the belief that he was already buried. Death came mercifully on November 19. Just before he passed away he had announced quietly: "Here, here is my end."

His end, yes. The end of his art? Never! But it took a number of years for the world to discover how immense a treasure Schubert had bequeathed it. When Schubert died, most musicians thought he had produced only a handful of works. This is why the inscription on his tombstone read: "The Art of Music has here entombed a rich possession, but even far fairer hopes." The prevailing belief was that Schubert's lifework consisted of some songs and a few other items, including the last symphony; that Schubert had died without fulfilling himself. It was only after the composer's death that his immense output was discovered.

The recovery of Schubert's works, a process that took years, compelled the world to give him a new evaluation as one of the greatest composers the world has known. The first discovery of Schubert's music was made a decade after his death by Robert Schumann, who on a visit to Vienna, paid a call on Schubert's brother Ferdinand, at whose home

Schubert had died. Ferdinand brought out a bundle of Schubert's manuscripts, of whose existence only he had known. Leafing through them, Schumann came upon the "great" C-major Symphony. Through Schumann's efforts and enthusiasm, that symphony was finally resurrected in Leipzig on March 21, 1839, with Felix Mendelssohn conducting.

The premiere of the *Unfinished* Symphony (already mentioned) took place in Vienna just about a quarter of a century later. The fact that two such incredible works had lain neglected and forgotten so long led two Englishmen to make an expedition to Vienna in a hunt for more unknown Schubert manuscripts. These two men later became renowned in English music. One was George Grove, who later edited the famous *Dictionary of Music and Musicians;* the other, Arthur Sullivan, the composer who achieved fame as a collaborator of W. S. Gilbert in writing such immortal operettas as *The Mikado* and *The Pirates of Penzance.* Both were young and unknown when they arrived in Vienna in 1867. At the home of a physician, and in the forgotten archives of a publisher, they discovered five symphonies, over sixty songs, a trio, the music to *Rosamunde,* a choral work, and other pieces of music. So thrilled were Grove and Sullivan at this amazing find that they proceeded to play a game of leapfrog around the room.

In the last year of his life Beethoven became acquainted with several of Schubert's songs. "There is a divine spark of genius in this Schubert," the master remarked. Had Beethoven known how much music Schubert had written, had he been able to see all the Schubert music that was recovered after Schubert's death, surely he would have referred to the bespectacled, round-faced, lovable composer not merely in terms of a divine spark but of a veritable conflagration.

It was almost as if it were an act of predestination, as if fate operated in a logical sequence, that Robert Schumann was the first musician to discover forgotten Schubert manuscripts after that composer's death. For it was Schumann who was destined to succeed Schubert as a major exponent of German-Austrian Romanticism in music.

Literature was a more potent force in Schumann's life than it had been with Schubert. Schubert, to be sure, had been affected by the German lyric poems that he set to music in his songs, but except for these songs, Schubert's music is not influenced by literature. Schumann, too, was stimulated by German lyric poetry in his songs. But Schumann also had a vast knowledge of and enthusiasm for Romantic literature, from
which spring the volatile moods and ardent and romanticized outbursts

that characterize most of his masterworks, as well as some of its subject matter.

Schumann learned to love literature early in life, as the son of a publisher-bookseller. Born in Zwickau, Germany, on June 8, 1810, Schumann was soon directed by a cultured father both to literature and to music. He avidly read the Romantic poets and Greek classics. His ambition was to become a writer, especially a poet. When he was thirteen, he had some of his articles published in a magazine put out by his father. He formed a literary society when he was fifteen. At about the same time he edited a volume of poetry (including several of his own poems), and between his fifteenth and eighteenth years he worked on another volume of verses, most of the poems original with him.

For the time being, music occupied a subsidiary role in his life, even though he had begun to study the piano when he was seven, had written his first compositions at about the same time, and by the time he was eleven had begun writing for orchestra.

When Schumann's father died in 1826, the boy's mother assumed the problems of raising her talented son. A practical woman, she was determined to have him become a lawyer. In 1828, Schumann matriculated as a law student at the University of Leipzig. He hated law and diverted his energies from the study of law books to the writing of poems and parts of an autobiographical novel. By late 1829 Schumann came to the conclusion that law was not for him. He had also decided that his principal talent lay with music and not literature. "If I were to achieve anything in the world," he wrote to his mother on November 11, 1829, "it would have been in music."

He rented a room at the home of Friedrich Wieck, a piano teacher, from whom he took lessons. At the same time Schumann studied harmony with another teacher. Wieck was thoroughly impressed with Schumann's possibilities as a piano virtuoso. "I pledge to turn him into one of the greatest pianists," wrote Wieck to Schumann's mother in 1830. Schumann, too, was thoroughly convinced of his ability. "With work, patience and a good master," he wrote to his mother, "I shall within six years be able to challenge any pianist. . . . Besides this, I also possess imagination, and perhaps aptitude, for individual creative work."

He forthwith went on to prove his creative aptitude by writing three highly talented compositions for the piano, which were published. He also tried his hand at a symphony, of which he completed three movements by 1832, one of which was performed. (That symphony was never completed and has not been heard since.) He was, in short, making headway as a composer. But his hopes of becoming a world-famous pianist were permanently destroyed when he became inflicted with an incurable paralysis of the hand, brought about through his insistence on using an artificial technique for his fingers to enhance his virtuoso capabilities.

The concert stage now denied him, Schumann immersed himself more passionately than ever in composition—working on ever larger, more ambitious, and more individualistic compositions. He also directed his musical energies into other channels. He founded a society of idealistic young musicians to fight false values and low standards in music, a group calling itself the Davidsbund. As a voice for this society, Schumann helped to bring into existence in Leipzig the first major music journal, the *Neue Zeitschrift für Musik,* which he edited and for which he contributed many penetrating articles.

By the time he reached his early twenties, Schumann was a dreamer, an introvert, a man of exquisite sensibilities and volatile moods. At times he was fired with animation and enthusiasms, at other times with despair. Once, in the fall of 1833, he tried to commit suicide. When seized by emotional crises he was convinced he was losing his mind, almost as if sensing what the future held in store for him! This instability became greatly intensified when he became involved in the one and only love affair of his life, whose tempests brought him years of anguish, and whose bliss brought him moments of ecstasy.

His beloved was Clara Wieck, the daughter of Schumann's teacher, and herself a remarkable piano prodigy. She was only twelve when Schumann (then twenty-one) recognized that she loved him. Schumann's reaction to the child was the gentle affection of a young adult for an attractive and highly gifted girl. By the time Clara was sixteen, her adoration of Schumann was matched by Schumann's now rapidly developing love for her.

Once Clara's father saw what was happening, his opposition to this love affair was tyrannical. He did not want a romance and marriage to interfere with his daughter's promising career as pianist, nor did he consider an impoverished composer a worthy candidate as the husband for his daughter. We need not elaborate here upon all the lies, threats, deceptions, and tempestuous outbursts of rage with which Wieck tried to keep the lovers apart. Nor need we dwell upon the subtle, secret ways the lovers managed to have furtive meetings and exchange love letters. It is

merely significant to note that the few moments of ecstasy the lovers experienced in their all-too-brief exchanges were far outweighed by the torment they suffered while separated. This situation went on for four years. Finally Schumann went to the law courts to sue for his right to marry Clara. The case turned out favorably for the lovers. On September 12, 1840, they were married. Happier than he had ever been in his life, Schumann needed his music more than ever as an outlet for his overwhelming emotions. Never was he more productive than in the first years of his marriage.

During the initial year of his marriage Schumann (who up to that time had concentrated mainly on writing works for the piano) turned to songs. A veritable avalanche followed, individual songs and song cycles, many of them filled with the sunshine of his great love for Clara. Here Schumann truly became Schubert's successor.

It was during the first year of Schumann's marriage that he completed his first symphony: the Symphony in B-flat major, op. 38 (1841). The name he gave this work was *Spring*. We find in this music all the exuberance and exhilaration that this most wonderful of all seasons inspires in a lover of nature. Indeed, a line of lyric poetry was very much on Schumann's mind when he wrote this music: "O turn, O turn thy course, the valley blooms with Spring." But what was in his heart, as he filled the four movements with romantic effusions, was not only his love of nature but his adoration of his young wife, his feelings for the woman who had taken him out of the winter of his despair into the springtime of his life.

The year of 1841 is sometimes described as Schumann's "orchestral year" (in the same way that the year of 1840 is designated as his year of songs). This is because he produced two other symphonic compositions, one of which is rarely heard (*Overture, Scherzo, and Finale,* op. 52), and another which frequently is (the Symphony no. 4 in D minor, Op. 120). The symphony is Schumann's second, but it bears the number "four" because it was published after the first three. Schumann became a pioneer in this symphony by requesting that the four movements be played without interruption. A motto theme (an appeggio figure at the beginning of the first movement), and the principal theme of the first movement, which recurs in later parts, unite the four movements into a cohesive unity. Even with changes of tempo and dynamics, a unifying mood pervades the entire symphony. This is music thoroughly Schumannesque in its lyrical beauty, always filled with an ardent romantic feeling, and sometimes with a gentle melancholy. It is the spirit of romanticism that led Schumann to call his slow movement a "Romanze"—a romantic piece of music highlighted by a nostalgic Italianate song for solo oboe and solo cello accompanied by plucked strings.

Before writing another symphony, Schumann worked on one of the most famous piano concertos in Romantic literature: the Concerto in A minor, op. 54 (1841–45). Its first version came during Schumann's symphonic year of 1841, when it consisted of just one movement and was designated as a fantasy instead of a concerto. Four years later, Schumann added two movements to the Fantasy, the Fantasy serving as the opening movement. Its fantasia character is one of several features that endow the concerto with its pronounced Romantic personality. Another is replacing the expected slow second movement by an intermezzo, into which another free fantasia section is introduced. But what places this concerto most solidly in the camp of the Romantics is the lyric-poetry quality of Schumann's principal melodies.

Schumann's Symphony no. 2 in C major, op. 61 (which, it must be remembered, is actually his third symphony, but the second to be published), arrived in 1846. When he wrote it he was suffering one of his "dark periods," as he called his attacks of nervous disorder. Much in this music is somber, much represents emotional upheaval, with only intermittent periods of tranquillity or suggestions of levity. To Schumann, this symphony appeared "more or less clad in armor. . . . music of light and shade, sunshine and shadow."

Schumann's only shorter orchestral composition to get a hearing today is his Overture to *Manfred,* op. 115 (1849)—one of several of his compositions inspired by Romantic poetry. In this instance, the stimulation came from Byron's poem of the same name, which would move Schumann to tears whenever he read it. Schumann wrote several musical episodes for Byron's *Manfred,* but only the deeply affecting music of the overture has gained a permanent place in the repertory.

Schumann's last symphony—listed as the third but actually his fourth—is the *Rhenish,* in E-flat major, Op. 97 (1850). The composer's romantic imagination was aroused by the landscapes along the German river Rhine, as well as by Rhenish festivals, and by a ceremony he attended at Cologne Cathedral where the archbishop was elevated to the rank of cardinal. This symphony differs from the three earlier ones in that it is often descriptive, and in that there are five movements instead of four. The first movement describes the composer's enthusiasm upon first seeing the Rhineland. In the second-movement scherzo, Schumann quotes a popular German folk song, "Rhine Wine Land." A gentle Romanza establishes a pastoral mood in the third movement. It is in the fourth that Schumann picturesquely depicts the ceremony at Cologne Cathedral. The finale recreates a festival along the Rhineland. But Schumann, apparently, was unable to forget the Cologne Cathedral ceremony, for just before the concluding coda of the finale he repeats the religious melody of the fourth movement, but with its character somewhat altered.

One more major work, and Schumann's principal contribution to orchestral music ends. It is the Concerto in A minor, for cello and orchestra, op. 129 (1850). Its writing came easily, Schumann completing the whole work in two weeks. But apparently he was displeased with it. Though a premiere had been set for 1852, he did not allow that performance to take place, nor was it performed or published during his lifetime. Yet it is a melodious work that takes full advantage of the capacities of the cello to sustain a long arched melody or to indulge in pyrotechnics.

Criticism has been leveled against Schumann's major works for orchestra for their weakness in counterpoint, his tendency to repeat melodic phrases rather than develop them, and the opaque texture and bland palette of colors of his orchestration. All this has an element of truth to it and would make for valid criticism if we were to discuss Schumann in terms of, say, Beethoven. But Schumann was in a class by himself, as indeed every genius is. The techniques and methods he used were those best suited for his romantic, poetic temperament, for a dreamer who always probes deeply within his soul.

The accusation about his orchestration is one that remains the most persistent. Through the years various conductors have assumed the burden of remedying this "defect" by doubling parts, introducing additional instruments, and so forth. Yet when we hear Schumann's orchestral works as he wrote them, we come to realize that what the textbook or the classroom might designate as a defect becomes an asset.

In avoiding contrapuntal complexities, in building up his orchestral music brick by brick with one enchanting melodic thought after another, in the economy, clarity, and simplicity of his instrumentation, Schumann was remaining true to his own nature. Others were dramatists. Schumann, by contrast, preferred to whisper treasurable confidences into the ears of his listeners. Accepted on this basis, Schumann's orchestral compositions reveal, as the American critic Philip Hale, once noted, "secrets of subtle and ravishing beauty." Mr. Hale then points to the listener's responsibility: "The hearer of Schumann's must in turn be imaginative and a dreamer."

The Cello Concerto was Schumann's first major work after he had assumed a post as musical director of the city of Düsseldorf, Germany, in 1850. His main job was to conduct orchestral concerts. By this time he had already resigned as the editor of the *Neue Zeitschrift für Musik* and had withdrawn as a teacher at the Leipzig Conservatory, to which he had been appointed in 1843, when it was founded. For five years before coming to Düsseldorf he had been living in Dresden, where he conducted two choral groups and did some teaching.

In Düsseldorf, Schumann was once again victimized by severe nervous attacks. Frequently he lost control of his powers of concentration. He was incapable of performing his duties adequately, so in 1853 he was politely asked to resign.

His mind began to give way completely after that. Strange voices and sounds harassed him. He plunged into pits of depression. He even lost his sense of reality. On several occasions he insisted that the master composers of the past had visited him to dictate melodies to him. In February of 1854 he tried to end his life by jumping into the Rhine. After that incident there was just one course his loving wife could take, terrible though it was: to confine him in an asylum at Endenich, near Bonn.

He remained in the asylum two years, tormented by apparitions and delusions and tortured by harrowing sounds in his head. He began to lose the power of speech and use of his limbs. Suddenly he had the appearance of a man made haggard by old age. Just before he died, Clara visited him. Though he was incapable of relating to anybody any longer, Schumann seemed to recognize her, for he took her in his arms. "Never shall I forget that moment," Clara recalls. "I would not give up that embrace for all the treasures on earth." It was Schumann's last gesture of love as well as a farewell. He died soon afterward in the asylum, on July 29, 1856. His life had been stormy, but death proved peaceful. With his beloved Clara at his side his end came so quietly that it was some time before Clara realized that Robert had left her forever.

Fate, which had treated both Schubert and Schumann so shabbily, seemed to have reserved all her gifts for Felix Mendelssohn. He was born with such an extraordinary precociousness in music that only Mozart surpassed him, and not even Mozart produced unqualified masterworks representative of his most mature style as early as Mendelssohn did. He was attractive in appearance. Wealth and culture were his heritage. His grandfather, Moses Mendelssohn, was so famous a philosopher that he was sometimes referred to as "the modern Plato," and sometimes as "the Jewish Socrates." Felix's father, Abraham, was a wealthy banker; his mother was an immensely cultured woman. No blessing seemed to have been denied this child.

When in his youth he became deeply involved in music, he received the full encouragement of both his parents, neither of whom had any objection to his making music his life's profession. His genius revealed itself early; by the time he was sixteen he had created masterworks. He never knew frustrations or setbacks as a musician, since fame came at once and kept growing from then on. He fulfilled his destiny as a musician in every possible way—not only as a composer, but also as a conductor and pianist (in both departments he was remarkable), and as the founder of Germany's greatest conservatory.

He inspired love as well as admiration: from his parents, to be sure, who burst with pride at his phenomenal achievements; from his brother and two sisters, especially his sister Fanny; from the woman whom he married and with whom he lived until the end of his life in marital happiness; and from all those with whom he came into contact either professionally or socially.

Surely, then, he had been rightly named. The word *felix* in Latin means "happiness." Felix Mendelssohn was for most of his life a thoroughly happy man.

He was born in Hamburg, Germany, on February 3, 1809. From the time he was three his family lived in a fashionable district of Berlin. His mother was his first teacher at the piano. When she soon came to realize that her boy was a genius, she sought more professional training for him. She chose wisely: Ludwig Berger, for piano; Karl Friedrich Zelter, for theory. Later on the boy also studied the violin and viola and acquired the finishing touches on the piano from Ignaz Moscheles, a noted virtuoso.

He was not allowed to devote himself exclusively to music, for his mother knew the importance of a well-rounded education. She hired the finest private tutors to teach the boy the sciences, mathematics, classical and modern languages, drawing, the arts. Felix's mind absorbed knowledge readily.

In music he proved to be one of a kind. He had an infallible ear, a retentive memory, innate musicianship, and wonderful muscular control on the piano and stringed instruments. He had to hear a piece of music only once to know every note of it. His gift at sight-reading was nothing short of phenomenal. By the time he was nine he was already able to perform on the piano in public and was creating ambitious compositions.

In 1819 Mendelssohn became a member of a chorus led by Zelter. Introduced for the first time to choral literature, the boy proceeded to write a choral psalm, which Zelter's chorus performed in 1819. By the time he was twelve, Mendelssohn had written piano quartets, fugues, two operas, several symphonies, and numerous short compositions. His creative output, two years after that, had increased to include no less than thirteen symphonies, five operas, several concertos, and choral and sundry other works.

Whoever came into contact with him was staggered by his ability: by his compositions, which, childish though they were in musical content, were nevertheless consistently melodious and neatly constructed; by his aristocratic piano playing; by his phenomenal gift at sight-reading; by his restless, inquisitive, searching musical intelligence. The celebrated Karl Maria von Weber, composer of the opera *Der Freischütz* and musical director of the German Opera in Dresden, was awed when he visited the Mendelssohn home in 1821 and heard Felix play the piano and conduct an ensemble. Incredulity and awe characterized the reactions of the great poet Goethe, and distinguished musicians like Ludwig Spohr and Johann Schelbe, when they heard Mendelssohn improvise. "This boy is one of God's own," remarked Schelbe. And when, on Mendelssohn's fifteenth birthday, his teacher heard a performance of the boy's opera *Die beiden Neffen, oder Der Onkel aus Boston,* he exclaimed proudly, if somewhat pompously, "You are no longer an apprentice but an independent member of the brotherhood of musicians. I proclaim you independent, in the name of Mozart, Haydn and the older Bach."

What we today regard as Mendelssohn's first symphony (even though he had previously written twelve) was completed in this same year, 1824, when the boy was fifteen. (The first twelve symphonies were never published, and are in discard.) In the Symphony no. 1 in C minor, op. 11 —the first of his symphonies he allowed to be published—we find the boy trying to steal Beethoven's thunder; Mendelssohn's gentle and placid nature was incapable of conveying in his writing the master's towering rages and Herculean struggles. This symphony is rarely given, but it is still well worth listening to.

It did not take Mendelssohn long to assert his own personality. When he did, he produced two of the most remarkable pieces of music ever 86 created by an adolescent. This happened in 1825, after the Mendelssohn family had acquired a palatial home of their own in Berlin. In its garden the Mendelssohns built a little concert hall, where concerts were given every Sunday morning. There, in 1825, eight string players played for the first time Mendelssohn's Octet in E-flat major, op. 20, the first composition where we can recognize Mendelssohn's mature personality and his graceful touch (especially in the mercurial scherzo movement). This is a masterpiece in chamber music literature, and it came from the hands of a mere boy.

It was also in this garden concert hall that, on August 6, 1826 (aided by his sister Fanny), Felix offered the premiere of his Overture to *A Midsummer Night's Dream* in its original piano-duet version. Shortly after that he orchestrated it, its premiere taking place in Stettin, Germany, in February of 1827.

The young Romantic had found his voice. Stimulated by Shakespeare's comedy and poetry, Mendelssohn invaded the world of fantasy and the supernatural world populated by fairies and elves. In his music the unreal world comes magically to life. Many years later (1843), Mendelssohn wrote twelve additional numbers for *A Midsummer Night's Dream* which, together with the overture of his youth, which he did not retouch, were heard in a presentation of the Shakespeare comedy in Berlin on October 14, 1843. Together with the overture, several of these numbers comprise an orchestral suite that must be numbered with Mendelssohn's foremost works. What is truly amazing about this suite, each time we listen to it, is the fact that there is no difference in inspiration, style, technical skill, or imagination between the overture (the work of a boy) and the rest of the suite (the fruits of Mendelssohn's full maturity).

The overture remains a thing of wonder, a masterpiece of German Romantic music. The world of elves, fairies, and forest spirits comes to life in music of the most sensitive orchestration and harmony, gentle lyricism, and lightness of touch. Four exquisite chords immediately carry us off to a world of fantasy. A rippling staccato figure for strings, and we see the fairies, elves, gnomes, and forest spirits at play. A melody of rare tenderness in the woodwind and a song in the horn carry the mystery of the forests. And so the overture proceeds without an interruption of its magic until it ends with the same four delicate chords with which it began.

The rest of the suite embraces a scherzo, nocturne, intermezzo, and "wedding march." The scherzo is in the diaphanous and light-fingered style of the overture. The nocturne is a romantic song for the horn. The intermezzo is music with a subtle interplay of a fast subject between strings and woodwinds, with the cellos occasionally intruding with an eloquent comment. And the "wedding march" is one of the two most famous such marches ever conceived (the other being that from Wagner's opera *Lohengrin*). Since Mendelssohn's time it has served as the joyous and at times sentimental music to whose strains many a young couple has marched from the marriage altar.

The first time Mendelssohn proved himself to be a conductor of the first importance was on March 11, 1829, when he directed a remarkable performance of Bach's mighty choral masterpiece, *The Passion According to St. Matthew*. This was now receiving its first hearing since Bach's death. It must be remembered that by 1829 Bach was a forgotten composer, except to a handful of highly discerning musicians, one of whom was Zelter. Zelter owned one of the rare existing copies of the *St. Matthew Passion*, was engrossed by its immensity, and passed on his own enthusiasm to Mendelssohn, whose dream was to present it in its entirety to a public unaware of its existence. He did so, and with such monumental success that the year of 1829 may well be considered as the one when the great revival of Bach's music began.

In 1829, Mendelssohn also visited England, where he conducted a performance of his First Symphony, among other works. The English music public took to him at once. In his nine subsequent returns to England, Mendelssohn became an idol in that country, such as no foreign musician since Handel and Haydn had been.

From England, Mendelssohn toured Scotland and later Italy, a visit that gave him ideas he would ultimately use in his *Scotch* Symphony, *Italian* Symphony, and *Fingal's Cave* Overture. Returning to London in 1832, Mendelssohn gave several more concerts to adulating audiences during one of which he offered the premiere of a new work for piano and orchestra, the *Capriccio brillant*, op. 22 (1832). This is a composition in two sections: a slow part with an appealing melody and a contrasting vigorous second section.

As if the fact that Mendelssohn's thirteenth symphony is now known as Symphony no. 1 were not enough to cause confusion, we are confounded by another difficulty: the way in which Mendelssohn's three most popular symphonies are numbered. His Symphony no. 3 is the *Scotch*, no. 4 is the *Italian*, and no. 5 is the *Reformation*. They are numbered that way because this is the order in which they were published. But in the sequence in which they were written the *Reformation* came first (1830), followed by the *Italian* (1833), and then the *Scotch* (1842).

The *Reformation* Symphony—in D major, op. 107—celebrated the tercentenary of the Augsburg Protestant Confession (the Confession being the Lutheran creed proposed to the Diet of Augsburg in 1530). In his first movement Mendelssohn used a famous passage common to both Lutheran and Catholic liturgy, the "Dresden Amen." (Years later Wagner also quoted it in his music drama *Parsifal*.) The "Dresden Amen" is initially presented by the strings in the beginning of the first movement. When it is repeated later in the movement, it is to suggest the victory of church over state, after a bitter struggle. In the finale yet another religious theme is heard, that of the famous Lutheran chorale "Ein' feste Burg." This is followed by another liturgical-sounding melody, one of Mendelssohn's own invention. Thus the religious element is pronounced in two of the three movements (there is no fourth movement).

It is easy to sense Mendelssohn's joy on first becoming acquainted with the beauty of Italy by listening to the first theme of the first movement of the *Italian* Symphony—in A major, op. 90. This melody bubbles with enthusiasm, and so does the entire first movement. The second movement, with its placid song first in woodwinds and violas and then in the violins, may serve as a tonal portrait of Italian landscapes. Italy comes through even more forcefully in the finale, where Mendelssohn introduces the saltarello, a lively Italian folk dance.

Mendelssohn expressed the wish that the four movements of his *Scotch* Symphony—in A minor, op. 56—be played without pause to maintain uninterrupted unity. He wrote down his first sketches during a visit to Scotland in 1829, but did not get around to developing them into a symphony until a dozen years later. The symphony opens with a solemn introduction, bringing up the image of a rocky Scottish coast as seen through a mist. This image must have touched Mendelssohn with melancholy, for that is the mood of most of the movement. Melancholy is dispelled by exuberance in the second-movement scherzo: Mendelssohn found more joy than sadness in the sights of Scotland. The third-movement adagio has much of the quiet pastoral beauty of a Scottish town bathed in sunlight. In the finale, Mendelssohn introduced a Scottish-type tune in the violins, and when the movement closes we hear a vigorous marchlike coda, which has been described as the gathering of the Scottish clans.

The years separating the *Reformation* Symphony (1830) and the *Scotch* (1842) brought several shorter works for orchestra, the best of which are the *Fingal's Cave* Overture, op. 26 (1832), sometimes also known as the *Hebrides* Overture, and the *Ruy Blas* Overture, op. 95 (1839). The picturesque caverns of Staffa in the Scottish Hebrides, which Mendelssohn admired in 1829, led him then and there to jot down a melody. Three years later he used it as one of the principal themes of his *Fingal's Cave* Overture, which opens with the gentle sound of lapping waters at the mouth of the cave. To Wagner this overture shows "wonderful imagination and delicate feeling." Wagner was also impressed by the important passage for oboes rising "above the instruments with a plaintive wail, like sea winds over the sea."

Fingal's Cave is termed an overture, even though the term *overture* generally refers to the musical preface to an opera, oratorio, or play and sometimes serves as the first movement of a suite. What *Fingal's Cave* actually is, is a "concert overture"—something new in orchestral music, a child of the Romantic era. This is a short piece of music (sometimes in sonata form) in the style of an opera overture. It is a self-sufficient work intended exclusively for concert use. *Ruy Blas,* however, is not a concert overture but one intended for a play by Victor Hugo. The music has in it a good deal of the romantic and at times melodramatic character of the Hugo play. Ruy Blas is a commoner who becomes the lover of a queen. Rather than dishonor and bring about the downfall of the royal lady, he poisons himself. The opening somber chords for brass and woodwind create an atmosphere of tragedy; and the poignant melody for first violins and flutes represents Ruy Blas's love for the queen.

It was during this same twelve-year period separating the *Reformation* and *Scotch* symphonies, specifically in the year of 1838, that Mendelssohn first began thinking of writing a violin concerto for Ferdinand David, a famous virtuoso. It took Mendelssohn six years to get this concerto (in E minor, op. 64) on paper, and even then he was not satisfied. Aided by David's advice and criticism, Mendelssohn revised it. Finally, in 1845, David introduced it in Leipzig. This is Mendelssohn's supreme work in the concerto form; it is one of his finest creations in any form; and it is one of the most cherished violin concertos. Rarely was Mendelssohn's melodic imagination poised so consistently on so lofty a level. Mendelssohn wanted the concerto to be played without pause between the movements. This is sometimes done, but the more usual practice is to make a pause between the first and second movements.

In Mendelssohn's best orchestral compositions we soar with him as he flies on wings of song. Through his melodies we glimpse wonderful landscapes, are transported into magical supernatural worlds, are tranquilized by the peace and comfort of his moods, are fascinated by the polish, culture, and refinement of his speech. And yet, and yet . . . We

seem to lack something basic, something important, something vital that keeps him from joining the company of Mozart or Beethoven, of Schubert or Schumann. What is lacking is passion and pain, strength and vigor. One American scholar (Daniel Gregory Mason) put his finger on the flaw in Mendelssohn's music: "Its reading of life, in which there is ugliness, crudity, violence, as well as beauty, is too fastidiously expurgated."

Mendelssohn had all the equipment with which to join the elect of composers: technique, imagination, discrimination, taste. Could it be that had he not been so fortunate in life—had he been less the darling of the gods and more the victim of fate and of man's inhumanity—he would have been able to sound strains of sorrow, melancholy, and despair like those that so pierce the heart of the music lover in the work of Mozart, Beethoven, and Schubert? Mendelssohn occupies a place in music history below theirs because he lacked their experience of suffering and thus was unable to transmit to us the fullness of human experience with all its bitterness and frustrations as well as joys and contentment. Could it be that fate, in having been so kind to Mendelssohn in the allotment of its favors, was in essence cruel, by denying him a place on music's Mount Olympus?

On May 22, 1836, Mendelssohn enjoyed a triumph with his oratorio *St. Paul* at the Lower Rhine Festival in Düsseldorf. On returning to his home in Leipzig, he stopped off to pay a visit to his friends, the Jeanrenauds. One of them was Cécile, aged seventeen. Mendelssohn and Cécile fell in love. They were married on March 28, 1837.

Now a happily married man, as well as an enormously successful one, Mendelssohn continued to make contributions to the music profession. About two years before his marriage he had been appointed musical director of the Gewandhaus Orchestra in Leipzig. This was one of Europe's most renowned symphonic organizations, which attained further distinction and significance during the five years Mendelssohn conducted it. Mendelssohn instituted rigorous rehearsals where no detail of a composition was neglected; he worked painstakingly to realize interpretations that he had carefully worked out beforehand; he subjected the orchestra players to severe discipline; he maintained the highest possible standards in his programming; his performances were consistently superlative. For all of these practices he is often looked upon as the first "modern" conductor.

He finally gave up this post in 1840 to head a music department (a branch of a projected Academy of Arts) that was formed in Berlin. Mendelssohn assumed this post officially, at the request of the king of Prussia, in 1841. But there was nothing for him to do, since the project never materialized. Mendelssohn withdrew as tactfully as he could to become music director of the city of Berlin, a post he much preferred since it carried with it no set duties or obligations and did not demand an extended presence in Berlin. His principal duty was to write music for special occasions from time to time—as he did, in 1843, when he wrote the additional incidental music for *A Midsummer Night's Dream.*

Returning to Leipzig, Mendelssohn brought back with him a dream. He had long hoped to see a conservatory in Leipzig to equal the best music schools Europe could offer. Mendelssohn used his influence, fame, and charm to win allies for his cause. He even induced the king of Saxony to provide funds. On April 3, 1843, the Leipzig Conservatory opened. Robert Schumann joined Mendelssohn in teaching piano and composition; Ferdinand David headed the violin department. The Leipzig Conservatory quickly became what Mendelssohn hoped—a world-famous institution for the training of talented young musicians.

Mendelssohn worked at an unprecedented pace. Besides his activities at the conservatory he also conducted the Gewandhaus Orchestra from time to time. He traveled frequently to give guest performances—one of them for Queen Victoria at her Buckingham Palace. And as a composer he was more productive than ever. In 1844 he completed the Violin Concerto we already discussed; in 1846, his monumental oratorio *Elijah,* with which he achieved a giant success when he introduced it in London. He refused to spare himself, to conserve his energies, to concern himself with the ravages exacted on his nervous system by exhaustion. Then, for one of the rare occasions in his life, a dark shadow obscured the sunshine in which he had so long been basking. His beloved sister Fanny died suddenly in 1847. This loss proved such a shock that Mendelssohn suffered a rupture of a blood vessel in his head. From then on, he was never again the same—no longer the happy, tranquil, productive musician for whom life had always been so kind. He aged overnight. Depression seized him. The pains he suffered physically warned him he did not have long to live.

He tried to find relief in card games with his wife, or by playing with his youngest daughter, Lili, and teaching her how to draw. One evening he visited a Leipzig hostess where one of his last pieces of music (a song, "Nachtlied") was performed. While accompanying this number he fell from his chair, a victim of a fit. He had another such attack the next day. "I am tired, terribly tired," he whispered to his wife when he regained consciousness. He died a few weeks later, early in the morning of November 4, 1847.

Romanticism in French Music

Hector Berlioz, Franz Liszt, César Franck,
Camille Saint-Saëns

History could hardly have selected a more representative candidate to inaugurate the Romantic movement in French orchestral music than Hector Berlioz. He was, both as man and musician, the essence of Romanticism. As a man he was a sentimentalist, egotist, and neurotic whose responses to given situations were as exaggerated as his behavior was often outlandish and unpredictable. He lived turbulently and loved passionately and quixotically. Like many Romantics, he took flights into fantasy and enjoyed the grotesque.

In music, too, he was the true Romantic. In the tradition of that new era he derived most of his subject matter for compositions from literary sources. The poetic idea was the prime force behind his creativity. Berlioz was a poet, dramatist, and tone painter all in one. He was thoroughly subjective, his music spilling over with personal reactions. Invariably he identified himself with the colorful romantic characters he was delineating in his compositions.

In the spirit of Romanticism, he was always experimenting. In orchestration he was an innovator and a master. He favored immense forces (introducing into the orchestra instruments that earlier composers and his contemporaries neglected, such as the English horn, the saxhorn, and various varieties of percussion instruments). He brought out, as none before him had done, the individuality of each instrument with remarkable clarity, combined them in the most unusual ways, and realized striking effects and colorations. His use of rhythm was so unusual and complex that his fellow musicians regarded it as eccentric. He brought new vividness to program music and evolved a new type of symphonic structure for which he devised new methods and techniques.

The musician becomes easier to understand when we uncover the details of his picaresque life—the man and the musician being indivisible. His life story reads as if he were the character of a Romantic novel. The son of a physician, he was born in La Côte-Saint-André, France, on December 11, 1803. The child (like the later man) was sensitive to the point of seeming to have exposed nerves. Whatever touched them made them quiver. When a passage in literature moved him, he burst into tears. An impressive church ceremony caused him to tremble uncontrollably. When he fell in love for the first time (he was twelve, and she eighteen!) he tended to overdramatize his reactions, spending his nights, as he later recalled, "in sleepless anguish."

His father early introduced him both to great literature (the Greek and Latin classics particularly) and to music. During early adolescence, Berlioz studied music with local teachers, while spending nights with his head deep in theory texts. With the primitive tools he acquired from such studies he fashioned his first compositions—some chamber music and songs.

The father wanted Berlioz to follow in his own footsteps by becoming a physician, and his will was not to be denied. Despite his own inclinations, which leaned so heavily toward music, Berlioz left for Paris in 1821 to begin medical studies. Before leaving home, almost as an act of renouncing his own musical ambitions, he destroyed all the compositions he had written.

His initial experiment in Paris in dissecting an animal so nauseated him that he jumped out of the classroom window, ran home, and locked himself in his room. Nevertheless, he continued with his medical studies, as his father insisted. But music became a refuge. He now devoted all his free time to memorizing scores at the Paris Conservatory library. Finally he asserted himself. Determined to become a musician after hearing a symphony by Beethoven, he informed his father he was giving up medicine. Bitter exchanges followed between father and son. But Berlioz could not be swayed. Early in 1823 he began studying composition privately with the composer Jean François Lesueur. The father eventually relented, consenting grudgingly to continue Berlioz' allowance if he was able to prove his talent for music. When Berlioz made his first attempt to enter the conservatory as a pupil, however, he was turned down.

In 1826 Berlioz finally managed to gain admission into the conservatory, where he continued to study composition with Lesueur. Berlioz was yet to have a successful accomplishment in music. An opera he was working on was discarded before completion. A cantata submitted for the coveted Prix de Rome (to which all gifted students of the conservatory aspired) was considered unplayable. The only way he could get some of his songs published was to pay for the printing. Nobody paid attention to them. Now convinced that music was not his son's vocation, Berlioz' father summarily discontinued the young man's allowance for good. Berlioz supported himself as best he could, by teaching the guitar, flute, and singing, and by accepting a miserable job as chorister in a minor Parisian theater. But he was content. He was making music, including some for orchestra. And though nobody else seemed to regard it with interest, his teacher, Lesueur, told him prophetically, "You are a genius, and I tell you so because this is the truth."

He was soon to justify the faith his teacher had in him by writing his first masterwork—the *Symphonie fantastique* (*Fantastic* Symphony), op. 14 (1830). The creation of this remarkable work is so inextricably bound up with a tempestuous, irrational romance with a woman that it is both relevant and illuminating to marshal the facts about that event.

In the fall of 1827, Berlioz attended in Paris a performance of Shakespeare's *Hamlet* given by a visiting English company. Ophelia was played by Harriet Smithson, with whom Berlioz fell immediately and madly in love from his seat in the auditorium. He went home in a daze. He resorted to every device he could contrive to meet her in person in the street, outside the theater, outside her apartment. All his efforts were in vain. As a last resort, he rented a room near her apartment, hoping their paths would cross. By the time he settled in his new home, Harriet Smithson had left Paris for London.

Heartbroken, frustrated, the chaser of an unattainable dream, Berlioz tried to sublimate his unrequited love in music: by writing a symphony where Harriet would be the central character, but portrayed as a reprehensible courtesan responsible for the suicide of a poet-hero. De Quincey's autobiographical book *Confessions of an English Opium Eater* provided Berlioz with a suitable program, which he himself summarized as follows:

A young musician of morbid sensibility and ardent imagination poisons himself with opium in a fit of amorous despair. The narcotic dose, too weak to result in death, plunges him into a heavy sleep accompanied by the strangest visions, during which his sensations, sentiments and recollections are translated in his sick brain into musical thoughts and images. The beloved woman herself has become for him a melody, like a fixed idea, which he finds and hears everywhere.

The "fixed idea" (*"l'idée fixe"*) became in the symphony a recurring musical motive representing Harriet. It is heard for the first time in the opening movement in first violins and flute, then returns, though often varied and transformed, in the subsequent movements, which are respectively entitled as follows: "Dreams, Passions"; "At the Ball"; "Scenes in the Country"; "The March to the Gallows"; and "Dream of the Witches' Sabbath." The last of these is a diabolic orgy in which, as Berlioz explained, "the fixed idea again appears, but it has lost its noble, timid character to become an ignoble, trivial grotesque dance. It is she who has come to the witches' Sabbath."

Harriet was back in Paris in 1829. With the conviction that a symphony in which she was portrayed must surely attract her curiosity, Berlioz had the work performed at the conservatory on December 5, 1830. Her failure to attend was a crushing blow; but Berlioz' pain was greatly relieved by the enormous enthusiasm with which the symphony was received—his first success.

The *Fantastic* Symphony is one of the most extraordinary symphonic compositions of the early nineteenth century. It represents such a complete break with the symphonic structure of Beethoven and Schubert that it sometimes becomes difficult to believe it was written only three years after Beethoven's death, and just two years after Schubert's great C-major Symphony. In dramatic and psychological interest (as well as structure) it was years ahead of its time. The vividness of its character portrayals, the outpouring of turbulent emotions, the excursions into fantasy and the grotesque and the diabolic, the realism of its programmatic writing, and its blazing orchestral sounds revealed its composer to be the first spokesman for musical Romanticism in France. Many a composer was influenced by this revolutionary work. The use of a recurring theme (*"idée fixe"*) was the source from which Richard Wagner got the idea of using leading motives in his music dramas. The symphony's pictorialism and the pliable structure of each of the five movements (deriving its shape and form from the musical content, rather than vice versa) led Liszt to originate the symphonic, or tone, poem, a new orchestral form that will be described later.

Hoping to forget Harriet, Berlioz involved himself in a new romance, this time with a pianist, Camille Moke, to whom he became engaged. But when late in 1830 Berlioz finally captured the Prix de Rome, he had to separate himself from his betrothed for a three-year period: the prize entailed that length of residence at the Villa Medici in Rome, where the winner could concentrate on composition and at regular intervals send back to the Paris Conservatory specimens of his work (called *envois*). Always the extremist in his emotions, Berlioz detested Rome violently. He was further disturbed to learn that his betrothed had been unfaithful to him. Impetuously, he decided to return to Paris and seek vengeance. Disguising himself as a lady's maid, he began the journey back to Paris for the purpose of murdering Camille and her mother, at whom he was also angry. By the time he reached Genoa, in Italy, he lost his disguise. And when he arrived in Nice the fires of vengeance had become dying embers. He changed his mind about committing murder, spent his time in Nice writing a concert overture based on Shakespeare (*King Lear,* op. 4), then returned to the Villa Medici. But since he still abhorred Italy he refused to complete the three-year stay. In 1832 he was back in Paris where he rented the same apartment Harriet had once occupied. Camille was permanently rejected from his heart, which once again belonged to Harriet.

Much to his delight he learned that Harriet was planning a return to Paris. In her honor he had his *Symphonie fantastique* repeated at the conservatory on December 9, 1832. Wonder of wonders! This time Harriet was in the audience. She was so enthralled with the music (or flattered that she had proved to be its inspiration) that she finally consented to meet Berlioz personally. Berlioz' personal magnetism, open and unashamed display of his passion, and perseverance finally won. On October 3, 1833, he and Harriet were married. "She was mine," Berlioz later wrote in his autobiography, "and I defied the world."

The victory did not prove as sweet as Berlioz had anticipated. Harriet was no longer the glamorous actress with whom Berlioz had so become infatuated. Her fame as a performer, as well as her financial resources, were in sharp decline. Away from the stage limelight, her beauty seemed faded and worn. She was now even suffering from a physical defect, a limp caused by an accident. As a soul mate, she proved hot-headed, temperamental, volatile, and unsympathetic, and Berlioz had his own ample supply of hypersensitivity, pride, temper, and changing moods. Clashes became inevitable. They quarreled almost from the first day of their marriage. Berlioz' once passionate love weakened rapidly into indifference, and indifference eventually turned into hatred. A few years after Harriet bore him a son (to whom both were always singularly attached), the Berliozes decided upon permanent separation; but they never got a divorce.

While still involved in marital difficulties, Berlioz worked on a second symphony, *Harold in Italy,* op. 16. This work assigned an important role to a viola solo because Paganini, the greatest violinist of his generation, had become interested in playing the viola and commissioned Berlioz to write a major symphonic work where Paganini could perform on that instrument. Paganini expected a virtuoso composition filled with pyrotechnics; what Berlioz intended writing was a giant symphony in which the viola would be a major element in a work concerned solely with dramatic and poetic values. Paganini lost all interest in the composition the moment he saw some of Berlioz' preliminary sketches. Berlioz was now free to write his music according to the dictates of his own personality and artistic conscience.

Ostensibly the symphony was based on Byron's classic *Childe Harold,* but in reality it describes Byron's wanderings through Italy as improvised by Berlioz himself. Around the viola, as Berlioz wrote, were woven "a series of scenes drawn from my memories of wanderings in the Abruzzi, which I called *Childe Harold* as there seemed to me about the whole symphony a poetic melancholy worthy of Byron's hero."

Berlioz once again evolved his own symphonic structure. All four movements are free in form, elastically adjusted to frame the descriptive program. The lengthy title for each movement provides us with the idea behind the music: I. Harold in the Mountains. Scenes of Melancholy, Happiness, and Joy. II. March of the Pilgrims Singing Their Evening Prayers. III. Serenade of a Mountaineer of the Abruzzi to His Mistress. IV. Orgy of the Brigands. Recall of Preceding Scenes.

The recurrent theme representing Harold is first heard in the opening Adagio of the symphony, played by the solo viola and repeated by the clarinets and violins. The scenes of joy and happiness involve the solo viola in a conversation with the orchestra. The second movement is march music, while the third has a scherzolike character (highlighted by

Harold's serenade, on the English horn). In the finale the composer indulges his love for the diabolic and the grotesque.

When the symphony was introduced at the conservatory on November 23, 1834, it made such a deep impression that one movement had to be repeated. Paganini was not in the audience. But when he heard the work four years later he was so moved that he sent Berlioz a gift of about four thousand dollars.

This gift provided Berlioz with the financial means with which to devote himself to the writing of an even more ambitious symphony on a subject that had been haunting him for years, from the time when first he saw Harriet Smithson appear as Juliet in Shakespeare's *Romeo and Juliet*. Though it became a composition of giant design and proportions, *Romeo and Juliet,* op. 17 (1839) took Berlioz only nine months to complete. Solo voices and a chorus supplemented the orchestra in this symphonic projection of Shakespeare's tragedy.

Yet again the symphonic structure is untraditional. The main purpose of the music was to translate into sound what Shakespeare had put into words. Avoiding any set pattern, Berlioz had to evolve a fluid form best suited to present and develop the story he was telling. The first movement describes the combat between the hostile Capulets and Montagues, the tumult that follows, and the prince's order that peace be restored. In the second movement Berlioz portrays Romeo's sad loneliness, then has him invade the Capulets' ball, where he meets and falls in love with Juliet; in this movement we also find the famous balcony love scene, and Mercutio's tale of how the queen of the fairies visited him in his sleep. The symphony ends with the death of the lovers, a tragedy that finally brings about a reconciliation between the Capulets and the Montagues.

Some of Berlioz' most inspired music is in this symphony, which is divided into two parts and a finale instead of the usual four movements. It is greatly to be regretted that the symphony as a whole is not performed as frequently as it deserves. But episodes from this huge score are perennial favorites at concerts. These include the wonderful love music of Romeo and Juliet as they exchange tender and ardent sentiments—Juliet on her balcony, Romeo on the ground below. Also popular is the gossamer music of the Queen Mab Scherzo, in which Mercutio tells of his dream about the fairy queen.

Another gigantic work best known to lovers of symphonic music more through excerpts than through its entirety is *La Damnation de Faust* (*The Damnation of Faust*), op. 24 (1846), based on Goethe's po-

etic drama. Although this work is basically an oratorio (Berlioz, however, referred to it as a "legend"), it does fall within the boundaries of
Berlioz' orchestral output. When presented without deletions, *The Damnation of Faust* is most often given in concert form, although from time
to time it has been staged as an opera. Three orchestral excerpts are performed at symphony concerts: the stirring Hungarian march, "Rakóczy
March"; "The Dance of the Will-o'-the-Wisps," a dainty minuet; and "The
Dance of the Sylphs," a graceful waltz. Berlioz introduced a Hungarian
march into *Faust* through the contrived expedient of bringing his hero
into Hungary. This rousing music builds up a tremendous effect through
the mounting of the sonority until the march music is thundered by the
whole orchestra. The minuet is intended to depict the will-o'-the-wisps
and evil spirits, conjured forth by Mephisto, encircling and protecting
the home of Faust's beloved Marguerite. And the waltz is the music to
which sylphs and gnomes dance as Faust lies asleep, dreaming about
Marguerite.

Though Berlioz tended to favor large symphonic structures, he did
not neglect shorter orchestral forms. Two of his overtures are among his
better-known compositions: Overture to *Benvenuto Cellini,* op. 23
(1837), and the *Roman Carnival* Overture (*Le Carnaval romain*), op. 9
(1844). The first was an overture for an opera that was a failure when
introduced by the Paris Opéra in 1838; its central character was the famous Renaissance sculptor Benvenuto Cellini, and the story tells how he
created one of his most famous statues (*Perseus*), and of his romance
with Teresa. The headstrong personality of Cellini is delineated in the
opening theme. The rest of the overture quotes some important passages
from the opera, including the love duet of Cellini and Teresa.

The *Roman Carnival* Overture was planned as a prelude to the second act of *Benvenuto Cellini.* When the opera was first performed, this
music had not yet been written. Berlioz then decided to make it into a
concert overture rather than part of his opera. The overture opens with
the hint of an Italian folk dance, the saltarello. The tender melody that
follows is part of Cellini's love song to Teresa. After that the music of
the saltarello—now presented in full and developed—takes over the
spotlight.

Berlioz had such enormous energy that writing major works did not
satisfy him completely. In 1835 he became a music critic; in 1839, an
assistant librarian at the conservatory; in 1842 he toured Germany and
Belgium as a conductor; in 1844 he published his *Treatise on Instru-*

mentation (a classic text in its field). He also wrote his autobiography, among other literary works.

His wife, from whom he had been separated for years, died in 1854, enabling Berlioz to marry Marie Recio, with whom he had for some time been in love. The second marriage was no more successful than the first, marked again by a continual conflict of fiery temperaments and volatile moods.

Berlioz' last works were an oratorio, *L'Enfance du Christ* (*The Childhood of Christ*), op. 25 (1854); a monumental opera in two parts and five acts, *Les Troyens* (*The Trojans*) in 1859; and a thoroughly delightful comic opera based on Shakespeare, *Beatrice and Benedict* (1862).

After 1862 Berlioz was stricken by profound depression and nervous disorders. He was convinced his creative life had ended. After the death of his second wife, in 1862, he lived alone in an apartment in Paris, withdrawing completely from the society of friends and fellow musicians. For a while he gathered his dissipating strength and succored his waning spirits and depleted energies by undertaking a few guest appearances as conductor; in 1866 to lead *The Damnation of Faust* and *Harold in Italy* in Vienna; in 1867–68 a concert of his works in Cologne and six concerts in St. Petersburg. The death of his only son in 1867 destroyed whatever meaning life still held for him. Almost as if conscious he did not have much longer to live, he destroyed all documents, letters, and criticisms that he did not want to survive. In March, 1868, he went for a cure to Nice, where he was attacked by cerebral congestion. He managed to return to Paris, where he died on March 8, 1869.

When Berlioz arranged for the premiere of his *Symphonie fantastique* to attract the attention of Harriet Smithson on December 5, 1830, she was not in the audience. But a celebrated musician was there: Franz Liszt. Liszt at that time had never heard of Berlioz, for the very good reason that up to that time Berlioz had written nothing to attract attention. But Liszt, ever curious about new musicians, had come to the concert, and what he heard was destined to become a highly crucial influence on his own development as a composer.

Liszt was nineteen years old at the time, having been born in Raiding, Hungary, on October 22, 1811. Already he had achieved recognition as an extraordinary pianist.

He had proved himself as a prodigy at the piano from his childhood. He began taking lessons at six, and at nine he gave some concerts in several Hungarian cities. A number of Hungarian aristocrats then raised a fund to send him to Vienna, where, for eighteen months (beginning in 1821) Liszt studied with Karl Czerny (piano) and Antonio Salieri (composition). On December 1, 1822, Liszt made a highly successful debut as pianist in Vienna. When he gave his second recital in that city, Beethoven came to the concert and embraced him after the performance.

In 1823 Liszt left Vienna for Paris to enter its conservatory. He had no trouble passing the entrance examinations. But the director of the conservatory, Luigi Cherubini, detested prodigies and was prejudiced against foreign musicians. He turned down Liszt. The young pianist now took lessons in composition from private teachers, but preferred to work out his technical and aesthetic problems at the piano by himself. On March 8, 1824, he caused a sensation at a concert in Paris. He then became the favored child of Parisian nobility and high society. Later the same year he performed in London, where the response to his playing was no less rapturous; he was invited to play for the king. Having become one of the most adulated pianists in Europe after several tours during the next two years, he suddenly and inexplicably formed the resolution to give up music for good and devote himself to literature, philosophy, and religion.

The *Symphonie fantastique*—and the awareness it gave him of the possibilities the new Romanticism had opened up for music—was one of several forces leading Liszt back to music. He was now determined to become the greatest piano virtuoso the world had known. After an extended period of intensive study, he returned to the concert stage a virtuoso of virtuosos, the idol of the concert world. Women adored him, and he responded. After a two-year love affair with the Countess d'Agoult, the countess left her husband and three children for him. Liszt and his beloved then lived together for four years, bringing three children into the world, one of whom was Cosima, later the wife of Hans von Bülow, the famous pianist-conductor, whom she eventually deserted for Wagner.

Liszt's next *grande passion* was for the Princess Carolyne von Sayne-Wittgenstein, whom he first met in 1847 and whose remarkable intelligence, knowledge of literature, and spiritual values gave appreciable stimulation to Liszt's evolution as a fully rounded musician. For up to the time when he met the princess he had devoted himself to concertizing and the writing of piano pieces. Remarkable though he was in both areas, these achievements did not satisfy the princess, who was convinced he was capable of far greater ones. And it was through her influence that he accomplished them.

In 1848 he became the music director of the city of Weimar, where for several years he led performances of operas and orchestral music. He was now the thoroughly dedicated artist, set on giving the most polished performances of which he was capable and ever concerned with promoting the work of new composers. It was through his high-minded idealism and intransigent will that Weimar became one of Europe's most progressive music centers.

He also expanded his horizons as a composer, becoming interested in larger and newer forms and directing his attention more than previously to the orchestra. His contributions to the orchestral literature of the Romantic period were of historic importance (even as his music for the keyboard helped to inaugurate a new era in piano music).

He popularized the form of the rhapsody, so that it became a medium favored by some Romantic composers. Liszt did not invent the form; that honor belongs to a now little-remembered Bohemian composer. But Liszt was the first composer to demonstrate how significant the rhapsody could be to instrumental music—a structure fluid and free in design in which popular melodies could be treated in a rhapsodic manner, with slow and sensuous passages alternating with fiery dramatic ones to create a theatrical effect. Between 1851 and 1886 Liszt wrote twenty rhapsodies for the piano, all made up of Hungarian tunes. He orchestrated twelve of these, with which the rhapsody makes its first appearance in orchestral literature. The most celebrated is undoubtedly the second, in C-sharp minor (1847). Here, as in his other rhapsodies, moods change continually to sustain fascinated interest. The fourteenth of these rhapsodies—that in F minor—has become known in its extended orchestral version as the *Hungarian Fantasy,* a transcription for piano and orchestra made by Liszt.

Liszt, then, established the rhapsody as a useful, popular form of orchestral music, though he did not devise it. But he did create as well as popularize another orchestral structure that has assumed far greater significance: the symphonic poem (also called tone poem). It is in this branch of composition that Liszt had been influenced by Berlioz' *Symphonie fantastique,* which was very much on Liszt's mind when he wrote his first tone poem, *Ce qu'on entend sur la montagne,* based on a work of Victor Hugo. He had first written the work for piano in 1840, and he turned it into an orchestral piece in 1848–49.

A tone, or symphonic, poem is a one-movement composition for orchestra without any definite established structural format. A story, poem, or any other kind of text, a painting or an idea is translated into musical sound. The tone poem, consequently, is program music, whereas most symphonies are absolute music with no pictorial or literary or ideological source.

Liszt wrote thirteen tone poems, the best known of which is *Les Préludes*. This is a musical interpretation of a poem by the French poet Lamartine whose opening line reads: "What is our life but a series of preludes to that unknown song of which death strikes the first solemn note?" The poem then points out various stages, or "preludes," of life: love, the destiny interrupting pleasure and dissipating illusions, the soul, nature. "But," the poem concludes, "when 'the trumpet has sounded the signal of alarms,' he hastens to the post of peril, whatever may be the strife which calls him to the ranks, in order to regain in combat the full consciousness of himself and the complete command of his powers." For each of these thoughts and suggestions Liszt finds an apt musical equivalent. The opening question is heard in a brooding subject for the strings that opens the tone poem; the happiness of love unfolds in a tender melody for the horns. The struggle, once the warning trumpet has sounded, is reproduced in exciting sonorities, dynamics, and chromaticisms; the recapture of man's consciousness and the command of his powers are evoked in a pastoral episode.

Tasso and *Mazeppa* are two more outstanding tone poems by Liszt. The first was inspired by Byron's poem *The Lament of Tasso* and Goethe's play *Torquato Tasso* and was written in 1843. Liszt provided his own program for this music:

Tasso loved and suffered at Ferrara; he was avenged at Rome; his glory still lives in the people's songs of Venice. . . . To express them in music, we first invoked the mighty shadow of the hero as it is now appearing, haunting the lagoons of Venice; we have caught a glimpse of his proud, sad face at the feats in Ferrara; and we have followed him to Rome, the Eternal City, which crowned him with the crown of glory and glorified in him the martyr and poet.

Mazeppa (1851) gets its program from a poem by Victor Hugo about a Polish nobleman (represented musically by a virile subject in trombones, cellos, and basses). Mazeppa, caught in a love affair with another noble's wife, is tied to an untamed horse, to be dragged across the plains of the Ukraine, the ride re-created in agitated music. In the end the horse collapses and Mazeppa is rescued and cared for by Cossacks, whose chief he eventually becomes. This story is all symbolized in the music, which also represents the struggles and triumphs of mortal men, especially artists.

Liszt wrote two symphonies, but (as had been the case with Berlioz) they are not symphonies in the original concept of that form, but a series of tone poems. Neither symphony is given frequent hearings, though each contains some of Liszt's noblest music. *A Symphony to Dante's Divine Comedy* (1856) requires a chorus of women's voices as well as orchestra. It is made up of two tone poems, "Inferno" and "Purgatorio." *A Faust Symphony* (1854), based on Goethe's poetic drama, was described by the composer as three character pictures, because each of the three movements is a tonal study of a major character in Goethe's drama: Faust, Marguerite, and Mephistopheles. Once again, what we have here is not a symphony but three tone poems.

Liszt also wrote some compositions for piano and orchestra. He worked on two concertos over a number of years, starting in the 1830s and finally completing no. 1 in 1856 and no. 2 in 1861. The first, in E-flat major, is the one more favored by audiences because the dramatics are sustained in two of the three movements, while the slow movement is unashamedly sentimental. The three movements are played without interruption. This concerto is at times spoken of as the "triangle" concerto because in the third movement Liszt uses this then rarely heard instrument, for which he was severely criticized by his contemporaries. The second concerto, in A major, in a single movement, is more consistently melodious and sentimental than the first.

In 1859 Liszt also completed a fantasy for piano and orchestra, *Totentanz,* or *Dance of Death.* Impressed by a church fresco in Pisa, Liszt was driven to write this extended work to express the spirit (but not the specific story) of the painting. In this composition Liszt makes extensive and effective use of a plainsong chant, dating probably from the thirteenth century, which has remained familiar through the years as a part of the mass for the dead. This sequence is known as the "Dies irae." (Berlioz had quoted it in the *Symphonie fantastique;* Liszt had not forgotten.) In *Totentanz,* the "Dies irae" theme is first suggested in the full orchestra and is heard in the low instruments to achieve a diabolical mood.

A reading of Austrian poet Nikolaus Lenau's *Faust* (a variation of the Faust legend) stimulated Liszt in 1861 to write two short orchestral pieces, the more famous of which is the *Mephisto Waltz.* This music has such theatrical interest, passion, and power that it must be numbered among Liszt's most distinguished works for orchestra. We can readily follow the course of the music by reading the program note (taken from Lenau) that Liszt quoted in his published score.

There is a wedding feast in progress in the village inn, with music, dancing, carousing. Mephistopheles and Faust pass by, and Mephistopheles induces Faust to enter and take part in the festivities. Mephistopheles snatches the instrument from the hands of a lethargic fiddler and draws from it seductive and intoxicating strains. The amorous Faust whirls about with a full-blooded village beauty in a wild dance; they waltz in mad abandonment out of the room, into the open, away into the woods. The sounds of the fiddle grow softer and softer, and the nightingale warbles his love-laden song.

In 1859, Liszt left his post in Weimar. From then on he lived mainly in Rome, where he embraced religion by receiving, in 1865, the tonsure, symbolic of admission to the clerical state, and later the minor orders, becoming an abbé of the Third Order of Saint Francis of Assisi, an honor that was conferred on him by Pope Pius IX. But religion did not keep him from working on various compositions or from teaching the piano (without fee) to a few gifted students. In 1875 Liszt was appointed president of the New Hungarian Academy of Budapest.

His old age was saddened by his total estrangement from his daughter, Cosima. Though Liszt had long recognized Wagner's genius and had been a passionate advocate of Wagner's art he could not forgive his daughter for having deserted her husband, Hans von Bülow, and their children, for Wagner. There developed hard feelings between Liszt and Wagner, but the two men eventually became reconciled. Liszt was present at, and deeply moved by, the first Wagner festival at Bayreuth in 1876. But Cosima stubbornly refused to have any further personal dealings with her father. She never allowed him to visit her home in Bayreuth either before or after Wagner's death. She did not even allow her father to attend Wagner's funeral in 1883.

Liszt was attacked by pneumonia while attending the Wagner festival at Bayreuth in 1886. The sickness proved fatal. He died in Bayreuth on July 31, 1886. Thus the last music Liszt was destined to hear was Wagner's, and that is probably the way he would have wanted it to be could he have chosen.

The Romantic movement launched so auspiciously in France by Berlioz was carried on until the end of the nineteenth century. The most famous symphony in French music springs from the soil of this Romanticism, the Symphony in D minor by César Franck (1822–1890). Franck was a humble, unpretentious, excessively kind and gentle man who failed to receive recognition for his music until the end of his life. He accepted this rejection stoically. His fame, in his lifetime, rested on his organ playing, done at his post at the Sainte-Clotilde Church in Paris, which he occupied from 1858 until his death. He went about his business—giving lessons, playing the organ, writing music—always maintaining the highest standards of which he was capable.

The thrice-familiar symphony of Franck (his only work in this form) came in 1888, when his life was almost over. Today we always respond to the majestic opening of the first movement. There follow several musical themes that either generate power or introduce moments of yearning. The middle movement (the symphony has only three) highlights a glorious melody for the English horn. The finale becomes a kind of summary, since main themes from the two earlier movements are repeated. This is in line with a technique developed by Franck, the "cyclical method," where in a large work he repeats in later movements material from earlier ones to achieve unity.

The symphony now has such an instantaneous appeal to audiences that it is impossible to believe that it was treated so harshly when it was first heard in Paris in 1889. Gounod, the composer of *Faust,* described it as "the affirmation of incompetence pushed to dogmatic lengths." Some of the conservatory directors were shocked to hear Franck use the English horn so prominently in the second movement. "Who ever heard of an English horn in a symphony?" they inquired hotly. The audience was either apathetic or abusive. Franck accepted such reactions with his usual calm. "It sounded well," he told his wife, "just as I thought it would."

Franck never wrote a piano concerto, but he did contribute a major work for piano and orchestra: *Variations symphoniques* (*Symphonic Variations*) in 1885. There are three sections, rather than movements. The first is an extended introduction where the main theme is at first suggested before being presented in full. The middle part consists of six variations on this theme. In the last section Franck creates a brilliant epilogue to the variations, including a wondrous melody for cellos based on the main theme.

Franck also wrote five tone poems for orchestra, which are given infrequently, and among which are *Les Éolides* (1876), *Le Chasseur maudit* (1882), and *Les Djinns* (for piano and orchestra, 1884).

Only in the last year of his life did Franck finally receive both public and critical approbation. This first happened on April 19, 1890, when the premiere of his string quartet aroused genuine enthusiasm. A few days later he was given an ovation at an all-Franck concert. "You see," he remarked quietly to a friend, "the public is beginning to understand me." It never occurred to him to grumble that he had had to wait so many years for the approval he had so long deserved.

That recognition arrived at the zero hour; Franck did not live long enough to enjoy fully his belated success. He was on his way to give a lesson in May of 1890 when an omnibus hit him. A fatal attack of pleurisy developed; complicated by his injuries. He died in Paris on November 8, 1890.

Camille Saint-Saëns (1835–1921) was the last of the French Romantics. He was a man of extraordinary culture whose mind imposed upon his emotions restraint and discipline, so that his music always had a beautiful sense of proportion, well-thought-out logic, and technical polish. He was a most versatile man outside music: a mathematician, astronomer, critic, archaeologist, traveler, author, painter, dramatist, philosopher. He was no less versatile as composer. His best larger works for orchestra are: Piano Concerto no. 2 in G minor, op. 22 (1868); Concerto no. 1 in A minor, for cello and orchestra, op. 33 (1873); Concerto no. 4 in C minor, for piano and orchestra, op. 44 (1875); Concerto no. 3 in B minor, for violin and orchestra, op. 61 (1880); and the Symphony no. 3 in C minor, op. 78 (1886), which requires an organ. All are in traditional Romantic style, filled with rich sonorities, with pleasing melodies, and with sentiment.

There was no area in music Saint-Saëns did not cultivate, and no style that he could not master. He wrote in a Portuguese, Spanish, Cuban, or Algerian style with equal felicity. And he could be witty as well as serious. One of his most delightful excursions into humor and satire is *Le Carnaval des animaux* (*The Carnival of Animals,* 1886). This work bears no opus number because Saint-Saëns had written it for his own pleasure and had no intention of publishing it or allowing it to be performed publicly. It was only after his death that it gained wide circulation.

This suite is made up of fourteen sections, opening with a regal march of the lions. After that come descriptions of hens and cocks, mules, tortoises, elephants, kangaroos, an aquarium, "personages with long ears," an aviary, a cuckoo in the woods, "pianists," fossils, and a swan. In the finale all of the above reappear briefly, almost as if for a final curtain call.

The loveliest movement of all is "The Swan," a solo for cello. This music has often been used as the accompaniment for a dance by a ballerina. In most of the other parts of the suite, Saint-Saëns' keen sense of fun comes to the fore. He puts pianists in the zoo full of animals. His music imitates the cumbersome walk of elephants and kangaroos. Musically, he uses mules to mock at pianists who play a composition as if by rote, following the printed music rigidly and inflexibly. In the kangaroo section he laughs at audiences who insist on talking during concerts. He quotes from the music of other composers, and even from his own works, to contribute droll contrasts. In the elephant part, for example, we are reminded of the delicate and graceful music of Berlioz' "Dance of the Sylphs" for the sake of amusing contrast. In "Fossils," a part of Rossini's *Barber of Seville* is interpolated, and so is a portion of Saint-Saëns' own *Danse macabre*.

The last-named composition is a tone poem, op. 40 (1874)—music far different from *The Carnival of Animals*. Here a grotesque dance of skeletons is described, with Death providing the ghostly music; the rattle of bones is simulated by a xylophone.

Saint-Saëns paid two visits to the United States, in 1906 and in 1915. He toured South America in 1916. As an old man he was still being heard as pianist and conductor, his last public appearance taking place in Dieppe when he was eighty-six years old. He died soon after that in Algiers on December 16, 1921.

Felix Mendelssohn, a caricature by Aubrey Beardsley.

Franz Schubert.

*Franz Liszt at the age
of twenty-one.*

Hector Berlioz.

An outdoor concert in London in 1848.

The Culmination of Musical Romanticism

Johannes Brahms

With most composers it is possible to hazard a guess on what kind of people they were from the music they wrote. Not so with Brahms! If you had been living in Vienna in the late nineteenth century and were to have seen him in the street or at a café, you would have been highly skeptical if you had been told that he was a composer, a very great composer. You might have ventured to suggest that he was a public official or the headmaster of a boy's school or a university professor. But a composer, never!—and, most assuredly, not the composer of those passionately dramatic outbursts, those sensuous moods in soaring strings, those deeply romantic utterances in the lower voices of his instruments that so enthrall audiences. For Brahms the composer and Brahms the man were opposites. An arch-romanticist, a sensualist, an exalted poet when he put notes down on paper, Brahms, in both appearance and daily habits, was, away from his music, as prosaic as a bookkeeper's ledger. Here once again we confront the mystery of genius: it appears in unexpected places under inexplicable conditions.

He was a dumpy little man, stocky, heavyset. His skin had a ruddy glow against a patriarchal beard and a thick head of hair worn down to his shoulders. He always favored the same kind of inexpensively priced and quixotically styled clothes. His trousers and jackets rarely matched, both usually out of fashion, and even more frequently failing to fit him properly. Walking in the street, he protected himself from Vienna's icy winter blasts with a blue-green shawl that he attached to his jacket with a large pin. He always carried hat in hand, instead of wearing it.

He lived simply (one might even say frugally). A very modest three-room apartment in the Karlgasse was his home during the last quarter-century of his life, when he was already famous and financially well off. Though he had a housekeeper, his place was in a perpetual state of disorder, with pictures, engravings, bronze reliefs, mementos from his many trips, books and music, and portfolios overcrowding the place. His square piano was overburdened with all kinds of odds and ends, and the closet where he kept his clothes was a mess. In the mornings he would brew his own coffee. He took his lunches and dinners in inexpensive restaurants, and whenever he visited a café, he kept a scrupulous eye on the bill he was accumulating. During his travels, he always bought a third-class ticket. He disliked spending money on himself and thus never allowed himself luxuries or extravagances. In his business dealings he was a hard bargainer. Yet, at other times, he could also be singularly careless about his finances. He was inordinately generous in giving out money to those in need, adding gruffly, "I have no use for it." He never knew how much he earned or how much he possessed. Bundles of uncounted bank notes were kept carelessly in cabinet drawers.

He was quite a different man when he sat down to work, to which he assigned special hours, usually in the morning. In his artistic habits he was as disciplined, methodical, and precise as he was careless about his extramusical activities. His manuscripts were always arranged in meticulous order and his musical notations were neat. For all the chaos in his household, he always seemed able to find any book or piece of music he wanted at any given moment. When he read a book or looked through somebody's music, he always corrected mistakes. Intellectually, as well as musically, this man's house was in order.

To outward appearance he seemed to be of even temperament, rarely permitting himself to get disturbed, seemingly at peace with himself and his personal world. But the process of creation, the birth pains producing a concerto or a symphony, was always accompanied by an inner hurricane. In the Austrian resort town of Bad Ischl, one of his favored summer haunts, he would wander off into the woods, his head bursting with music, to all appearances looking like a man driven by de- mons. Sometimes while composing he would weep bitterly.

But once the birth pangs ended, once he stepped out of the role of composer into that of an ordinary Viennese, he stopped being the genius and gave the appearance of a bourgeois government official and school-master.

Johannes Brahms was born in a tenement on the waterfront of Hamburg, Germany, on May 7, 1833. He was the son of a doublebass player in the Hamburg Opera and a slightly deformed mother who added to her husband's meager salary by doing needlework. Johannes was a musical child who began inventing his own melodies (and a system of putting them down on paper) before he could read or write. He began studying the piano when he was seven. Within two years he helped to support his family by playing the piano in disreputable inns and cafés at the waterfront.

One of Hamburg's highly revered piano teachers, Eduard Marxsen, took Brahms on as pupil when he was ten. So carefully did Marxsen nurse Brahms's gifts, both as pianist and composer, that in his fourteenth year Brahms made his debut simultaneously as pianist and as composer by including his own variations on a folk melody in a piano recital. Poverty, however, made it impossible for the boy to devote himself as seriously and completely to music as he would have liked. He had to earn money, and he did so by writing hack compositions (about one hundred and fifty of which were published under pen names), teaching the piano, and doing arrangements. The continual pressure imposed upon him by these assignments—or was it the wear and tear hack work imposed on his artistic conscience?—combined to undermine his health. He would probably have suffered a nervous breakdown had not a generous relative rushed him off to the country for a prolonged rest period.

By 1851 he had produced the Scherzo in E-flat minor, for piano, op. 4 and in 1852 a piano sonata. One year later he finally found a job that not only did not rob him of his self-respect but even advanced his career as a serious musician. He became the piano accompanist for Eduard Reményi, a distinguished violinist, with whom he toured Germany. With Reményi he was now able to perform the music of the masters. He was also given the opportunity to meet personally some powerful and highly esteemed musicians. One was Liszt, who, after hearing Brahms play his own music, presented the young musician with a cigarette case. Another

The Culmination of Musical Romanticism

115

was Joseph Joachim, already a violinist of considerable eminence, whom he met in Hanover. Most significant (in view of their impact on Brahms's life from that time on) were Clara and Robert Schumann. Brahms visited them in Düsseldorf, played for them one of his piano sonatas, and won them over completely as admirers and friends. In his diary, describing this visit, Schumann referred to Brahms as a "genius," then went on to write a special article about the young, unknown composer in the *Neue Zeitschrift für Musik*. The Schumanns were so taken with Brahms that they had him for a while as a permanent guest at their home, the better to give him the benefit of their experience, criticism, and advice. At the same time, Robert Schumann used his reputation and influence to get a German publisher to issue three of Brahms's piano sonatas and to arrange for Brahms to give a piano recital in Leipzig.

To such generosity Brahms responded with a heart full of love and gratitude. He soon had an opportunity to reciprocate. When, in 1854, he learned of Schumann's physical and mental disintegration, he rushed to Düsseldorf to be with Schumann and his family and help them as best he could. And when Robert Schumann was confined to an asylum, Brahms rented an apartment in Clara's house, where he lived for two years to bring her solace and help. He took care of Schumann's children as if they were his own. He visited Schumann regularly at the asylum up to the time of Schumann's death in 1856. After that—for the next forty years—he never wavered in his love and devotion to Clara, who probably meant more to him than any other woman except his own mother, whom he had always adored.

Why Brahms never married Clara after Schumann's death (since the love was mutual) raises the problem of Brahms's lifelong resistance to marriage. Both before and after he became so strongly attached to Clara, Brahms had been interested in many women. Some of these relationships were mild flirtations, some intense love affairs. Once when his friendship with a girl approached the dangerous boundary line beyond which stood the marriage altar, he exclaimed, "Chains I cannot wear!" Instead of marrying her, he sublimated his feelings by writing a sextet. On another occasion he explained lamely that the reason he refused to marry was his fear of bringing his wife news of failures. "Failures, they do not hurt me," he said. "But if I had been obliged to meet the questioning eyes of a wife and to tell her that once again I had failed—that I could not have endured." He was, to be sure, not penetrating to the heart of his problem (and he probably knew it). Biographers have offered various reasons to explain his fear of marriage, if fear it was. Whatever the reason, though he was thoroughly capable of loving a woman and being loved in return, he remained a bachelor.

While he had produced much chamber and piano music in which he was arriving at creative maturity, Brahms did not make his first attempt to write for orchestra until about 1857, when he was employed part-time as house musician for the prince of Lippe-Detmold in Hamburg. That work was his Piano Concerto no. 1 in D minor, op. 15, which took him four years to write and which he finally completed in 1858. It started out as an idea for a symphony but was completed as a sonata for two pianos. Only late in 1857 did he decide to rewrite the sonata into a piano concerto, using the first two movements of his sonata, to which he provided orchestral backing. "I am only experimenting and feeling my way," was the modest manner in which Brahms referred to his concerto. He was, to say the least, guilty of understatement. That first concerto is a masterwork, remarkable for its completeness of concept, maturity of thought, and sureness of technique. The music has power and passion, brilliance, and in many pages profound meditation. Strength is continually contrasted with introspection. The elegiac slow movement has some of the depth of feeling encountered in Beethoven. This movement bears the inscription, "Benedictus qui venit in nomine Domini" ("Blessed is he who comes in the Name of the Lord"), a fact leading some critics to infer that his music was inspired by Robert Schumann's death.

The continual conflict between strong statements and mellow ones, between defiance and moody introspection, is a quality characterizing Brahms's later orchestral works—particularly his four symphonies. Another later characteristic of Brahms found in the first piano concerto is his respect for classical structure, however much he may bend or expand it. This marriage of the Romanticist on the one hand and the Classicist on the other sets Brahms apart from most of the other orchestral writers of the Romantic era. Brahms's heart is Romantic, but the mind that controls the heart is Classic. In his subsequent compositions Brahms repeatedly demonstrated his interest in the traditions of the past: in his use of polyphony; in his revival of such old structures as the orchestral serenade, the passacaglia and the concerto grosso; in his avoidance of programmatic music or music inspired by literary subjects and his allegiance to absolute music; in the way he remained faithful to the basic form of the symphony or concerto or overture as Beethoven had left them.

It was the Classicist in Brahms (which revealed itself early) that led him to write two orchestral serenades in the old Baroque style when he next used the orchestra, this time without a solo instrument. The two serenades appeared between 1858 and 1859. The first, in D major, op. 11, imitated the rococo style of the days of Haydn and Mozart. In the second, in A major, op. 16, a Romantic spirit tries to assert itself within the constricted confines of a Classical form.

Through the time of writing these two serenades, Brahms had been living in his native city of Hamburg, where from 1860 to 1863 he led a chorus. After 1863 his home was in Vienna, to which he came in 1863 bearing several masterpieces (two piano quartets, some songs, and the *Variations on a Theme by Handel* for piano). "This is Beethoven's heir," said Joseph Hellmesberger, the leader of a famous Viennese string quartet. This was not the first time Brahms's name was linked with Beethoven's, nor was it the last.

It took Brahms fourteen years after his second serenade to write another work exclusively for orchestra. But what an outpouring of masterworks took place in that interim: chamber, piano, and choral music, including the majestic *A German Requiem,* for soprano and baritone solos, chorus, and orchestra, and the autumnal beauty of the *Alto Rhapsody,* for alto voice, male chorus, and orchestra. All these works came from the hands of a master who now well deserved a place in that royal line of masters who had lived in Vienna since the time of Gluck. This fact was recognized. In 1872 Brahms was appointed director of one of Vienna's most honored musical institutions, the Gesellschaft der Musikfreunde, a position he retained for three years.

Brahms had used the orchestra in *A German Requiem* and the *Alto Rhapsody,* but it occupied a supplementary role to the voice. Hypercritical of himself and awed by the shadow of Beethoven that continually hovered over his consciousness, he was reluctant to invade the field of symphonic music that Beethoven had dominated. "You will never know," he told a friend, "how the likes of us feel when we hear the tramp of a giant like Beethoven behind us."

His first new work exclusively for orchestra had been germinating in his mind for about a decade: the *Variations on a Theme by Haydn,* op. 56a. Once again, as had happened with his first piano concerto, the *Variations* started out as a composition for two pianos, which Brahms completed in 1873. (This work bears the opus number of 56b and became his last major work for the keyboard.) Brahms then rewrote the composition for orchestra.

The title indicates that the melody Brahms used is by Haydn, but this is not strictly true. The theme actually is an old hymn known as the

"Chorale St. Antoni" which Haydn had borrowed for use in a long-un-published divertimento in or about 1782. (The more pastoral Haydn piece was finally published in 1932.) This theme is heard in the Brahms work without introduction, presented by the woodwinds over a string ac-companiment. Eight variations and a finale follow, covering a wide gamut of styles and moods. At the end of the work, the original chorale theme is repeated forcefully in the brass and woodwinds to decorative treatment by the strings.

But Brahms's ambition to write a symphony could not be perma-nently denied, no matter how many years he delayed in getting to work on it. Writing that first symphony proved a Herculean undertaking, since Brahms always felt he was trying to walk in Beethoven's giant footsteps. So taxing did the labor of completing his symphony prove that when fi-nally, in 1876, the last notes were scratched on his manuscript he vowed never again to write another symphony. Fortunately that vow was soon broken.

Brahms was forty-three when he finished the Symphony no. 1 in C minor, op. 68. Few composers come to the writing of a symphony so late in life. Brahms was at the peak of his creativity. This is undoubtedly the reason why what he accomplished was a masterwork of master-works; the greatest first symphony ever written; a work that was by no means overshadowed by the immensity of Beethoven's symphonies; a work so immense in structure, technique, and material that it was once referred to as "Beethoven's Tenth Symphony." In dubbing it thus, the speaker or writer was underlining the truly Beethovenian personality of this work: its heroic style, its high-minded speech, its muscular strength, its conflicts, its grandeur, and its poetry. James Gibbons Huneker, a fa-mous American music critic of the past, once wrote that Brahms was "the first composer since Beethoven to sound the note of the sublime." Sublime, indeed, is the first-movement introduction, where the violins soar ecstatically over a background of throbbing tympani; sublime, too, is the second movement, which is carried to a pitch of emotional delir-ium before settling down to the introspective calm with which it had begun; and sublime is the word for the finale, whose heart is a majestic song for strings that bears a slight resemblance to the "Ode to Joy" mel-ody in Beethoven's Ninth Symphony.

Despite his original intention to write no more symphonies, a second one—in D major, op. 73—followed the first by only a single year. In his new symphony Brahms is the pantheist, the lover of nature. The music breathes a serenity or a bucolic joy, a pastoral beauty or re-

119

strained exhilaration all inspired by the lovely Austrian lake resort (Pört-schach) where it was written.

The Symphony no. 3 in F major, op. 90 (1883), on the other hand, presents a bold, heroic personality. It opens strongly with three chords in the woodwinds with trumpets and horns, followed by a vigorous down-sweep of the violins that is the movement's first subject. Those three pre-liminary chords are a kind of motto that is heard throughout the move-ment, sometimes as a discreet background to the main theme, sometimes as subsidiary material, and sometimes given principal treatment. The second movement has a kind of religious quality to it, with a choralelike melody and a sensitively lyrical subsidiary subject. This movement is typical of the reflective Brahms, as is much of the third movement, where Brahms dispenses with the expected scherzo to replace it with a romanza. But in the finale we are in the presence of a conflict whose forces are put under control to permit a wonderful song to rise from the cellos and horns.

Brahms wrote only one more symphony—no. 4 in E minor, op. 98 (1885). He was now fifty-two years old. The passions of his youth and early manhood have subsided. He is now given to quiet reminiscences, to melancholy reflections, to the sadness of approaching the threshold of old age. So melancholy is the pervading mood of this symphony that one Brahms biographer has designated the work as "elegiac." A simple two-note phrase is the germ of the theme that opens the first movement; after each two-note sequence the woodwinds reply with the same two-note pattern. This, too, can be regarded as a kind of motto, for it is repeated in the development, helps to usher in the recapitulation, and becomes material for the coda. The solemnity of the motto theme, however, finds a contrast in a flight into sensuality as the strings ascend ecstatically to a high register. A similar outburst of passion erupts midway in the second movement, whose main melody has an exotic character (built from one of the old church modes rather than from a major and minor scale), and whose secondary theme is an elegy for woodwinds. There is sprightlier music in the third movement. Then comes the finale, which brings the symphony to an epic ending. In this movement Brahms takes a back-ward glance at music's past by using the Baroque form of the passaca-glia: an instrumental structure in which the treble furnishes variations to a theme stated and restated in the bass. In the Fourth Symphony the theme is heard first in brass, woodwind, and tympani and is treated to thirty variations in the high, middle, and low voices. Never was Brahms's skill in the science of thematic transformation, his gift for reaching ever new heights of eloquence more forcefully evident than here. The variations ended, the full orchestra sounds the basic theme (in a free adaptation) to begin a momentum carrying the symphony to a grandiose conclusion.

Between the second and third symphonies, Brahms completed his only violin concerto (the Concerto in D major, op. 77 in 1878), his Piano Concerto no. 2 in B-flat major, op. 83 (1881), and two concert overtures, the *Akademische Festouvertüre* (*Academic Festival* Overture) op. 80 (1880) and the *Tragische Ouvertüre* (*Tragic* Overture) op. 81 (1880).

In both his violin and second piano concerto Brahms the symphonist is ever present. Each is a giant structural projection, the piano concerto even more so than the one for violin. In each, Brahms passes from turmoil to repose and back again to turmoil. In each, the solo instrument is never used to glorify the performer, but rather the music itself.

Though Brahms wrote his violin concerto with the advice and criticism of one of the greatest violinists of his time—that same Joseph Joachim whom Brahms had met when he was an accompanist—it is not always written gracefully for its instrument. Some facetious critic commented that Brahms had written a concerto not *for* the violin but *against* it. The truth is that Brahms did not always accept Joachim's suggestions. The composer was so concerned with his symphonic texture, and with his dynamic and electrifying melodic material, that the niceties of writing music suitable for violin assumed for him secondary importance. Nevertheless, this concerto is one of the greatest ever written; if it is undisciplined, it is because of its fiery spirit, which often assumes a Hungarian identity. Only in the second movement, with its idyllic song, is the lyrical quality of the violin catered to.

Concerning his Second Piano Concerto, Brahms wrote to a friend, "I have written a tiny, tiny piano concerto with a tiny, tiny wisp of a scherzo." His tongue was in his cheek. This concerto is one of the hugest monuments in the literature. It has four instead of the usual three movements, each so spacious in design and breadth that the entire work has sometimes been referred to as a symphony with piano obbligato. Serenity rather than struggle predominates in most of this music, almost as if Brahms had come to terms with life and with himself. Much of the greatness of this wonderful concerto lies in its poetic melodies, or what Brahms himself referred to as an "adagio mood." But the work is also rhapsodic and at times, as in the finale, filled with animal energy.

Brahms wrote only one more concerto after that (his last work to use a symphony orchestra): the Concerto in A minor, op. 102 (1887). It is a curious work. For one thing, it is a concerto for two instruments, the violin and the cello; for another, the composer reverted to the old Baroque structure of the concerto grosso, with the solo instruments as the *concertino,* and the orchestra as the *ripieno.* Essentially, however, this composition (popularly known as the "Double Concerto") is Brahmsian in its lyrical and romantic appeal and in the grandeur of its architectonic design.

Brahms's two concert overtures were produced in 1880. The *Academic Festival* Overture was a token of gratitude to the university of Breslau, in Germany, for bestowing on Brahms the honorary degree of Doctor of Philosophy. Brahms used as his principal thematic material college songs popular throughout Germany and even Europe, including the celebrated "Gaudeamus igitur." Brahms often referred to this overture as "a very jolly potpourri of students' songs." The climax comes with a resounding presentation of "Gaudeamus igitur."

It is a good-humored man who speaks in the *Academic Festival* Overture, but a brooding, unhappy one in the *Tragic* Overture. "I could not refuse my melancholy nature the satisfaction of composing an overture for a tragedy," he explained to his publisher. As one of Brahms's friends commented about the two overtures, "One of them laughs, the other weeps." Brahms had no specific tragedy in mind in writing the *Tragic* Overture. This is one of the most deeply moving of his shorter works for orchestra, the tragic mood growing ever darker and deeper as the overture progresses.

The honorary doctorate conferred on Brahms by the university of Breslau was one of several tributes conferred on him in recognition of his magisterial position in the world of music. In 1886 Brahms became Knight of the Prussian Order. Three years after that, the city of his birth, Hamburg, gave him the freedom of the city, and that same year the emperor of Austria confered on him the Order of Leopold.

His life followed an established pattern. Winters were spent in Vienna at his Karlgasse apartment, with the mornings usually devoted to composition, and evenings at coffeehouses with his friends. During the summer Brahms went to Austrian resorts, his work periods relieved by walks along lakes and on mountain paths. Occasionally his routine had to be altered to allow him to make guest appearances as conductor of his works in various European cities.

In the summer of 1883 Brahms abandoned his habit of vacationing in Austria by going to the German city of Wiesbaden. There he fell in love with a young and comely girl, a singer named Hermine Spies, whom he described as "my gay and pretty Rhineland girl." He became engaged to her and during this period wrote some lovely love songs to her. But Brahms had not outgrown his weakness for fleeing from a woman he loved when he was threatened with matrimony.

His love for Clara Schumann remained deep and all-abiding until her death in 1896. Brahms attended her funeral, where he caught a cold that aggravated a serious physical condition (cancer of the liver) from which he was then suffering. Though ill, he insisted on attending a performance of his Fourth Symphony in Vienna on March 7, 1897. Both the members of the orchestra and the audience sprang to their feet as slowly and painfully he made his way to the artist's box. After each movement, there was a demonstration; at the end of the symphony, pandemonium was let loose. Here is how Brahms's first significant biographer, Florence May, described the scene that she herself had witnessed:

The applauding, shouting house, its gaze riveted on the figure standing in the balcony . . . seemed unable to let him go. Tears ran down his cheeks as he stood there, shrunken in form, with lined countenance, strained expression, white hair hanging lank; and throughout the audience there was a feeling of a stifled sob, for each knew they were saying farewell. Another outburst of applause, and yet another. One more acknowledgement from the master. Then Brahms and his Vienna were parted forever.

Less than one month after that, early in the morning of April 3, 1897, Brahms passed away in Vienna.

Musical Nationalism

The Russian Five, Antonín Dvořák,

Edvard Grieg

A significant development in Romantic music was the spread of musical nationalism during the second half of the nineteenth century. The Napoleonic Wars and their aftermath, the revolutions of 1848, the tides of liberalism and political upheavals felt far and wide, the restlessness of small countries dominated by large ones all gave rise to a swelling national consciousness. People became interested in their country's culture, heritage, customs, ideas. Since the Romantic movement in music sought out untried subjects for musical treatment, composers began reaching into folklore, history, geographical location, and people's lives for material for compositions. Composers with nationalistic tendencies became fascinated with their country's folk songs and dances, which they either quoted or imitated. In writing program music, these composers preferred subjects or characters indigenous to their own countries.

The stir of musical nationalism had already been felt early in the nineteenth century: with Karl Maria von Weber (1786–1826), when in his folk opera *Der Freischütz* he based his arias and choruses on German folk music and used a text derived from German legend; with Frédéric Chopin (1810–1849), when in 1817 he began writing polonaises for the piano, and in 1824 mazurkas, both of which are types of Polish dances; with Mikhail Glinka (1804–1857), who went to Russian history and poetry for the texts of his two operas (*Russlan and Ludmilla* and *A Life for the Czar*), which he filled with music modeled after old Russian songs, dances, and church music. Glinka also wrote an orchestral composition of national identity: *Kamarinskaya* (1848), a fantasy based on two Russian folk songs. There were also indications of nationalism in Liszt's *Hungarian Rhapsodies,* the first of which came in 1846.

But it was really in the latter half of the century, and in Russia, that there emerged for the first time a clearly defined, carefully directed movement to have composers concentrate on a national musical art. In Saint Petersburg (now Leningrad), there appeared a group, or "school" of composers called "the Russian Five" or "the Mighty Five." Their leader was Mili Balakirev (1837–1910). It was he who clarified the ideal governing the creativity of Russian composers, that of bringing into existence an authentically Russian music. Pride in country was not Balakirev's sole stimulus. He wanted Russian composers to free themselves completely from the influence of Western European music, from imitating Brahms or Wagner, for example. Balakirev felt that the only way this could be done was to have Russian composers derive their style and materials not from European but from Russian sources. Putting theory into practice, Balakirev wrote an *Overture on Russian Themes,* for orchestra (1858), in which he quoted three folk songs; *Tamara,* a tone poem using a text by M. Lermontov (1882); and *Russia,* another tone poem elaborating on three Russian folk songs (1884).

Balakirev influenced four other Russian composers to follow his lead: Alexander Borodin (1833–1887); Modest Mussorgsky (1839–1881); Nikolai Rimsky-Korsakov (1844–1908); and César Cui (1835–1918). Because of Balakirev's persuasive arguments all four were induced to join him in a common cause. What a curious gathering of personalities these five men represented! Balakirev was a driven man—harassed by hypochondria, a victim of superstitions that governed his life, and eventually a man obsessed by religious mania. Borodin was one who divided his immense talents and interests equally between music and science; he was an authority on chemistry, a professor at the Academy of Medicine, and a dedicated research worker. Mussorgsky was born to wealth, lost his property when Russian serfs were liberated in 1861, then earned a meager living as a government clerk. He degenerated into an alcoholic in his last years and lived in squalor and degradation. He was as uncouth and undisciplined in his musical writing as, in his later years, he was in his personal appearance and habits. In spite of this he was the greatest composer of this group. He evolved his own style and was the creator of one of the greatest folk operas ever written, *Boris Godunov*. Rimsky-Korsakov was trained for the navy and for three years was a midshipman aboard a Russian vessel that sailed around the world. He left the navy for music, eventually becoming renowned as a professor at the Saint Petersburg Conservatory as well as a composer; of the Five, he was the scholar. And finally there was Cui, the most normal of the group, who led a disciplined and productive musical life, wrote abundantly, and ended up as a total mediocrity. Together, this strange mixture of five radically different personalities was responsible for the first full flowering of musical nationalism.

Borodin's most famous work is his folk opera *Prince Igor*, begun in 1869 and completed after his death in 1887 by Rimsky-Korsakov and Alexander Glazunov. Its central theme is the conflict between the Tartars of Central Asia (known as the Polovtsi) and the Russian army headed by Prince Igor. Out of this opera come the exotic, exciting *Polovtsian Dances* (often played in symphony concerts). But this opera was also indirectly responsible for another of Borodin's major orchestral works: the Symphony no. 2 in B minor (1877). The six years it took Borodin to write his symphony was also a period when he was involved with his opera. Some of the music Borodin had planned for his opera was finally used in the symphony, so that the symphony has the same kind of epic and oriental character as the opera. This four-movement work has such an ambitious design and such a heroic personality that it is sometimes identified as "Bogatyr"—a *bogatyr* being a giant of old Russian epics. Though it has no program, the symphony has been interpreted as a tonal picture of feudal Russia. It describes the assembling of ancient Russian princes, and Russian heroes celebrating a banquet. Many of the melodies simulate the songs of old Russian troubadours.

Borodin's tone poem *On the Steppes of Central Asia* (1880) is as famous as his symphony. This is the program found in the published score:

Out of the silence of the sandy steppes of Central Asia come the sounds of a peaceful Russian song. Along with them are heard the melancholy strains of Oriental melodies, then the stamping of approaching horses and camels. A caravan, accompanied by Russian soldiers, traverses the measureless waste. . . . It continues its long journey. . . .

The songs of the Russians and those of the Asiatic natives mingle in common harmony. The refrains curl over the desert and then die away in the distance.

Mussorgsky produced a frequently heard orchestral fantasy, *A Night on Bald Mountain* (1860–66). Its program is an old Russian legend about the revel of witches, sorcerers, and other evil spirits on Saint John's Eve on Bald Mountain near Kiev. Mussorgsky actually never wrote the fantasy as it is today heard. He had left behind numerous sketches, which, after his death, were assembled by Rimsky-Korsakov into an integrated composition and then orchestrated by him and first performed in 1866.

Rimsky-Korsakov is the composer whose orchestral works most often represent the Five on our concert programs. And Rimsky-Korsakov's most beloved work is the suite *Scheherazade,* op. 35 (1888). Despite their preoccupation with things Russian, the Five were sometimes drawn to colorful subjects and backgrounds of exotic lands. In *Scheherazade* Rimsky-Korsakov reveals his fascination for *The Arabian Nights* by using some of its stories as subjects for his music. The title of each of the four movements discloses the story it is telling: "The Sea and Sinbad's Ship," "The Tale of the Kalandar Prince," "The Young Prince and the Princess," and "The Festival of Bagdad." Rimsky-Korsakov explained that he tried to present "a kaleidoscope of fairy-tale images and designs of oriental character." Recurring musical motives identify the principal characters throughout the composition: quiet chords for the brass suggest the Sultan, and a sinuous theme for solo violin, Scheherazade. The Scheherazade theme appears in all four movements, then carries the suite to a gentle conclusion after a brilliant description of a festival in Bagdad.

The lure of the exotic is also present in Rimsky-Korsakov's most famous symphony, the Symphony no. 2, op. 9 (1868), dubbed the *Antar*. The subject is based on an old Arabian legend, whose entire plot unfolds in the first movement. Antar, man's enemy, saves a gazelle's life. In a dream, Antar finds himself in the palace of the queen of Palmyra, a fairy who turns out to be the gazelle Antar has saved. The queen compensates Antar by enabling him to realize life's three greatest pleasures: vengeance, power, and love. Antar and the queen fall in love, a love of which Antar soon grows weary and for which he pays with his life. This story told, the symphony goes on in the next three movements to describe each of the three pleasures of life Antar was privileged to enjoy. The

127

symphony ends with the pleasure of love that is responsible for Antar's death.

Two of Rimsky-Korsakov's shorter works for orchestra deserve attention: *Capriccio espagnol (Spanish Caprice),* op. 34 (1887) and the concert overture, *Russian Easter* Overture (*La Grande pâque russe*), op. 36 (1888). The first is a five-movement composition allowing experiment with orchestral timbres. Spanish-type melodies and rhythms further allow the composer to exploit orchestral effects. The five movements, played without interruption, begin with an "Alborada," or "morning song," whose music has more of a dance than lyric character. The second movement, "Variations," consists of a melody (on the horns) and five variations. The "Alborada" is repeated in the third movement, but in a changed key and in a different orchestration. In the fourth movement, "Scene and Gypsy Song," five orchestral cadenzas are featured. The suite concludes with "Fandango of the Asturias"—a fandango being a rapid Spanish dance performed by a couple and accompanied by guitar music and the rhythm of castanets.

Russian Easter Overture portrays a Christian-pagan ritual in Old Russia. Ecclesiastical melodies of the Russian Orthodox Church are quoted to provide the composition with a liturgical character.

Nationalism infected composers outside Russia, too. In many instances, composers with nationalistic ideals became the most important their respective countries produced.

From Bohemia (today part of Czechoslovakia) came Antonín Dvořák. He was the first Bohemian composer to gain recognition outside his own land and today is acknowledged as his country's greatest composer. But he was not the founding father of Bohemian musical nationalism. That distinction goes to Bedřich Smetana (1824–1884), composer of Bohemia's greatest folk opera, *The Bartered Bride,* with which Bohemian musical nationalism can be said to have emerged. His orchestral masterwork, *Má Vlast (My Fatherland,* 1874–1879), is a set of six tone poems, each of which displays a facet of Bohemia: ancient Bohemia (in "Vitesgrad"); the river Vltava, or the Moldau (in "The Moldau"); a rock valley near Prague, setting of an old Bohemian legend (in "Sárka"); Bohemian landscapes (in "From the Fields and Groves of Bohemia"); and Bohemian patriotism (in "Tábor" and "Blanik").

"The Moldau," or "Vltava"—the second in the set—is a classic. Here is its program:

*Two springs pour forth their streams in the shade of the Bohemian
forest. . . . Their waves, gaily flowing over their stony beds, join and
glitter in the sun. The woodland brook, chattering along, becomes the
river Moldau which, as its waters hurry through the valleys of Bohemia,
becomes a mighty stream. It flows through the dense wood in which
the joyous sounds of the chase resound, and the call of the hunter's
horn is heard ever nearer. It flows through verdant meadows and low-
lands where a marriage feast is being celebrated in song and dance. At
evening . . . wood nymphs and naiads hold revels, and in these
waters many a fortress and castle are reflected which bear witness to
the bygone splendor of knight-errantry. . . . At the rapids . . . the
stream speeds onward . . . cleaves a path . . . into the wide river
bed in which it rolls on, in majestic calm, towards Prague where it
disappears from the poet's gaze far on the horizon.*

As a young man Antonín Dvořák played the viola for almost a
decade in the orchestra of the opera house of which Smetana was director. Up to this time, in his own compositions Dvořák had copied the
German Romantics (mainly Wagner and Liszt). The influence of Smetana, however, weaned him away from German models. Aroused by
Smetana's ideals, Dvořák aspired to write Bohemian music, a decision
responsible for sweeping him from mediocrity to greatness.

Born in Nelahozeves, near Prague, on September 8, 1841, Dvořák received his first musical training from local teachers until 1857, when he
went to Prague for a ten-year training in all facets of music at the organ
school. During this period he supported himself by playing the viola in
the opera orchestra and became a convert to Bohemian nationalism.

His first national composition was a cantata, which was received enthusiastically when introduced in Prague in 1873. This was followed by
a symphony, also in a national idiom, which won the Austrian State
Prize in 1875, together with a delightful set of vocal duets, *Airs from
Moravia,* which in 1876 brought its composer a yearly pension of about
$250. While this process of nationalization was taking place in his music,
Dvořák was employed as church organist, a post to which he was appointed in 1873, the same year when he married Anna Cermakova, a
young member of the opera-house chorus. They raised six children, but
the death of their three firstborn children, in 1876 and 1877, which for
the time being left them childless, led Dvořák to create his first major
composition, the *Stabat Mater,* op. 58, for solo voices, chorus, and or-

chestra, which is sometimes referred to as "the foundation stone" on which all later Bohemian choral music rests.

Dvořák attracted the notice of Brahms. Through Brahms's influence, Simrock, the publisher, commissioned Dvořák to write a series of Slavonic dances. Dvořák completed a set of eight in 1878 (op. 46) for piano duet. They proved so successful that Simrock not only called upon Dvořák in 1886 to write eight more such dances (op. 72) but had Dvořák orchestrate all sixteen. It is with these dances that Dvořák's name first became known in Europe and the United States. And it was in these dances that Dvořák became recognized as Smetana's successor as Bohemia's foremost national composer (Smetana having died in 1884).

Between the first and second sets of these dances, Dvořák further expanded his national horizons by writing *Three Slavonic Rhapsodies* for orchestra, op. 45 (1878), the Violin Concerto in A minor, op. 53 (1880), and the Symphony in D major, op. 60 (1880). All are thoroughly Bohemian. In the three rhapsodies Dvořák evokes the Bohemian past: in the first rhapsody through a description of a tournament of knights; in the second with a Bohemian love idyll; and in the third with a picture of a Bohemian hunting scene.

The concerto form was introduced to Bohemian music (and Bohemian music was introduced to the concerto form) with Dvořák's A-minor Violin Concerto. Rhapsodic in feeling, with the violin often indulging in passages improvisational in character, this music is rich with folk material. There are three folklike melodies in the second-movement romanza, and the closing-movement rondo has several more Bohemian folklike tunes, including one in the style of the popular Bohemian folk dance known as the "furiant."

For a long time the Symphony in D major, op. 60, has been numbered as Dvořák's first symphony, not because Dvořák had not written symphonies before this one, but because this was the first of his symphonies to be published and to be accepted by critics as a product of his maturity. Four symphonies came after that, so that for years Dvořák was officially credited with having written five symphonies. Since 1960, however, attention was drawn to four early Dvořák symphonies through recordings and performances. To avoid confusion, the publishers of Dvořák's music decided to renumber the symphonies to embrace not five but nine works. Thus what was once identified as the Symphony no. 1 is now Symphony no. 5.

The Symphony no. 5, and its successor, the Symphony no. 6 in D minor, op. 70 (1885) are delightfully lyrical, fresh in spirit, unmistakably Bohemian in style. Through this music there breathes "the sweet fragrance and the unspoiled beauty of Bohemian woods and meadows," as one Bohemian critic has remarked. Even more national is the Symphony no. 8 in G major, op. 88 (1889), often called the *Bohemian* Symphony. It alternates between cheerful moods and pastoral ones, projected with a disarming simplicity and naturalness of expression.

The best-known of Dvořák's shorter orchestral compositions is the *Scherzo Capriccioso,* op. 66 (1883). It has two sections, beginning with an energetic one in which a horn theme (repeated in the rest of the work) is prominent. The second part is made up of two folklike melodies.

Dvořák also wrote three concert overtures, one of which is particularly favored: *Carnival,* op. 92 (1891). The composer himself prepared the program on which this music is based: "A lonely contemplative wanderer reaches the city at nightfall where a carnival of pleasure reigns supreme. On every side is heard the clangor of instruments, mingled with shouts of joy and unrestrained hilarity of the people, giving vent to their feelings in song and dance."

Dvořák's nationalistic tendencies ultimately took a strange turn away from Bohemia toward America. This was because between 1892 and 1895 he lived in New York and held the office of musical director of the then newly founded National Conservatory. One day, one of his pupils, H. T. Burleigh, sang for him several Negro spirituals. So taken was Dvořák with these poignant melodies that he published an article emphasizing that songs like these could provide the American composer with the material to create an authentic American musical art. As if to prove his point he went on to write two masterpieces whose thematic material was modeled after Negro spirituals. One was the ever-popular Symphony no. 9 in E minor, op. 95 (1893), so well known as the *Symphony from the New World*. The other was the Concerto in B minor for cello and orchestra, op. 104 (1895).

For years musicologists have argued the question as to whether the *Symphony from the New World* is stylistically American Negro or Bohemian. Unquestionably, basic melodies in the first and second movements have the unmistakable physiognomy and personality of Negro spirituals. But, just as undeniably, there are pages in these movements—and more especially in the third and fourth movements—that echo with the melodic ripples and rustles that float from the Vltava rather than from the Suwanee (or as Stephen Foster preferred to call the Florida river,

Swanee). Actually, had those opposing critical forces bothered to look at the title page of Dvořák's score they would have found the answer to their questionings. Dvořák did not identify his work as *The New World Symphony* (that is, a symphony about and a voice of the new world). He took special care to name it *Symphony from the New World,* by which he intended to make it perfectly clear that this music is the work of a Bohemian composer writing *in* the new world rather than about it. However much he was influenced by the American Negro folk song—and it was considerably—he also retained his Bohemian identity. Certainly the American Negro influence is felt strongly in the second theme of the first movement, which sounds like the spiritual "Swing Low, Sweet Chariot"; and this Negro influence is even more pronounced in the elegiac melody for English horn, the principal melody of the second movement, which was used by Williams Arms Fisher for his Negro spiritual-like song "Goin' Home."

The Negro identity of the cello concerto is also prominent. We recognize it in the second theme of the first movement, a lament for solo horn accompanied by strings. There is also a strong Negro feeling throughout the deeply moving slow movement. In the lively finale, Dvořák remembers some of his principal themes from the first and second movements.

During Dvořák's stay in America he also came into contact with, and was impressed by, the melodies and rhythms of American Indian music. Once again he was driven to imitate the esoteric style of these songs and dances—but in chamber rather than orchestral music.

Homesickness drove Dvořák to resign from his position with the conservatory in 1895 and go back to his native land. In 1901 he assumed there the post of professor at the Prague Conservatory, where he soon became full director. When his sixtieth birthday was celebrated that same year, he received tributes from all over the world.

In his closing years Dvořák suffered from arterial degeneration and a heart broken by the miserable failure suffered by his last opera, produced in 1904. He died in Prague on May 1, 1904, of an apopleptic stroke, five weeks after the premiere of that opera.

When the story of Edvard Grieg's life was made into a Broadway operetta in 1944, then in 1970 adapted into a motion picture, both bore the title *Song of Norway.* It was an apt title. For Grieg's music is truly "the song of Norway." Not until he began singing about his land and people in musical accents and inflections lifted from Norway's folk songs and dances did Grieg acquire for himself an identifiable artistic profile and enter into music history as Norway's greatest composer of all time.

The "song" of Norway was far different from that of Bohemia. A southern people, Bohemians have a capacity for gaiety and joy that has continually filtered through their songs and dances. Bohemian folk dances (notably the furiant and the polka) are full of energy and a heady spirit, while those of Norway are gentler and more restrained. Bohemian folk songs have vigor even when they are lyrical, while those of Norway are as soft-spoken as a whisper and, more often than not, elegiac. And the restraints that keep a check on Norwegian folk music are also found in Grieg's most familiar orchestral compositions.

Grieg was born in Bergen, Norway, on June 15, 1843. His principal training in music took place at the Leipzig Conservatory in Germany, from which he was graduated with highest honors in 1862. His Leipzig schooling partly explains why his earliest works were so greatly influenced by Mendelssohn and Schumann.

In 1862 Grieg presented in Bergen a concert of his works, which did nothing to enhance his reputation or advance his career. Disheartened, he went to Copenhagen, where he befriended Rikard Nordraak, a young Norwegian who, despite his youth, had already written Norway's national anthem and had become a scholar of Norwegian folk music. Nordraak inflamed Grieg with his own patriotism and with his passion for Norwegian folklore and folk songs and dances. From him, Grieg discovered (to use his own words) "what the Norwegian folk song was . . . and to learn to know my own nature." Grieg became a voracious reader of books about his country and its culture and art. Into his own musical writing he now started to assimilate some of the more characteristic elements of Norwegian folk music. The first piece to show such qualities is a *Humoresque,* for piano, op. 6 (1865), dedicated to Nordraak.

While in Copenhagen, Grieg became engaged to his cousin, Nina Hagerup, with whom he had for some time been in love. Marriage, however, was not to be considered, since Nina's parents refused to allow her to marry an indigent musician. Grieg's most famous love song, "Ich liebe dich" ("I Love You") was written for Nina at the time of their betrothal.

Grieg went to Italy for an extended visit in 1865. There he wrote his first work for orchestra, a concert overture, *In Autumn,* op. 11 (1866), which captured first prize in a competition conducted by the Swedish Academy of Music. The joy of his first success was totally obliterated by the death of his young friend and inspiration Nordraak (who was only twenty-three). Grieg collapsed physically from grief. After his recovery he was determined to carry on his friend's lifework in furthering Norway's national art.

Grieg's first act in this direction was to arrange a concert devoted exclusively to Norwegian composers, in Christiana (now Oslo). The date of this concert is historic—October 15, 1866—since it marked the first time a concert of all-Norwegian music had ever been given. A few months later Grieg founded the Norwegian Academy of Music to help train talented musicians. He also became conductor of a symphony orchestra to provide performances for Norwegian music.

He now managed to convince Nina's father he was capable of supporting a wife and children. On June 11, 1867, Nina and Grieg were finally married. Their happiness was unblemished until two years after their marriage, when their thirteen-month-old daughter died. They had no other children, and Grieg turned to his work for solace.

Grieg's first masterpiece, and the one that is still his most admired composition, is the Piano Concerto in A minor, op. 16 (1868). When it was first performed in Copenhagen in 1869 it achieved such a triumph that the audience, unable to contain its enthusiasm, burst into shouts during the first-movement cadenza. One annotator has interpreted the first movement as Grieg's self-portrait—bubbling, as it does, with the joy of living and loving, and of having fulfilled himself creatively. The slow movement is the jewel of the work, a pastoral song for muted strings that seems to spring from the very heart of Norway. There is no pause between this movement and the energetic finale that follows, whose principal material consists of two folklike tunes. Grieg brought the manuscript of this concerto to Liszt in Rome in 1870, and Liszt played it at sight and expressed unqualified enthusiasm.

In his role as a musical nationalist, Grieg often used the works of Scandinavian writers as material for compositions. For *Sigurd Jorsalfar,* a drama by Björnstjerne Björnson, an outstanding Norwegian poet, novelist, and playwright, Grieg wrote some incidental music in 1872, three parts of which were assembled into an orchestral suite, op. 56. Three years later Grieg wrote incidental music for the Norwegian classic *Peer Gynt,* by Norway's foremost dramatist, Henrik Ibsen. Peer Gynt is a legendary character who is deceitful, immoral, and irresponsible. He deserts his mother, Aase, abducts the lovely Ingrid on the day she is to be married to another man, abandons her, and then goes through various experiences, including an adventure with the daughter of the troll king in the mountain hall. After travel in far-off lands he comes home for good, now old and weary, and finds that the sweetheart of his early manhood, Solveig, has been faithfully waiting for him. Through her constancy, Peer achieves redemption.

Grieg's music fully realized the spirit of fantasy created by Ibsen. The production of the play with Grieg's music proved an enormous success in Christiana (Oslo) in 1876. But more successful by far are the two suites for orchestra—opp. 46 and 55 (1876)—in which Grieg used the best parts of his incidental music. The first suite is a sturdy staple in light classical music. Its four movements are "Morning" (a beautiful nature study), "Aase's Death" (a tender elegy), "Anitra's Dance" (an Oriental dance), and "In the Hall of the Mountain King" (music recreating the exotic dwelling place of trolls and gnomes of Norwegian legend). Of the second suite, only one movement has remained popular, the tender "Solveig's Song," based on an old Norwegian folk song. This is preceded by "Abduction of the Bride and Ingrid's Lament," "Arabian Dance," and "Peer Gynt's Homecoming."

Ludvig Holberg was the father of Danish literature. When the bicentennial of his birth was celebrated throughout Scandinavia, Grieg made his own contribution by writing the *Holberg* Suite, op. 40 (1884–85), both for solo piano and for orchestra. Keeping in mind the age in which Holberg lived and worked, Grieg revived the Baroque suite; the *Holberg* Suite consists of a Prelude, Sarabande, Air, Gavotte, and Rigaudon, with the "Air" as the only movement through which flows a Norwegian strain.

Some of Grieg's short pieces for orchestra are of musical value. The *Two Elegiac Melodies,* for string orchestra, op. 34 (1880), are transcriptions of two Grieg songs, "The Wounded Heart" and "The Last Spring." *Two Norwegian Melodies,* for string orchestra, op. 63 (1895), are thoroughly nationalistic, since both melodies are derived from actual folk songs. Nationalistic, too, are the *Four Norwegian Dances,* op. 35 (1881), which Grieg first wrote as a piano duet, then transcribed for orchestra. The second of these, in A minor, is the one most often heard.

From the mid 1870s on, Grieg's stature as one of Europe's major composers was acknowledged. The Norwegian government gave him a pension that made him financially secure for life. He received appointments to the Swedish and Leyden academies, membership in the French Academy, and honorary degrees from Cambridge and Oxford universities. His sixtieth birthday was declared a legal holiday in Norway.

In 1885 Grieg acquired a country home, six miles from Bergen, called "Troldhaugen." It was secluded in a wooded area overlooking a fjord. Grieg loved this place, and here he lived for the rest of his life. To the present time, Troldhaugen is a shrine to which music lovers of the world come to pay tribute to Grieg's memory.

In May of 1906, Grieg made his last public appearance when he conducted a program of his music in London. Returning home, he suffered a heart attack from which he never recovered. He died in Bergen on September 4, 1907.

Johannes Brahms.

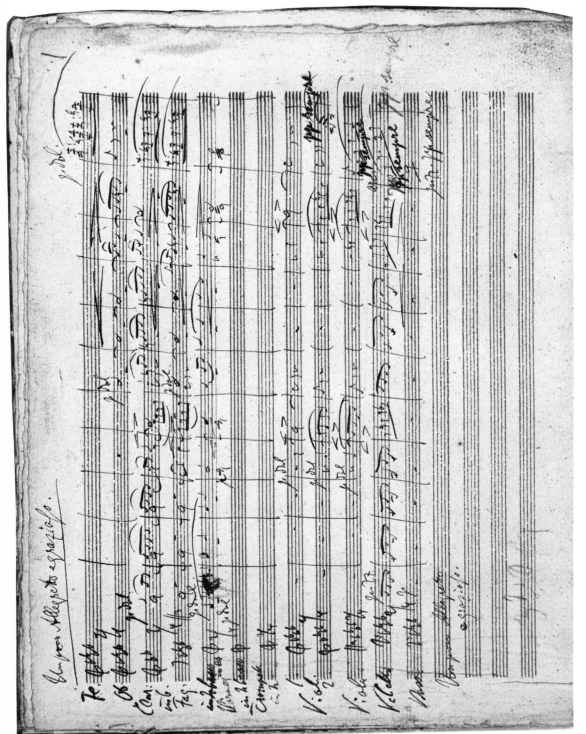

A page from the manuscript score of Brahms Symphony No. 1, 3rd movement.

Nikolai Rimsky-Korsakov.

Edvard Grieg.

The Russian Soul

Peter Ilitch Tchaikovsky,

Sergei Rachmaninoff

The music of Tchaikovsky is his emotional autobiography. It was Tchaikovsky's way of opening his heart; a symphony, as he put it, was "a musical confession of the soul." In his best works he laid bare, for all to see, his own inner life of frustrations, torment, self-incrimination and self-contempt, tortured conscience, deep-rooted pessimism, and psychoneurosis.

His music is also thoroughly Russian. He was profoundly influenced by Russia's first great nationalist composer, Mikhail Glinka, whose operas he learned by heart in his boyhood. (Only Mozart continued to hold a higher place in Tchaikovsky's esteem than Glinka.) Some of Tchaikovsky's major works are based on Russian plays, poems, backgrounds, historical events, and characters. In many compositions he quotes Russian folk songs, dance tunes, and liturgical melodies; in most compositions, his own melodies and rhythms betray the way folk music had shaped his own musical thinking and writing. "I am a Russian through and through," he confessed, "passionately devoted to every expression of the Russian spirit."

Yet the Russian Five and Tchaikovsky were at odds with each other, even though each reached toward the single goal of authentic Russian musical art. The Russian Five in Saint Petersburg felt that Tchaikovsky's music was too concerned with the wringing of hands in personal grief, too deeply involved with personal torments, and too little concerned with Russian culture and folk art. They accused Tchaikovsky of being too European, and too little Russian, because his style was so well groomed and neatly manicured and paid too much obeisance to classical structures and to absolute rather than programmatic music.

For his part, Tchaikovsky, in Moscow, also held the Russian Five in disdain. Their barbaric style (with emphasis on complex, changing rhythms and brilliant orchestration) was objectionable to a man of his sophistication and taste. He had no sympathy for their interest in orientalism, exoticism, and fantasy, nor was he at all taken with their partiality for programmatic realism. He felt that the Russian Five had become slaves to theories and dogma, rather than their inmost feelings.

Certainly it was with his inmost feelings that Tchaikovsky was most concerned when he worked on his masterpieces. This, no doubt, explains his sustained popularity with so many music lovers. In the pathos and the sentimentality of his melodies, and in the disturbed outburst of his stormy passages and climaxes, a direct emotional communication takes place between composer and listener. The listener does not have to seek through the mazes of sound to uncover what Tchaikovsky is telling them; it is openly revealed.

There are, of course, many Tchaikovsky compositions in a light mood: his delightful waltzes, for example, or the enchanting pages of his music for *The Nutcracker*. But Tchaikovsky of the towering masterworks is a man obsessed with melancholia, a neurotic whose nerves quivered like leaves on a tree in a storm. He was tormented by obsessive fears, some real, others imagined. When he conducted an orchestra, he sometimes held up his chin with his left hand for fear that his head would fall off. An emotional imbalance that persisted throughout his life was already evident in his childhood when he reacted to his mother's death with a hysteria far in excess of the grief a normal youth of fourteen experiences at such a tragedy. Tchaikovsky became excessively shy and timid after that. Making close friends was difficult for him, and strangers so upset him that in their presence he experienced, as he said, "acute suffering." He became a terribly lonely man, which further heightened his misery. "None but the lonely heart can know my suffering," he sang sadly and sweetly in one of his loveliest songs (words by Goethe). Tchaikovsky sought escape from loneliness by frequent restless wanderings from place to place. At other times he sought escape in reminiscences, a habit he had formed when he was quite young.

A slight remark or incident subjected him to such an exaggerated disturbance that he would burst out weeping. Disappointments or tragedies overwhelmed him to a point where he suffered a nervous breakdown, or tried to commit suicide, or was convinced he was going mad. He once wrote, "A worm continually gnaws in secret in my heart. . . . I suffer from torments which cannot be put into words."

Yet through all these interior upheavals and tempests, he kept on writing music—music that pierces the hearts of audiences because it rises from so troubled a heart and from so anguished a soul.

Tchaikovsky's birth took place in Votkinsk, Russia, on May 7, 1840. In his tenth year, the family moved to Saint Petersburg. There, four years later, his mother died of cholera, a tragedy that had a shattering effect on his always delicate nervous system. But this did not keep him from continuing his academic schooling. He was a student at the School of Jurisprudence until his nineteenth year. Up to this time his musical training had been highly sporadic; none of the world-famous composers came to formal, disciplined training so late in life. Such musical activity as had involved his interests before his nineteenth year had been improvising at the piano or reading the scores of Glinka, or attending concerts and opera performances.

Between 1859 and 1862, Tchaikovsky worked as a clerk in the Ministry of Justice. Music first now began to absorb him completely. At the advice of Nicolai Zaremba, with whom he was then privately studying harmony and counterpoint, he deserted his clerk's job (which he hated) to enroll in the Saint Petersburg Conservatory from which he was graduated in 1866 with a silver medal. At school Tchaikovsky wrote his first two orchestral works, a set of dances and a concert overture; they were also his first pieces of music to be performed.

In 1866 Tchaikovsky was appointed professor of harmony at the then newly established conservatory in Moscow directed by Nicholas Rubinstein (brother of the famous pianist-composer Anton Rubinstein). This period was creatively productive for Tchaikovsky, since it resulted in the writing of his first tone poem, his first opera, and his first symphony. All this music was done under the duress of Tchaikovsky's doubts about his talent and the obsessive fear that death would prevent him from finishing his symphony. He became afflicted with headaches and depressions that led to a nervous breakdown. After a rest cure, his spirit and energies were sufficiently revitalized to allow him to complete his first symphony, in G minor, op. 13, *Winter Dreams,* which was praised when it was heard in Moscow on February 15, 1868.

These early pieces were the preparatory exercises of a potential master about to produce his first masterpiece: the overture-fantasy for orchestra *Romeo and Juliet.* He wrote it at the suggestion of Balakirev, who also worked out its format. Tchaikovsky followed Balakirev's suggestions. As Balakirev had indicated, Tchaikovsky opened the composition with a religious hymn in the style of a chorale (descriptive of Friar Laurence); a fiery section pointed up the hostility between the houses of Montague and Capulet; a romantic episode served as the heart of the composition, the wondrously lyrical love music of Romeo and Juliet; and a concluding section portrayed the death of the lovers.

When this overture-fantasy was first performed (Moscow, March 16, 1870) it was a failure. Tchaikovsky then revised it extensively, and a decade after that rewrote it a third time. It is this third version that is heard today and that has become for concertgoers everywhere a favorite among Tchaikovsky's shorter orchestral compositions.

At about this time Tchaikovsky fell in love (or thought he had) with Désirée Artôt, an opera singer whom he hoped to marry. Actually, though, he had never been physically attracted to women; he never would be. Apparently, Désirée recognized this failing, for she decided to give up Tchaikovsky and marry a Spanish baritone. The extent of Tchaikovsky's emotional attachment to this woman can be gauged by the fact that when he heard of her marriage he described his own involvement with her as "amusing" and "ridiculous."

Tchaikovsky's second symphony, in C minor, op. 17 (1872), has the name of *Little Russian* because its themes are based on folk songs from the Ukrainian area known as Little Russia. The Symphony no. 3 in D major, op. 29 (1875), is called *Polish,* since a Polish dance form, the polonaise, is prominently featured in the finale. Both works are strangers to our symphony halls.

Not so with Tchaikovsky's Concerto no. 1 in B-flat minor, for piano and orchestra, op. 23 (1874), one of the most frequently played works in the repertory. It had such an unfortunate beginning that at first it seemed doomed for oblivion. When Tchaikovsky had finished writing it, in 1874, he played it for Nicholas Rubinstein, who hurled at the composer a tirade of abuse and insults. As Tchaikovsky described Rubinstein's reaction: "It appeared that my concerto was utterly worthless, absolutely unplayable; passages were so commonplace and awkward that they could not be improved; the piece as a whole was bad, trivial, vulgar. I had stolen from this and from that and from this one." Tchaikovsky's reply to Rubinstein's devastating attack was, "I shall not change a single note." And he stuck to his word.

Nobody in Russia seemed at first to want to play the concerto, whose world premiere finally took place in Boston on October 25, 1875, with Hans von Bülow as soloist. The performance was crowned with success. Von Bülow then performed it all over Europe, and so did many other pianists, including Nicholas Rubinstein, who by this time had changed his mind about the quality of this music. From then on the popularity of this concerto kept mounting. A performance of this work by a world-famous pianist now guarantees a sold-out auditorium.

This concerto is unusual in that it opens with an extended introduction of more than one hundred measures, none of the thematic material of which is ever used again. This is particularly strange in view of the powerful (and highly familiar) opening: four thundering measures exchanged by orchestra and piano, followed by a resounding melody for the strings accompanied by piano chords. This is the kind of exciting material a Romantic composer can exploit in many different ways during the progress of the movement. Yet Tchaikovsky deserted it once the main part of the movement was presented, with a first theme said to have been based on a folk tune the composer had heard a blind beggar sing in the Ukraine. The melancholy mood that is established in most of the first movement comes to even greater prominence in the second with an elegiac melody first played by the flute before it is adopted by the piano. The finale opens with a Russian folk-type dance to set the stage for dynamic music in which rhythmic energy rather than beauty of melody is of prime interest.

Undoubtedly heartened by the success of his concerto in Boston late in 1875, Tchaikovsky proved remarkably fertile in the year that followed. In 1876 he completed his first ballet score. It has often been written that the golden age of Russian ballet began with the three works for which Tchaikovsky wrote the music, of which *Swan Lake* (*Le Lac des cygnes*), op. 20, was the first. Tchaikovsky did not live to see this stage work assume the imperial position it has since acquired in ballet literature. The premiere was a fiasco; not until the ballet was revived after Tchaikovsky's death did it begin to enjoy that universal approbation it deserved. Tchaikovsky's score is made up of thirty-three numbers.

About a dozen of these have provided material for symphonic suites often given at orchestral concerts. One of these numbers is among Tchaikovsky's most famous waltzes.

Two short orchestral compositions and a work for cello and orchestra also date from the year of 1876. *Marche slave,* op. 31, expressed the composer's sympathy for the Slavs in the war between Serbia and Turkey. This march was written for a benefit concert for wounded Serbian soldiers. The solemn stately melody with which the piece opens is an old Serbian folk song. Two other folk tunes are featured after that, and the composition reaches a climax with the Russian national anthem.

Francesca da Rimini, op. 32, is an orchestral fantasy based on the fifth canto from Dante's *Inferno.* Tchaikovsky provided his own program for this music. The first section is devoted to the sufferings of victims consigned to Inferno. After that unfolds the love story of Paolo and Francesca, whose romantic element is underlined with a tender melody for clarinet accompanied by plucked strings. The composition ends with a return to the horrors of Inferno.

In *Variations on a Rococo Theme,* for cello and orchestra, op. 33, Tchaikovsky pays homage to his beloved Mozart. The melody on which the variations are based (heard in the solo cello after a sixteen-measure orchestral introduction) has rococo grace and charm, even though the lyricism we have here is Tchaikovskian rather than Mozartean. Seven variations in a simulated Baroque style follow, one variation separated from the other by a short orchestral interlude.

In 1877 Tchaikovsky became involved with two women. One brought him excruciating mental torture. The other was, for thirteen years, a limitless source of solace, understanding, inspiration, and love —not to speak of bountiful financial assistance.

We have already spoken of Tchaikovsky's indifference to women. The truth is that Tchaikovsky was homosexual. This is not speculation; it is a fact stated in his letters and diaries. He referred to his abnormality as "The." Repeatedly he revealed that this disposition disgusted him and that he sought to free himself of it. The reason why he had wanted to marry Désirée Artôt years earlier had been the hope that marriage would provide a cure. Marriage continued to be very much on his mind as his sole hope of ridding himself of his aberration. "From this day on," Tchaikovsky wrote to his brother in 1876, "I will seriously consider entering matrimony with any woman. I am convinced that my *inclinations* are the greatest and insuperable barrier to my well-being, and I must by all means struggle against my nature." In another letter to his brother the same year he added, "What a dreadful thought that people close to me may be ashamed of me! In a word, I am determined by means of marriage or public connection with a woman to shut the mouths of sundry despicable creatures whose opinions I despise but who may cause pain to people I love."

Unfortunately he married the wrong woman. She was one of his pupils, Antonina Miliukova, a distraught, erratic, overemotional young woman who one day fell on her knees before Tchaikovsky and pleaded for the privilege of serving him all her life. This was the girl Tchaikovsky decided to make his wife. They were married on July 18, 1877. When they were alone for the first time Tchaikovsky "was ready to scream" (to use his own words). Night after night he roamed the streets of Moscow to avoid coming home. His mental anguish became so acute that one night he stood in the cold waters of the Moscow River hoping to contract pneumonia and die. In a state of mental collapse, he finally deserted his wife, resigned from the Moscow Conservatory, and spent a year in travel. The marital experience had proved such a nightmare that for years he avoided Moscow. For a while, soon after his flight from marriage, he lived in Clarens, on Lake Geneva. "I do not want to see anyone," he wrote. "I am afraid of everyone and I can hardly work." Then he made it a practice to spend summers on his sister's estate near Kiev, and winters traveling in Europe.

His relationship with a second woman had happier consequences. In 1877, Nadezhda Filaretovna von Meck, a wealthy and highborn widow who was a patroness of music, wrote to Tchaikovsky of her admiration for his music. He replied gratefully. From such unpretentious beginnings there developed an exchange of correspondence that lasted thirteen years. Mme von Meck provided Tchaikovsky with an annual allowance of six thousand rubles, more than enough to support him well while he concentrated exclusively on composition. Of no less importance is the fact that a great love developed between the composer and his patroness as the letters went winging back and forth. Yet, curious to relate, during all those years Tchaikovsky and Mme von Meck met face to face only once, by accident, and then without exchanging a single word. This had been the condition imposed on Tchaikovsky by his patroness from the beginnings of their friendship. She may have been conscious of the social gap separating them; she may have been trying to avoid possible emotional entanglement that would have had an unhealthy reaction on her children; or she may have realized that this was the most satisfactory way for her to know Tchaikovsky. Such an arrangement served Tchaikovsky well. He had a "beloved friend" to whom he could come with problems (personal and creative) even if only by letter; he had a woman to love who would make no physical demands on him.

Under the warm sun of Mme von Meck's love and sympathy, generosity and lavish appreciation, Tchaikovsky flourished. The wounds of the spirit sustained by his brief unhappy marriage were being healed. Surely it is no coincidence that at this time he began to create some of his best music: the fourth and fifth symphonies; the opera *Eugene Onegin;* the violin concerto; the *Capriccio Italien* and the Overture *1812,* for orchestra; and a library of songs.

First came the Violin Concerto in D major, op. 35, and the Fourth Symphony in F minor, op. 36, both in 1878. Apparently Tchaikovsky did not have much luck with concertos. The Violin Concerto was rudely rejected by the artist for whom it was written and to whom it was dedicated: Leopold Auer, distinguished violinist and teacher. Auer insisted that the music was not violinistic, that parts were even unplayable. Auer even used his influence to keep a French virtuoso from performing it. It took three years for the work to be heard. When this happened, in Vienna on December 4, 1881, many in the audience hissed, and the critics were annihilating. One of them described the music as "barbarously terrible." The most vituperative report came from Vienna's most powerful critic, Eduard Hanslick. "Tchaikovsky's violin concerto," he wrote savagely, "brings us face to face for the first time with the revolting thought: May there not . . . exist musical compositions that we can hear stink?"

But just as Tchaikovsky lived to see his faith in his first piano concerto fully vindicated, so he was to see his first violin concerto rise above its initial defeat to resounding victory. Adolf Brodsky's performance in London in 1882 was "a tremendous success," as the violinist reported back to Tchaikovsky. Soon afterward, the concerto was acclaimed in Russia. Only after Tchaikovsky's death did Leopold Auer revise his estimate radically. He not only played the concerto himself, and expressed unqualified admiration for it, but trained a generation of the world's greatest violinists in its performance.

Consistently romantic as it is, the concerto poses no greater listening problems to present-day audiences than it does technical difficulties to performers. Melodious from beginning to end, with some themes that are soft and sentimental and others that are lively, this concerto is always a joy to listen to.

The Fourth Symphony (the first such work by Tchaikovsky to be in the permanent orchestral repertory) was written under the influence of his then rapidly growing friendship for Mme von Meck. He confessed that she was very much on his mind when he wrote every measure of the work. He discussed details with her through his letters. He dedicated it to her and always referred to it as "our symphony."

To Mme von Meck Tchaikovsky explained that the first-movement introduction was "the kernel, the chief thought of the whole symphony. This is Destiny. . . . This might is overpowering and invincible. There is nothing to do but to submit and vainly to complain." The passion and torment that follow, however, represent not submission but the struggle of a man to achieve joy and peace with Fate. Then comes the second theme as an aftermath of the struggle, which Tchaikovsky interpreted as follows: "It is better to turn from the realities and to lull oneself in dreams. Happiness! Happiness! Happiness! No, they are only dreams, and Fate dispels them."

The second movement, with its opening sad, sweet melody for oboe, presents to us, as Tchaikovsky explained to Mme von Meck, "another phase of sadness. Here is that melancholy feeling which enwraps one when he sits at night alone in the house, exhausted by work." To Tchaikovsky the third movement is filled with "capricious arabesques, elusive images which pass in the imagination when one has tasted a little wine and experiences the first phase of intoxication." In this movement Tchaikovsky introduced a novel effect that he explained as follows: "At first the strings play alone, and pizzicato throughout. In the trio the woodwind instruments enter and play alone. At the end . . . [the] choirs toss short phrases to each other. I believe that the effect of sounds and colors will be most interesting."

Tchaikovsky described the finale by saying, "If you find no pleasure in yourself look about you. Go to the people. . . . There is a picture of a folk holiday. . . . There is still happiness, simple native happiness." In the finale Tchaikovsky quotes a famous Russian folk song, "In the Fields There Stands a Birch Tree."

Before going to work on his next symphony, Tchaikovsky completed his opera *Eugene Onegin,* op. 24 (1879), its libretto based on a poem by Pushkin; and sundry compositions for orchestra of which only the *Capriccio Italien (Italian Caprice),* op. 45 (1880), and the *Ouverture solennelle* (Overture *1812*), op. 49 (1880), need concern us.

Capriccio Italien is a fantasy on popular Italian folk songs with which Tchaikovsky became familiar during a trip to Italy in 1880. The

opening fanfare is a motive Tchaikovsky heard in Rome every evening played by a bugler at a nearby army barracks. After the fanfare two Italian melodies are presented and elaborated upon. The fantasia ends with a frenetic Italian folk dance, the tarantella.

The *Ouverture solennelle,* or the *1812* Overture, as it is popularly called, was commissioned as part of the celebration of the consecration of a cathedral in Moscow in 1881. The building of the cathedral was in commemoration of the defeat of Napoleon in Russia at the Battle of Borodino. In the opening of the piece, a Russian hymn is played, but the main part of the overture is a vivid description of the battle, its music containing excerpts from the Russian hymn and the French *Marseillaise* to identify the opposing forces. The overture comes to a grand climax with a triumphant statement of the Russian national anthem, a token of Russia's victory over France. Tchaikovsky's original version called for the boom of actual cannon at various parts of the work, which was intended to be played out of doors. Several adventurous conductors still employ cannon in the orchestra in outdoor concerts (though not frequently).

Tchaikovsky wrote little of major importance between 1881 and 1888. He was convinced that his musical well had gone dry. "I am beginning to fear that my muse has flown far, far away," he told Balakirev. What he did write had more charm than powerful invention, more grace than sentiment: his Suite no. 3, for orchestra, op. 55 (1884); a series of four tone poems inspired by Byron's *Manfred,* known as the *Manfred Symphony,* op. 58 (1885), though it is never numbered with Tchaikovsky's symphonies; and an orchestral suite, *Mozartiana,* op. 61 (1887), orchestral transcriptions of various pieces by Mozart.

Then with the writing of the mighty Symphony no. 5 in E minor, op. 64 (1888), came creative renewal. The theme of Fate runs through this symphony as it had done in the Fourth. Fate is symbolized by a motive in the clarinet with which the first movement begins and which courses throughout the entire symphony. This continual repetition of the Fate motive is not the only way in which this symphony is unified. The first theme of the finale is derived from the first main theme of the opening movement. The symphony ends with a grandiose final presentation of the Fate theme. Structurally, this symphony is unusual in that a waltz replaces the usual third-movement scherzo. This is the only place where the pessimistic character of the symphony finds relief in light, graceful music; but this lightness is in the end dispelled by the intrusion of the Fate motive.

Though the Fifth Symphony was an immense success from its first performance in 1888, Tchaikovsky was not as yet convinced that he had not come to a creative dead end. He was dissatisfied with what he had written, certain that the only reason his symphony was so enthusiastically received was because the audience and the critics remembered and respected his previous achievements. "Am I really played out?" he asked Mme von Meck in one of his letters. "Last night I looked through our symphony [no. 4]. What a difference! How immeasurably superior it is! It is very, very sad."

His confidence in himself was strengthened in 1888, when he received a handsome life pension from the Russian government as a token of its high esteem, and when he enjoyed a succession of triumphs as a guest conductor of his own works throughout Europe. He found the will to write his second ballet, *The Sleeping Beauty* (*La Belle au bois dormant*), op. 66 (1889), several of whose passages are gathered into suites at symphony concerts. He also wrote an important opera, *Pique dame* (*The Queen of Spades*) in 1890.

Then this brief period of contentment was crushed by a sudden blow. While traveling in the Caucasus in 1890 he received a short, coldly worded letter from Mme von Meck explaining that because of financial reverses she was compelled to end her annual subsidy to him. The loss of the money did not mean anything to Tchaikovsky, who no longer needed it. But the frigid tone of her letter upset him. He quickly responded to reassure Mme von Meck that he deeply regretted her reverses and that he hoped that nothing would interrupt or break up their precious friendship. Mme von Meck did not reply, nor did she respond to the other letters Tchaikovsky sent her. When Tchaikovsky returned to Moscow and discovered that Mme von Meck's financial troubles were over, he decided that she had used finances as a pretext for ending their epistolary affair. This conviction brought an unhappiness from which his spirit never recovered.

Nobody has given a definitive explanation of why Mme von Meck decided to break with Tchaikovsky after thirteen years. Was she bored with all this letter-writing and so artificial a friendship? Had her children insisted that she end this strange relationship that was being gossiped about in Moscow? Was Tchaikovsky's homosexuality becoming an embarrassment to her and her family? Was she the victim of a nervous disorder? Whatever the reason, this strange love affair was over. Depression, pessimism, and despair once again seized Tchaikovsky, this time to retain a permanent hold.

He sought escape from his torment by touring the United States in

1891. At that time he participated in the gala opening of Carnegie Hall in New York by conducting his *1812* Overture. He was flattered by the fuss made over him wherever he went and particularly by the ovations his concerts inspired. But nothing could dispel the gloom enveloping him. "I enjoy all this," he wrote, "like a person sitting at a table set with marvels of gastronomy devoid of appetite."

His anguish notwithstanding, he was nonetheless able, following his return to Russia, to conceive his most delightful score, the music for the ballet *The Nutcracker* (*Casse-noisette*), op. 71 (1892). Never before had his touch been so aerial, his writing so spontaneous, his treatment so enchanting. The ballet scenario concerns itself with a Christmas party where little Clara gets as a gift a German nutcracker shaped like a man. Late that night, the room becomes filled with mice and with toys come to life. A battle royal ensues between the mice and the toys, ending with a duel between the king of the Mice and the Nutcracker. With Clara's help, the Nutcracker is victorious. He is now transformed into a handsome prince who conducts Clara to the Kingdom of the Sweets ruled by the Sugar Plum Fairy. A grand entertainment takes place for the visitors. Spanish, Arabian, and Chinese dancers represent chocolate, coffee, and tea. Other colorful spectacles and dances take place.

The orchestral suite draws from this ballet score some of its most delectable pages, to have become a perennial favorite with young and old. It opens with a "Miniature Overture" followed by "March," "The Dance of the Sugar Plum Fairy" (with its exquisite melody played on a celesta), "Trepak" (an electrifying Russian dance), "Arabian Dance," "Chinese Dance," "Dance of the Flutes," and "Waltz of the Flowers."

In writing this bright, lovable music Tchaikovsky was wearing a mask behind which was concealed a face twisted with anguish. It was a man no longer able to raise himself from the bottomless pit of despond who now went to work on his last symphony, the Symphony no. 6 in B minor, op. 74 (1893), that bears the name of *Pathétique*, or *Pathetic* (a title invented by Tchaikovsky's brother a day after the first public performance). Its writing proved such a drain on Tchaikovsky's nerves that even while putting his notes down on paper he often gave way to tears. Did he suspect that in creating this masterpiece (and particularly the last movement) he was producing his own requiem? There are some musicologists who suspect this may have been the case. We know that when Rimsky-Korsakov asked Tchaikovsky if he had a program in mind while writing the symphony, Tchaikovsky replied that he did but refused to divulge what it was. The music apparently had far too personal a meaning for its composer to reveal what that meaning was. Since the tragic implications of this music are so strong, since Tchaikovsky introduced a fragment from a Russian funeral service in the first movement, and since the symphony ends with perhaps the most funereal music in all symphonic literature, the temptation is irresistible to believe that Tchaikovsky was, indeed, creating his own elegy.

That the symphony had a highly personal meaning for its composer is underlined by its becoming his favorite work. "I love it as I have never loved a single one of my offsprings," he told a friend. And to his publisher he wrote, "On my honor, never in my life have I been so pleased with myself, so proud, so happy in the knowledge that I have really created something good."

The solo bassoon that sets the first movement into motion immediately creates a lugubrious atmosphere that is maintained even when the tempo later grows faster and a change of key takes place. There is an emotional upheaval, then a melody of surpassing pathos. Grief turns to resignation, resignation to agitation, until a feeling of utter desolation is projected. After this first movement, Tchaikovsky has two movements of a character never before encountered in a symphony. The second, instead of being slow and melodic, is a lively scherzo in which, however, the composer's pessimism cannot long be denied, obtruding as it does in the middle section. The third is a march built up sonorously and dynamically until it becomes a thunderous statement.

Unusual, too, is the way the symphony ends, with an adagio lamentoso, the first time a symphony is made to end with a slow movement. This is a lamentation beginning with an outcry of grief in which Tchaikovsky's lifetime of fears and terrors culminates in music of black despair.

Tchaikovsky himself conducted the world premiere of the *Pathetic* Symphony, on October 28, 1893. Was he consciously and deliberately performing his own requiem? The question has troubled some Tchaikovsky biographers, because only five days later, during a cholera epidemic, Tchaikovsky drank some unboiled water and contracted the dread disease. Since Tchaikovsky's mother had died of cholera, it might be expected that when an epidemic was raging he would have taken special precautions. To have drunk unboiled water was the height of recklessness, unless the one so doing was courting disease and death. After studying all the relevant facts, most historians and biographers have come to the conclusion that Tchaikovsky *was* reckless, but that he was not trying to commit suicide. But whenever we listen to the *Pathetic* Symphony it is difficult to suppress the suspicion that, having had enough of life, Tchaikovsky was submitting to total defeat. Infected with cholera, he died in Saint Petersburg on November 6, 1893.

When Sergei Rachmaninoff (1873–1943) conducted the American premiere of his Symphony no. 2 in 1909, one unidentified critic pointed out how close was the spiritual and emotional kinship between Tchaikovsky and Rachmaninoff.

Like Tchaikovsky, Rachmaninoff was a man sagging under the accumulation of sorrows. Those sorrows were real, not imagined. Rachmaninoff had suffered maladjustment as a conservatory student, so much so that, in spite of his obvious brilliance as a musician, he proved to be a lackadaisical and shiftless student for a long time. Early in his manhood he suffered a nervous breakdown. Despite his first triumphs as pianist and composer he was victimized by violent melancholia. And during his last two decades, he was a man without a country, the result of a self-imposed exile from his native land, Russia, which he could not understand when a new regime overthrew the old order and introduced new political and social values. His homesickness for Russia assumed the dimensions of a disease as the years passed and as, pathetically, he tried to adjust himself to a new environment, language, and customs—first in Switzerland and finally in the United States, where he died.

In his nervous makeup, emotional upheavals, and unshakable despair he reminds us continually of Tchaikovsky. So does his music, which has as vivid a Russian identity as does Tchaikovsky's and is filled with Tchaikovsky-like melodies and sentiments, music to which pathos clings tenaciously. To Rachmaninoff, too, as to Tchaikovsky, music had to come from the heart and not the mind; it had to search into the deepest recesses of the heart.

Rachmaninoff's most celebrated orchestral works reveal the Tchaikovsky-like qualities described above: the Concerto no. 2 in C minor, for piano and orchestra, op. 18 (1901), possibly the most popular piano concerto of the twentieth century; the Symphony no. 2 in E minor, op. 27 (1907); the grim tone poem *The Isle of the Dead* (*Die Toteninsel*), op. 29 (1907); the Concerto no. 3 in D minor, for piano and orchestra, op. 30 (1909); and the *Rhapsody on a Theme by Paganini*, for piano and orchestra, op. 43 (1934).

The writing of the one work above all others that made Rachmaninoff's name glow so luminously in our symphony halls—the Second Piano Concerto—has a dramatic history. The terrible failure suffered by Rachmaninoff's First Symphony at its premiere in 1897 proved devastating to his nervous system. A nervous breakdown followed, from which Rachmaninoff emerged with chronic melancholia, physical inertia, and the conviction that never again would he write any music. He sought the help of a Moscow physician who specialized in autosuggestion, Dr. Dahl. Slowly, painstakingly, Dr. Dahl worked on Rachmaninoff to restore the young man's self-confidence. Again and again, Dr. Dahl kept repeating to Rachmaninoff, "You will write a piano concerto and it will be a great work." The treatment took effect. Rachmaninoff went to work on a piano concerto that he dedicated to Dr. Dahl. It was the now world-famous Second Piano Concerto, whose premiere in 1901 was a triumph. Rachmaninoff now had the self-assurance with which to continue his career as composer. He went on to become one of the world's greatest piano virtuosos and a distinguished conductor, and to write several compositions carrying into the twentieth century the traditions of Tchaikovsky and thereby enriching the Romantic orchestral repertory with music the world has come so to love.

The Post-Romantics

Gustav Mahler, Anton Bruckner,

Richard Strauss

Brahms had his followers and imitators. Even more so did Richard Wagner (1813–1883), whose artistic goals and means were completely opposite to those of Brahms. Wagner wrote few compositions exclusively for orchestra, of which only two are of general interest. *Eine Faust Ouvertüre* (*A Faust* Overture) already carries identifications of Wagner's mature stylistic characteristics, even though it came so early in his career (1840). *A Siegfried Idyll,* for chamber orchestra (1870), is one of the gentlest and most tender orchestral lullabies—a birthday gift to Wagner's wife Cosima. Most of the melodies come from Wagner's music drama *Siegfried.* One, however, is a German lullaby interpolated as Wagner's token of gratitude to Cosima for having borne him a son, Siegfried.

Most of the orchestral pieces representing Wagner on symphony programs, however, are either the overtures or preludes to, or significant excerpts from, his best operas and music dramas: *The Flying Dutchman, Tannhäuser, Lohengrin, The Ring of the Nibelungs, Tristan and Isolde, The Mastersingers,* and *Parsifal.* (Wagner used the term *opera* for his earlier works through *Lohengrin,* and *music drama* for the later ones.) Orchestral music is all the richer for this wonderful repertory. Listening to this music, even outside the opera house, we can readily understand why only two courses were left to composers after Wagner: to accept both his style and methods, or to reject them for totally new ones.

Wagner's world was essentially the theater. His ideal was to create a musical drama that would be a super-art in which music, poetry, drama, scenery, costuming, and acting would coalesce into a single unified artistic concept. To achieve this synthesis of the arts, Wagner wrote his own poetic dramas, filling them with symbolism and allegorical allusions pointing up his social and political thinking. To voice these thoughts and ideas he had to expand the expressiveness of music far beyond anything previously attempted. For his works from the *Ring* cycle on, he used an immense orchestra: sixty-four strings, four each of the woodwinds, eight horns, four trumpets, bass trumpet, three trombones, bass trombone, eight tubas, contrabass tuba, and extra harps and percussion instruments. He invented the "Wagnerian tuba" to bridge the color gap between horns and the ordinary tubas, using two of each in two different keys. He assigned to the orchestra an importance it had never known in opera, using it with the virtuosity of a supreme violinist or pianist handling his instrument. The orchestra became as important as the voice in projecting the music, at times even assuming the dominant roll. Writing for the orchestra (as for the stage), Wagner was first and foremost the dramatist. He was partial to big sonorities, powerful dynamics, grandiloquent statements, and breathtaking climaxes, with particular emphasis on the brass instruments. His orchestra never failed to achieve the theatrical effect he was seeking.

He created an inextricable bond between music and text, mainly through the complex network of what are known as "leading motives." Called *Leitmotiv* in German, each theme represents a mood, situation, character, emotion, idea, or object, and recurs in the music whenever its subject is referred to. Some leading motives are melodious, some just fragments. With some Wagner achieved a descriptive literalness that no program music had previously approximated. Hundreds of these leading motives were used in seemingly infinite permutations and combinations to build up a giant orchestral scheme: melody piled on melody, sound on sound, color on color with the most extraordinary polyphonic, harmonic, and instrumental technique. Ever seeking to allow the music to flow freely through continual modulations (changes of key) and avoidance of cadences (chords closing a section), and to realize the appropriate musical equivalent for programmatic details, Wagner enriched his har-

monic language with new kinds of chords and evolved a vague tonality
through chromaticisms (sharps and flats).

He thought in gigantic terms, worked in gigantic molds. It took him
a quarter of a century to complete *The Ring of the Nibelungs,* a cycle of
four music dramas: *Das Rheingold (The Rhinegold), Die Walküre (The
Valkyrie), Siegfried,* and *Götterdämmerung (Twilight of the Gods).*
Each (with the exception of the first, the prologue to the remaining three
dramas) lasts for about four hours. Thus this giant work requires four
evenings of performances.

With the vastness of his artistic concept, with the newness of his musical vocabulary and language, with the independence of his musical
thought, with his concentration on musical realism and symbolism, with
his emphasis on the theatrical, and in the way he used orchestration, polyphony, harmony, and tonality, Wagner became an irresistible force to
the younger generation of composers of his and a later day. Though
their field of activity may have been the symphony rather than the stage,
these younger composers worshiped him, were influenced by him, and in
some details imitated him. These followers of Wagner have come to be
identified as post-Romantics.

Two such in Vienna were Gustav Mahler (1860–1911) and Anton
Bruckner (1824–1896), each of whom is credited with nine symphonies.
(Mahler began a tenth that he never finished; Bruckner's ninth symphony is without a finale.) Like Wagner, Mahler used large structures, so
much so that some of his symphonies take up a whole program. The
Symphony no. 5 in C-sharp minor (1902), for example, is of such dimension and has such elaborate orchestration that it has been named the
Giant. Like Wagner, Mahler chose to employ large forces. His Symphony
no. 8 in E-flat major (1907) is called the "symphony of a thousand" because it is scored not merely for an immense orchestra but also for eight
solo voices, a double chorus, a boy's choir, and organ. The human voice
is added to three other Mahler symphonies: no. 2 in C minor, the *Resurrection* (1894), no. 3 in D minor (1895), and no. 4 in G major (1901).

But what links Mahler most closely to Wagner is his determination to
express extramusical ideas and philosophic concepts through music. Vitally concerned with cosmic problems, Mahler continually tries to give
them voice and to seek solutions in his symphonies, transmuting his
moral search into musical terms in much the same way that Wagner had
done through symbolism. More consciously than any other orchestral
composer (more even than Beethoven), Mahler sought to give intellec-

tual content to his symphonies, wrestling continually with the meaning of life and death, universe and nature, eternal love and fate, birth and resurrection, suffering and resignation. Wagner had glorified the hero (Nietzsche's Superman) in his character Siegfried; Mahler, who also admired Nietzsche profoundly, likewise did so in his very first symphony, in D major, the *Titan* (1888).

Bruckner's symphonies differ from Mahler's in that they make no effort to expound ideas, dogmas, or philosophies. His music has a sturdy peasant quality, often given to overemotional rhetoric and garrulousness. It has the same kind of passion for grandeur and expansiveness that characterize both Wagner and Mahler. Wagner was Bruckner's musical god, whom he worshiped with the same piety he lavished on his religion. He humbly dedicated his Symphony no. 3 in D minor (1873) to Wagner. Soon after Wagner's death he wrote a monumental dirge for him: the slow movement of the symphony no. 7 in E major (1883). He imitated Wagner in the way he used his brasses and in his chromaticisms; in his partiality for monumental climaxes; and, in some instances, in the use of melodies that seem to have stepped out of the pages of the Wagnerian music dramas. In his Seventh Symphony he added Wagnerian tubas to his orchestration. Wagnerian tendencies can easily be recognized in two of Bruckner's most familiar symphonies: the Symphony no. 4 in E-flat major, the *Romantic* (1874) and in the symphony no. 9 in D minor (1894), which ends with a long slow movement in which Bruckner reaches sublimity. (He did not live to write a finale.)

But the most exciting, the most influential, and the most frequently performed and recorded orchestral music carrying on the traditions of Wagner is that of the remarkable tone poems of Richard Strauss.

Strauss started out imitating Brahms and not Wagner, and with good reason. His father—a distinguished horn player who was a member of the orchestra in Munich when Wagner's music dramas were performed under Wagner's direction—was a passionate admirer of Brahms and at the same time a virulent and active antagonist of Wagner. He passed on both his enthusiasm and his prejudice to his impressionable son.

Born in Munich on June 11, 1864, Richard Strauss proved to be a remarkable prodigy in music. After pursuing music study with various Munich teachers, he wrote several compositions thoroughly Brahmsian in their adherence to classical forms, to absolute music, and to the kind of melodic and harmonic beauty for which Brahms had become famous. By the time he was nineteen, Strauss had published a *Festival March* for orchestra and had had some songs, a string quartet, a symphony, and a violin concerto performed in Munich. In 1884 his second symphony received its world premiere in New York City.

In 1882 Strauss had gone to Bayreuth to hear Wagner's latest (and last) music drama, *Parsifal*. This experience stirred him profoundly—not profoundly enough for him to desert his allegiance to Brahms, but sufficiently so as to make him reevalute his own judgment about Wagner's importance.

Strauss became the assistant conductor of the Meiningen Orchestra in Germany in 1885, rising to the post of full conductor a year later. In Meiningen he suddenly leaped out of the camp of Brahms into that of Wagner. He had been given a powerful push in that direction by a friend, Alexander Ritter. Ritter was a poet, philosopher, and musician all in one. A nephew of Wagner by marriage, Ritter was a true believer in Wagner's aesthetic and musical credo, and a passionate admirer of Wagner's works. Ritter convinced Strauss that Wagner was the spokesman for the musical future and and that Strauss should embrace Wagner's principles and techniques; he should turn from absolute to program music and discard the conventional classical forms of orchestral music for the Lisztian tone poem.

Strauss wrote his first programmatic composition in 1886, with which once and for all he broke the cord that had bound him to Brahms. The work was a symphonic fantasy, *Aus Italien (From Italy)*, impressions of Strauss's then recent visit to Italy. To inject realism into his description of the hubbub in the streets of Italy, Strauss used discords more freely than any composer before him. The audience found this music formless and noisy and hissed with disapproval when Strauss conducted its premiere in Munich in 1887. Strauss's father expressed contempt and dismay.

But having discovered a structure and a language best suited to his own temperament—and having become a member of the Wagner cult—Strauss went on to write his first tone poem, *Macbeth* (1887). In the ensuing decade he completed a series of tone poems that startled and electrified the music world with their daring techniques and realism, extravagant orchestral colors, lush harmonies, rapidly changing tonalities and rhythms, and the complexity with which thematic subjects followed one another and were transformed and developed. These tone poems were violently attacked. Strauss became the most notorious composer since Wagner. "This is not music," exclaimed César Cui in Russia, "but a mockery of music." One of the tone poems was described by Debussy in

France as "an hour in an insane asylum." Today these are the only orchestral compositions by Strauss to have become classics.

First in the new group came the passionate music of *Don Juan* (1888), based on a poem of Nikolaus Lenau. The sensuality of the famous lover erupts from the orchestra in an electrifying upsweep of the strings in the opening measures, while Don Juan himself is later portrayed in a romantic melody for the horns. His escapades find detailed description in music so richly pictorial that it is possible to follow his pursuit of one woman after another until (in the shimmering, shuddering figures with which the tone poem ends) he recoils in disgust.

The music of *Tod und Verklärung (Death and Transfiguration)* in 1889 is a detailed musical treatment of the following program provided for Strauss's music by Alexander Ritter:

In a little room, dimly lighted by only a candle end, lies the sick man on his bed. He has just now wrestled despairingly with Death. Now he has sunk exhausted in sleep. But Death does not long grant sleep and dreams to his victim. Cruelly he shakes him awake, and the fight begins afresh. . . . Neither bears off the victory, and all is silence once more. . . . The sick man now sees his life pass through his inner eye. First the morning red of childhood. Then the saucier play of youth, till he ripens to the man's fight, and now burns with hot lust after the higher prizes of life. . . . And so he pushes forward, so he climbs. Then clangs the last stroke of Death's iron hammer. . . . But from the heavenly spaces sounds mightily to greet him what he yearningly sought for here: deliverance from the world, transfiguration of the world.

The tone poem begins with an introduction marked "Sleep, Illness, Revery." This is followed, without interruption, by sections respectively entitled "Fever and Struggle with Death," "Dreams, Childhood, Memories and Death," and "Transfiguration."

Till Eulenspiegels lustige Streiche (Till Eulenspiegel's Merry Pranks) in 1895 uses an old German legend as its program. In describing this tale, Wilhelm Mauke also provides a road map with which to travel through Strauss's descriptive music:

Once upon a time there was a prankish rogue . . . named Till Eulenspiegel. Now he jumps on his horse and gallops into the midst of a crowd of market women, overturning their wares with prodigious clatter. . . . Disguised as a priest, he "drips with unction and morals," yet out of his toe peeps the scamp. As a cavalier he makes love, at first in jest, and soon in earnest, and is rebuffed. He is furious and swears vengeance on all mankind, but meeting with some philistines he forgets his wrath and mocks them. At length his hoaxes fail. He is tried in a court of justice and is condemned to hang for his misdeeds; but he still whistles defiantly, as he ascends the ladder. Even on the scaffold he jests. Now he swings; now he gasps for air; a last convulsion. Till is dead.

There are two themes to portray Till. The first is heard initially on the horn, and the second in the strings—both showing him to be an impudent scoundrel. Piercing discords reveal how he throws the marketplace into pandemonium, and with a violin glissando the false monk's clothes are torn from Till's body to reveal who he really is. The same kind of realistic writing prevails throughout the tone poem. A roll on the drum spells Till's doom. A descending interval tells us that Till has been executed. We even hear Till's dying gasps.

Also Sprach Zarathustra (*Thus Spake Zarathustra*) in 1896 is music with philosophical implications, since the program is based on Nietzsche's philosophical tome of the same name. "I want to convey by means of music," Strauss explained, "an idea of the development of the human race from its origin, through the various phases of development, religious as well as scientific, up to Nietzsche's idea of the Superman." The work tries to represent man's eternal struggle to conquer death and achieve immortality, tracing the steps by which he can become a Superman. The introduction is Zarathustra's invocation to the sunrise. A motto theme of three notes (C, G, C) that identifies the will to live is followed by two shattering chords (one in the major, the other in the minor). The eight sections after that are given the following titles: "Of the Dwellers of the World in the Rear," "Of Great Longing," "Of Joys and Sorrows," "Song of the Grave," "Of Science," "The Convalescent," "Dance Song," and "The Song of the Wanderer." The first two are religious in spirit, and quote Gregorian chants. The third and fourth turn from asceticism to physical passion. In the fifth, to indicate science, Strauss uses fugal writing. The sixth explores science further (fugal writing is amplified) to seek a solution to life's riddle. The seventh describes earthly pleasure, and the last attempts to provide a key to life's riddle. Man has reconciled himself to being mortal. But the repetition of the three notes of introduction (C, G, C) gives us a hint that there still stirs in man the ambition to overcome death, to rise to be a Superman. (In 1967 the music from *Thus Spake Zarathustra* was used with extraordinary effect on the soundtrack of the motion picture *2001: A Space Odyssey*.)

Don Quixote (1897) relates some of the picaresque adventures of the knight-errant in the Spanish classic by Cervantes. Strauss called his tone poem "fantastic variations on a theme of knightly character." But before this principal theme is heard, there is a brief introduction. The theme of knightly character is then given by the solo cello. The adventures of Don Quixote and his squire, Sancho Panza, unfold in ten variations on this knight theme: an attack on the windmills, which the don believes to be giants; the battle with the sheep, which the don mistakes for robbers; the fight with two monks, whom the don suspects of being magicians come to abduct a princess; the struggle with the Knight of the White Moon in which the don meets his doom, and so forth. The work ends with the knight theme sounding like an elegy, for the don is dying peacefully in his own house. For this work Strauss invented a wind machine to suggest the sweep of the wind as the don and his squire think they are flying through the air on a wooden horse. This is one of the earliest successful attempts to use an actual noisemaker with serious musical intent in orchestral music.

Strauss's last tone-poem masterpiece is *Ein Heldenleben* (*A Hero's Life,* 1898). This work tells of the struggle of a hero to overcome his enemies in his effort to build a new world. The "hero" theme— appropriately vigorous—is given in the opening section, marked "The Hero." As this theme is developed, so is the hero's personality: his will, idealism, pride, and ambition. A brass fanfare announces that our hero is ready to go into action. The sections that follow tell of his confrontation with his enemies ("The Hero's Adversaries"), his wooing of his beloved ("The Hero's Courtship"), his involvement in battle ("The Hero's Battlefield"), and his achievements in peace ("The Hero's Works of Peace"). In his tone poem Strauss identifies himself as his hero— Strauss who had to fight against and overcome the prejudices and hostilities of his enemies and critics. In the part in which the hero's peacetime achievements are reviewed, Strauss interpolates quotations from several of his earlier works. The tone poem ends with "The Hero's Retreat from the World and Fulfillment," in which the hero reminisces about his past. Here the opposition of the enemy is recalled by the tubas. But in the end there is tranquillity, even solemnity, as our hero finally finds peace and rest in death.

The tools with which these tone poems were carved are basically
Wagner's, but Strauss contributes some of his own: a supreme mastery of

orchestration and the capacity to bring out the fullest potentiality and individuality of every instrument of the orchestra, such as we do not encounter even in Wagner; a gift of storytelling that has few parallels; an endless source of sensuous, luscious melodies; a grandiloquence of poetic concepts. Once the novelty of Strauss's iconoclastic methods wore off, once the shock of his heresies lost their impact, the music world came to realize that in these tone poems the post-Romantic movement had produced some of its finest treasures. And the formerly greatly abused composer became one of the most highly honored composers of his time, one of music's outstanding contributors.

In 1904, Strauss paid his first visit to the United States to tour with a German orchestra in concerts of his own music. One of these (in New York on March 21) featured the world premiere of a new work, the *Symphonia Domestica,* or *Domestic Symphony* (1903). This was even more autobiographical than *A Hero's Life* had been. Structurally a tone poem and not a symphony, it details the events in the life of Strauss's family during a single day. One of its parts even describes Strauss's son taking a bath, while another reproduces a dispute between Strauss and his wife. This work is rarely performed.

In fact, though Strauss continued to write for the orchestra virtually until the end of his life, he was unable to produce a single work as consistently inspired, and as consistently performed, as his tone poems. This does not mean that after 1900 his musical powers were on the decline in other areas. After 1900 his creative genius found its most grateful outlet in opera, indeed in three of the greatest the twentieth century has yielded: *Salome* (1905), *Elektra* (1908), and *Der Rosenkavalier* (1910). He was also acclaimed one of the great conductors of his generation both in the opera house and the concert hall, particularly in performances of his own works and those of Mozart and Wagner.

His fame as Germany's foremost musician appeared to be so firmly established that it seemed nothing could possibly undermine it. But undermined it was, by the turbulent political upheaval in Germany in the early 1930s, with the rise of Hitler and Nazism. For a short time Strauss identified himself with the new regime, determined as he was to allow nothing to dethrone him from the imperial position he had assumed in German music. But in time he came to grips with the Nazis officials: first, when he wrote an opera to a text by a Jew; next, when he allowed his son to marry a Jewess; finally, when he openly opposed the Nazi *Blitz* on Poland that started World War II. Strauss was placed under house arrest in his villa at Garmisch-Partenkirchen in the Bavarian Alps near

Munich, he and his family subsisting on the barest necessities during the war years. He kept on composing, however. One of his late orchestral works was a dirge to the dying Germany: *Metamorphosen* (1945), scored for twenty-three solo strings. The two words "In memoriam" appear at the end of the piece.

After the war Strauss once again received the honor due an elder statesman of music. London held a one-week Strauss festival, which he attended. After a denazification court in Munich in 1948 cleared Strauss of collaborating with the Nazis, the rest of the world stood ready to pay him homage, particularly on the occasion of his eighty-fifth birthday, which brought celebrations in many music capitals.

Strauss died of uremia in Garmisch-Partenkirchen on September 8, 1949. He had been a man of colossal vanity, selfishness, opportunism, and parsimony. But some of these unpleasant traits, together with many others, had also blemished the personality of Wagner. Both, as human beings, left much to be desired. But in his music Strauss, like Wagner, was a genius, and that is the way we will always remember him.

Peter Ilitch Tchaikovsky.

Моему дорогому и глубокоува-
жаемому другу Антону Доренку
и искреннюю почитателя
И. Чайковски
20 февр. 88

Natalia Makarova and Ivan Nagy (*American Ballet Theatre*)
in Tchaikovsky's Swan Lake.

Madame von Meck.

Gustav Mahler.

A concert in New York City in the 1870s, with Hans von Bülow as pianist.

II

The World of Impressionism

Claude Debussy, Maurice Ravel

Some of the most significant new movements in twentieth-century music developed in revolt against Wagner. The first such movement was Impressionism, the leader of which was Claude Debussy. He called himself a "French musician" to emphasize his freedom from Germanic (specifically, Wagnerian) influences. He sought a characteristically French music: clear, precise, and economical; music that made its effect through understatement rather than overstatement; whose orchestral colors were subdued and subtle rather than garish; that made an effort not to overpower listeners with sonority, dynamics, and sweeping climaxes but to woo them gently with delicate sounds. These are the qualities of musical Impressionism.

Impressionism is a term that was used, at first in a derogatory sense, for a kind of French painting prominent in the second half of the nineteenth century. Impressionistic painting represented an open rebellion against the work of the traditional French Romantic painters, who favored heroic figures or sentimental landscapes as subjects. Such Impressionists as Manet, Monet, Renoir, Cézanne, and Degas were not interested in putting images on canvas with photographic realism but, rather, wanted to convey the impression gained from the direct observation of nature. To achieve their artistic ideal, Impressionist painters emphasized neither substance, nor form, nor subject matter, but, instead, the effects that light and shadows had on the theme being portrayed, particularly the variations in color caused by different lighting conditions.

The artistic ideas of these Impressionist painters fell like seeds on fertile soil when Debussy first heard of them. From his boyhood he had aspired to write a new kind of music, totally freed from the bondage of formal harmony, counterpoint, melody, and structure. His sensitive nature reached out for new sounds, colors, and effects that could be fused into a restrained musical art. The aesthetics and techniques of the Impressionist painters gave him the theories he needed to bring into existence the kind of music best able to express his own temperament and personality. And so he evolved Impressionist music: music with new harmonies, new concepts of melody, new ways of orchestration; music rid of the emotional outpourings, dramatic force, programmatic realism, and large architectural designs of the Romantics. Debussy's interest lay in color, nuance, subtle sensations and sounds, atmosphere, mood.

He was born in Saint-Germain-en-Laye, a suburb of Paris, on August 22, 1862. When he was two years old his family moved to Paris. Poverty compelled his parents to turn over four of their children to an aunt. The fifth, Claude, remained with his mother. He began taking piano lessons when he was eight. In his eleventh year he entered the Paris Conservatory, where he stayed to study for eleven years. He was from the beginning a brilliant student, but one driven by inexplicable inner forces to make music according to his own tastes rather than school rules. He introduced discords into his exercises; he moved chords in unorthodox or forbidden progressions. In one such exercise he imitated the cacophonous sounds of buses as they rushed through the streets of Paris. When his fellow students and some of his teachers expressed dismay at the kind of music Debussy was evolving, he commented hotly, "Look at them. Can't they listen to chords without knowing their names?"

Debussy began composing (songs) in 1876 and from 1880 to 1884 produced some excellent ones inspired by his love for a woman who was married and several years older than he. In 1884 he won the Prix de Rome with the cantata *L'Enfant prodigue.* This award carried with it a three-year period of residence at the Villa Medici in Rome. The first composition (or *envoi)* he dispatched back to the authorities of the Paris Conservatory was *Printemps,* so advanced in its harmonic idiom, so free in its tonality, and seemingly so formless that it was denounced as "Impressionistic." In using this term for Debussy's work, the conservatory academicians were expressing contempt. These authorities would have been amazed to discover they were prophets. For this was the first time the word *Impressionism* was applied to Debussy—at a time when Debussy had not yet actually come under the influence of that movement.

Debussy was unhappy in Rome. He detested everything Italian. The strict regime at the Villa Medici, and the severe way in which his second *envoi* was received ("bizarre, incomprehensible, and impossible to execute" is the way it was described) made matters still worse. He yearned for Paris, for freedom to write his music without academic restrictions. Without waiting for his three-year term to end, he suddenly left Italy in the spring of 1887 to return to the French capital. His last *envoi,* the cantata *La Damoiselle élue*—which he dispatched to the conservatory after he had returned to Paris—was also condemned. The conservatory refused to perform it. It met with considerable favor, however, when it was finally given in 1893 at a concert of the Société Nationale de Musique, an organization founded in Paris in 1870 to promote new French music. "The spirit of Wagner—the Wagner of *Parsifal*—hovers over the entire score," French music critic Leon Vallas wrote.

For after returning to France from Italy, Debussy had become infatuated with Wagner's music and then a full convert to the Wagnerian cause after having studied the score of *Tristan and Isolde.* In Wagner he found some of his own rebellious attitudes against tradition. In 1888 and again in 1889 Debussy went to the Wagner Bayreuth Festival, one more pilgrim come to worship at the shrine of a musical god. But as he involved himself more deeply with Wagner, his sensibilities, his French nature, and his own instinctive partiality for refinement and delicacy made him grow intolerant of Wagner's kind of music. "Don't you see," he now said, "that Wagner with his formidable power—yes, in spite of his formidable power —has led music astray into sterile and pernicious paths?" Debussy now found his models in old French music and his ideal in trying to realize a thoroughly French style.

He arrived at these goals by way of Impressionism, having learned of the new ideas of painting firsthand from Manet and Renoir, among others. Debussy was also influenced by the theories of the Symbolist poets (Mallarmé and Verlaine, for example), who believed that poetic techniques should be used to express the subtle states of human emotions and to evoke subjective response. Again, this group was rebelling against the traditional line of development, in this instance, in French literature. Debussy drank in their theories and absorbed their ideas. He suddenly

171

knew that what these men were trying to accomplish in painting and poetry he must try to do in music. Only then would he be able to arrive at
a music thoroughly French but modern in idiom and spirit.

His first Impressionist masterworks were not slow in coming. Between 1893 and 1894 he wrote a string quartet and his first composition
since *Printemps* exclusively for orchestra, *L'après midi d'un faune* (*The
Afternoon of a Faun*).

The full title of his first Impressionist classic in orchestral music is
Prelude to the Afternoon of a Faun—and yet it is no prelude. Debussy
originally planned to use Mallarmé's poem (on which this composition is
based) for an orchestral triptych comprising a prelude, an interlude, and
a finale. He wrote only the prelude, retaining this term in the title, and
releasing the composition as an independent work. He never attempted
to write the other two sections.

The Prelude is a sensitive tone portrait about the dreams of a faun
lying in a half-asleep state. Drowsy, he recalls the visions of nymphs he
had seen in his dreams. Then he lapses languidly further into drowsiness
and succumbs once more to the world of dreams. A solo flute (a slow
melody in whole tones) immediately brings up the half-real world of the
faun. A passionate song for the oboe and a monologue for solo violin
maintain a nebulous atmosphere that, toward the end of the composition, dissolves like scattered mist.

In Debussy's initiation into orchestral music we encounter some of
the elements that characterize all his later orchestral works. Most important is his use of the whole tone scale: a six-tone scale made up entirely
of whole tones—for example, C, D, E, F sharp, G sharp, A sharp—
capable of realizing a new kind of sensitive and exotic melody. (In some
compositions Debussy further emphasized exoticism by occasionally also
employing the five-tone scale—the Oriental pentatonic scale—or the sev-
en-tone scale of the old church modes.) His music, moving freely without concern for a tonal center, evoked a world of shadows and mystery.
Intervals forbidden by texts, the avoidance of formal cadences, the use
of rapidly changing meters and rhythms all combined to realize the most
delicate moods, while discords introduced novel sensations. In later
works subtle images and colorations were produced by the flutes and
clarinets in the low register and by the shimmering high register of the
violins, by muted trumpets and horns, and by the delicate tones of a
harp and such percussions as the celesta, triangle, glockenspiel, muffled
drums, and cymbals tapped lightly by a drumstick. In combining the

various instruments, Debussy arrived at a transparency of texture in which the basic timbre and individuality of every instrument is defined with wonderful clarity. He loved also to produce blotches of orchestral color in the same way that the Impressionist painters splashed colors on their canvases.

Debussy did not try to reproduce vast panoramas but concentrated on small vistas, as, for example, in the *Three Nocturnes,* for orchestra (1893–99). The titles of these three nocturnes are "Clouds," "Festivals," and "Sirens." It is the effect that the idea of clouds, festivals, and sirens made upon the composer that is found in these atmospheric compositions, not a representation of these subjects. In the closing nocturne, eight sopranos and eight mezzo sopranos enter with a wordless chant.

Debussy's notoriety (among those who failed to comprehend his strange kind of music) and his fame (with those who recognized how important his contributions were) were greatly enhanced after the turn of the twentieth century, mainly through the production of his only opera, the greatest in an Impressionist style: *Pelléas et Mélisande* (1902). This opera made Debussy one of the most talked about, fought over, and exciting musical figures in Paris. Before long the opera was responsible for making the Impressionist style a cult among some of France's younger composers.

In his favorte cafés, Debussy became a familiar figure. He dressed like a Bohemian, with his broad-brimmed hat and flowing cape. But his swarthy complexion, black hair and beard, and high cheekbones gave him an exotic appearance. He had unusual interests: a passion for the circus, for example, and for cats. He enjoyed playing a card game called bezique. He smoked continually both cigarettes and a pipe, with the result that he developed chronic hoarseness.

For about a decade after returning from Rome he lived with the woman he loved, Gabrielle Dupont. She dedicated her life to Debussy, becoming his mistress, companion, housekeeper, helpmate, and inspiration all in one. But Debussy grew tired of her, and in 1899 he deserted her to marry a poorly educated and thoroughly unmusical dressmaker, Rosalie Texier. It was to his new wife that he dedicated his three orchestral nocturnes as "proof of the deep and passionate joy I have in being her husband." But this deep and passionate joy in Rosalie began to dissipate by 1902. Debussy now fell in love with Emma Bardac, wife of a banker. After Emma and Debussy had broken their respective marriages through divorce (in 1904), they were married the following year. They had one child, a daughter whom Debussy playfully nicknamed "Chouchou."

During the first year of his second marriage Debussy completed his most ambitious score for orchestra: *La Mer* (*The Sea,* 1905). Though each of its three sections is a completely realized tone poem, there is such a close relationship among them that a unified symphonic design, not to be found in any other of Debussy's larger works for orchestra, was realized. One movement carries on musically where the other left off, and the first two movements are played without pause. Where the separate parts of the nocturnes, preceding *La Mer,* and *Images,* for orchestra, following it, can be played independently, and often are, the three parts of *La Mer* must be heard in their entirety for full appreciation. Its impact comes from the accumulation of states of feelings built up subtly from the beginning of the first movement and carried through to the end of the last movement. The first movement, "From Dawn to Noon on the Sea," suggests the unfathomable mystery of the sea, and its changing personality at different times of the day. In the second part, "Play of the Waves," the waves indulge in capricious sport, prancing like dolphins. Melodic fragments, continually altered by changes of tone color and rhythm, and sinuous figures portray the gaiety of the waves, just as they describe the gentle flow of the waters caressed by breezes in the final part, "Dialogue of the Wind and the Sea."

Debussy's last important work for orchestra was *Images* (1912). The most celebrated of its three movements is the second, "Iberia," often played by itself. "Iberia" is an impressionistic rather than pictorial representation of Spain. This movement is made up of three parts. The first, "In the Streets and Byways," is an animated picture of the colorful and noisy streets of Spain. More poetic and dreamlike is "The Odors of the Night," for night in Spain brings with it the suggestion of mystery. The third part, which comes without pause, is "The Morning of the Festival Day," a brilliant evocation of the sights and sounds, the songs and dances of a Spanish holiday. The two less frequently heard movements from *Images* are "Gigues" and "Rondes de printemps."

In the second decade of the twentieth century, Debussy was to experience the bitterness of neglect, together with physical suffering. A victim of cancer, he underwent a number of operations that left him, as he confessed, "a walking corpse." The outbreak of World War I added financial problems to his other troubles. Nevertheless, he kept on writing music. He died in Paris on March 25, 1918. Because the war was on

everybody's mind at the time, and the fear of a German invasion of
Paris appeared imminent, few knew or cared that France's greatest composer of the twentieth century had just died. Only fifty people attended
his funeral service, and a mere handful followed the coffin to its final burial place in Paris.

By the time Debussy died, Maurice Ravel had already achieved recognition as his logical successor, both as the leader of the Impressionist
movement in music and as France's major composer. He had not won
such recognition without a battle. About a decade earlier, in 1907, he
was the center of a musical storm that raged throughout Paris. At that
time he was being attacked by the critics as an imitator of Debussy, as a
plagiarist. Pierre Lalo, an eminent French critic, detected in everything
Ravel wrote "the unmistakable echo of Debussy's music." While there
were a number of instances where Debussy and Ravel stood on common
ground—both in the subjects they used for their music and in their style
—the points of difference between them were far more pronounced than
the similarities. Debussy's was music of shadows, while Ravel's was of
sunlight. Ravel had concern for well-defined structures. Debussy emphasized fragmentary themes, while Ravel often spun out full melodies. Debussy's orchestration was exquisitely sensitive, while Ravel's was luminous. Debussy was a master in using the whole-tone scale, which Ravel
avoided.

In short, if Debussy was a powerful factor in Ravel's development
—and he was—he was also just the starting point from which Ravel
progressed in Impressionism through his own methods and personality.
By the time Debussy died, Ravel's individuality as an Impressionist became an acknowledged fact. The French critic Jean Marnold now wrote
that Ravel had created a language that belonged exclusively to him,
while another French critic, Émile Vuillermoz, found that in his music
Ravel was "a painter, a goldsmith, a jeweler."

Today we refer to Ravel as a post-Impressionist, rather than Impressionist, to point up the truth—what these and similar critics finally
accepted—namely, that Ravel was an extension of Debussy rather than
an echo.

Ravel was born on March 7, 1875, in Ciboure, in the Basque region
of southern France close to the Spanish border. After studying piano
and harmony with private teachers, Ravel entered the Paris Conservatory in 1889. There, like Debussy, he was both brilliant and rebellious.
One teacher, however, understood him and was sympathetic to his indi-

vidual thinking. That teacher was the highly esteemed French composer Gabriel Fauré (1845–1924). Fauré had a profound influence on Ravel, encouraging the young man in his independence. Under Fauré's guidance, Ravel completed two compositions, the first of his works to be performed, one of which was an orchestral overture, *Shéhérazade* (1898).

Success first came to Ravel with two piano pieces, each of which is still extremely popular. The first was *Pavane pour une Infante défunte* (1899), the other, *Jeux d'eau* (1901). Since the *Pavane* is often given in Ravel's own orchestral transcription, a descriptive word or two is in order. A pavane is a slow, stately old French court dance with three sections, and an Infante is a Spanish princess. The picturesque title has tempted some writers to give a programmatic interpretation to the music, but Ravel always insisted he had no extramusical subject in mind in writing this piece. He chose his title because he liked the way it sounded.

A masterwork in a larger form made its appearance in 1904, the String Quartet in F. Some writers were now beginning to refer to Ravel as a leading composer in France. For this reason several musicians caused a furore in 1905 when Ravel was turned down for the Prix de Rome for the fourth time, feeling young musicians far less gifted than Ravel had been chosen because they were more traditional and far less original. The battle of words, pro and con, that followed (which came to be known as "the Ravel affair") grew into a scandal that finally led to the resignation of the director of the Paris Conservatory; he was succeeded by the more progressive Fauré. When this furore finally died down, Ravel was better known than ever.

The second time Ravel became enmeshed in public dispute was in 1907, when his satirical and amusing songs *Histoires naturelles* were introduced. It was on this occasion that several critics accused Ravel of being Debussy's imitator. The violent exchange of opinions between those who condemned Ravel and those who admired him once again served as valuable publicity.

It did not take Ravel long to justify the opinion of these who had lined up solidly on his side. Even while the argument over Ravel's indebtedness to Debussy was in white heat, he was proving his capacity to write in a vein far different from that of his predecessor. He wrote a one-act comic opera, *L'Heure espagnole (Spanish Hour, 1907),* a gay escapade about the illicit affairs of the wife of a Spanish clockmaker. Both text and music were uninhibited in their indulgence in wit, comedy, and

at times even in burlesque. A work such as this could never have come
from Debussy.

In *L'Heure espagnole* Ravel betrayed his lifelong fascination with Spain, and not for the first time. In 1905 he had included a Spanish number in his piano suite *Miroirs*—the "Alborada del gracioso," which Ravel orchestrated in 1912 and which has become one of his better-known short symphonic pieces. The world *Alborada* means "morning serenade," and *gracioso* suggests mockery. This composition therefore adds to its Spanish identity ironic overtones.

The year Ravel wrote *L'Heure espagnole* he returned to the Spanish scene with a major symphonic work, the *Rapsodie espagnole (Spanish Rhapsody)*. Its premiere in Paris on March 15, 1908, was so successful that the second of its four movements had to be repeated. This rhapsody is both atmospheric and pictorial. It opens in a tranquil mood with "Prelude to the Night." Two characteristic Spanish dances follow, a Malagueña and a Habanera (the latter an orchestral adaptation of a piece for two pianos Ravel had completed in 1895). The rhapsody ends with a highly rhythmic, percussive, and sonorous section called "Feria," ("Fair").

One of Ravel's most lovable orchestral works came in 1908: *Ma Mère l'Oye (Mother Goose)*, based, of course, on several famous tales from that classic in children's literature. Originally Ravel conceived this suite for piano, four hands, and only then adapted it for orchestra. There are five sections, beginning with the stately "Pavane of the Sleeping Beauty," which consists of just twenty measures. For the second part, "Hop o' My Thumb," Ravel contributed the following program note: "He believed that he would easily find his path by means of his bread crumbs, which he had scattered whenever he had passed; but he was very much surprised when he could not find a single crumb; the birds had eaten everything up." The story of Laideronnette is told in the third section, the title of which is her name. She is a princess who is made ugly through the powers of an evil princess, but whose beauty is restored through the love of a prince. The fourth part, "Conversations of Beauty and the Beast," features a delightful little waltz alternating with a more vigorous melody. The closing movement, "The Fairy Garden," presents a beautiful melody in the strings.

In 1910, under the stimulus of Franz Schubert's piano waltzes, Ravel wrote *Valses nobles et sentimentales (Noble and Sentimental Waltzes)*, first as a suite for piano, and then, in 1912, for orchestra.

The published score of the orchestral version (the more familiar one) bears the following dedication: "To the delicious pleasure of useless occupation." The suite has eight movements in which Schubertian waltzes assume a French rather than Viennese identity through the refinement and delicacy of Ravel's characteristic melodic material and orchestration.

Before World War I broke out, Ravel's finest hour as a composer came with what is generally regarded as his greatest score: the music for the ballet *Daphnis et Chloé*. He had been commissioned to write this music in 1909 by Sergei Diaghilev, the artistic director of the then recently organized Ballet Russe. Ravel spent two years on this project. The ballet was introduced in Paris on June 8, 1912. Ravel's music came in for its deserved share of the honors. *"Daphnis and Chloé,"* wrote Jean Marnold, "really consists of a 'musical drama' which offers the coherence and unity of a symphony. All of this music holds itself together and lives its own autonomous existence to such an extent that the preliminary introduction of the leading motives would make even a blind man understand and follow the scenic action."

The scenic action was based on an old Greek pastoral describing Daphnis, as, lying in a grotto of nymphs, he dreams of his beloved Chloé. Chloé and her shepherdesses appear. She is wearing a crown Pan has given her as a token of the nymph Syrinx, the beloved of the gods. Daphnis and Chloé now mime the story of Pan and Syrinx, their dance growing ever more agitated. Then Daphnis performs a melancholy tune on a flute he has fashioned from a stalk. Chloé falls into Daphnis' arms before the altar of the nymphs. A frenetic dance celebrates Daphnis' vow of eternal fidelity to Chloé.

To his score Ravel brought technical wizardry, an extraordinary facility at tone painting, and an extreme sensitivity in creating the most subtle moods and sensuous sounds. This wonderful music, surely one of the finest fruits of post-Impressionism, is best known to us through two symphonic suites (Ravel preferred to call them orchestral series) derived from the ballet score, of which the second is the more famous. The first section, "Daybreak," carries the action from the time Daphnis lies in the grotto dreaming of Chloé to her appearance with the shepherdesses. "Pantomime" is pastoral music for the episode in which Daphnis and Chloé mime the story of Pan and Syrinx. In "General Dance" Daphnis swears his fidelity to Chloé, which inspires an exciting dance of celebration.

During World War I, Ravel became a member of a motorized corps serving at the front, since he had been rejected for active duty because of physical unfitness. The gruesome spectacle of the dead and the dying was a nerve-shattering experience he never forgot. A civilian again, in 1917, he paid tribute to friends who had been killed in the war in a six-movement suite for piano, *Le Tombeau de Couperin,* four parts of which were later orchestrated by the composer. François Couperin-le-grand (1668–1733) was one of France's major composers in the Baroque era. Ravel's *Tombeau de Couperin* borrows the structure used by Couperin for his own suites. The dead are honored not with sorrowful music but rather with tranquil tenderness. The six movements are typical of the Baroque suite: prelude, fugue, forlane, rigaudon, menuet, and toccata. The fugue and the toccata were omitted in the orchestration.

A more important work, however, is *La Valse,* for orchestra (1920). Where Schubert's waltzes had been the point of origin for Ravel's *Valses nobles et sentimentales,* those of Johann Strauss II, the composer of *The Blue Danube Waltz,* and Vienna's waltz king, were the source of *La Valse.* Ravel wanted this work to be, as he explained, "a kind of apotheosis of the Viennese waltz, linked . . . with the impression of a fantastic whirl of destiny." The published score provides the following explanation of the music. "Whirling clouds give glimpses, through rifts, of couples dancing. The clouds scatter little by little. One sees an immense hall peopled with a twirling crowd. The scene is gradually illuminated. The light of the chandeliers bursts forth fortissimo. An Imperial court, in or about 1885."

First we hear the fragment of waltz music before the waltz itself is fully developed. There is buoyancy and gaiety in this waltz, which slowly and subtly degenerates into grimness. The lilting waltz music becomes discordant. For though Ravel was writing about Vienna of 1855, he was thinking of Vienna of 1914, a city whose love of life was destroyed by the outbreak of war followed by postwar problems.

Ravel left Paris in 1921 and found a new home, which he occupied for the remainder of his life; it was a villa, Le Belvédère, in the little town of Montfort l'Amaury. He was happiest in quiet and seclusion, removed from the turmoil of big-city life. At Le Belvédère he relaxed by gardening and tending devotedly to his favorite pets, a family of cats. (He always insisted that he understood cat language, and that cats understood him.) The house, managed by a devoted servant, reflected Ravel's fastidiousness about order and cleanliness. He always dressed with the most meticulous neatness, and the same neatness prevailed throughout his home. Ravel never married, but he was saved from loneliness by his many friends, who kept his home alive with vital conversation and who were continually entertained by his remarkable gift of mimicry and his seemingly inexhaustible fund of amusing anecdotes.

Ravel's only visit to the United States took place in 1928. He made his American debut with the Boston Symphony on January 12, 1928, after which he gave concerts of his works in many other cities. When he arrived in America, he told interviewers what he was most eager to see and do (besides presenting his works): to visit Harlem, to see the birthplace of Edgar Allan Poe, and to meet George Gershwin. He did all three. With his concerts a huge success, and with himself the center of numerous parties in his honor, Ravel had good reason to look upon his American experience with satisfaction.

He was not long back in Paris when Ida Rubinstein, a famous dancer, asked him to write for her music in the Spanish style. Ravel complied with *Bolero* (1927), a composition that took the world of music by storm after Ida Rubinstein had danced to it in Paris late in 1928 and it was performed as a symphonic work by the foremost orchestras of America and Europe. What made this music so exciting, even at first hearing, was the way in which Ravel took a Spanish-style melody and its countersubject in the rhythm of a Spanish dance, the bolero, and kept repeating it throughout the work without variation or development. The effect arises by having the theme and countertheme pass from one group of instruments to another, while all the time the sonority and dynamics are built up. In the end both melodies are given a thunderous climactic presentation by the full orchestra.

In America, particularly, *Bolero* became the rage. It was heard not only in concert halls all over the country, but also in movie theaters, over the radio, on recordings, and even in a Broadway revue. It was transcribed for every possible instrument or combinations of instruments. Hollywood paid a handsome price to use the word *bolero* as the title of a motion picture, which justifiably caused Ravel considerable bewilderment, since his music was not being used in the movie and the word *bolero* was in common usage so that anybody could use it for any purpose.

Three years after *Bolero* Ravel finally worked upon the concerto form, for the first time in his career. In fact he completed two concertos that year. One was for piano and orchestra, the Concerto in G major; the other was for only the piano left hand and orchestra, the Concerto in D major. Ravel conceived the first in the spirit of Mozart and Saint-Saëns. The second had been commissioned by a concert pianist, Paul Wittgenstein, whose right hand had been lost in the war; the pianist made it a practice to commission famous composers to write for him works for the left hand alone, so that he might have a repertory to use at his concerts. In his first concerto, for both hands, Ravel is faithful to the classical structure. In both compositions we can detect the interest Ravel always had in American jazz, and especially in the music of George Gershwin.

Hardly had he finished these two concertos in 1932 when Ravel became partially paralyzed, the result of an accident while he was riding in a taxi in Paris. Physical disintegration was accompanied by creative inertia. "I no longer have any music in my head," he told a friend. "I am finished."

Ravel remained an invalid for several years. Then, in December of 1937, he was operated on for a tumor of the brain. He died in hospital soon after the operation, on December 28, 1937. With him went, as one French critic, Émile Vuillermoz, said in an eulogy, "the greatest French composer of our age" in whose hands "the torch of our national art was kept alight."

Gustav Mahler

Maurice Ravel

Sir Thomas Beecham   *Pablo Casals*

Arturo Toscanini

Bruno Walter

Leonard Bernstein   *Seiji Ozawa*

12

The World of Expressionism

Arnold Schoenberg, Alban Berg,
Anton Webern

Impressionism and post-Impressionism are the first significant trends in twentieth-century music. They represent a reaction against Wagnerism and post-Romanticism. Expressionism, which followed Impressionism as a major twentieth-century movement in music, reacted against both Wagner (and post-Romanticism) *and* Impressionism.

Where the Impressionist was concerned with what he perceived in, and how he responded to, the exterior world, the Expressionist divorced himself from the world around him to find reality in his inner experiences. He looked inward, where the Impressionist looked outward. The American musicologist Paul Henry Lang explains that the Expressionist "seeks to cast into musical forms the most mysterious, intimate, and uncontrollable movements of the creative process, as independent of external influences as possible." Abstraction and compression became the guidelines for the Expressionist composer as he rejected reality and former concepts of beauty.

The Expressionist composer concerned himself with a precise musical logic, since thought processes were more important to him than emotional ones. In this concern he arrived at a totally new kind of melody, avoiding any semblance of lyricism and substituting for it combinations of isolated tones. Consonance was replaced by dissonance. The music began in, moved to, and ended in any key (atonality). Working in restricted structural areas, rather than in large designs, and making the most economical use of orchestration, harmony, counterpoint, and melody became the core of an Expressionist's music.

The apostle of this new music was Arnold Schoenberg, one of the most revolutionary figures music history has known. Schoenberg dared to depart completely from all the standards and traditions previously guiding the creation of music through Wagner and Debussy. Perhaps there is no better way to comprehend what Expressionism in music is, how it developed, and why, than by following Schoenberg's evolution as a composer, step by step.

Schoenberg was born in Vienna, September 13, 1874. At age eight he started to study the violin. While attending elementary school he wrote his first composition, at the age of twelve. His first creative efforts were an imitation of the German Romantic composers, with whose music the boy had been fed and nurtured. Those studies, however, were haphazard. Whatever Schoenberg learned about composition and playing instruments (which later included the cello) came from self-study. Not until his teens did he finally get a teacher, Alexander von Zemlinsky, who gave him lessons in theory. This was the only *formal* instruction Schoenberg ever received.

Zemlinsky welcomed Schoenberg into his household almost as a member of his own family. (Eventually, in 1901, Schoenberg did indeed become a member of the Zemlinsky family by marrying Zemlinsky's sister, Mathilde.) With a highly competent and experienced musician to guide him, Schoenberg was able to make music systematically. He not only composed, but also played the cello in an orchestra conducted by Zemlinsky, and directed a chorus in 1895.

A now neglected string quartet written before the op. 7 in D minor (called no. 1) was Schoenberg's first composition to be performed, in Vienna in 1898. It was liked because it followed the well-established examples of Brahms and his post-Romantic successors. But writing in the Brahms manner soon lost its appeal for Schoenberg. Before the nineteenth century ended, he had come upon Wagner's work, which swept over his musical consciousness like a tidal wave. Like so many of the younger composers in Vienna at that time, he looked upon Wagner as a prophet and an idol. Wagner's principles became Schoenberg's creative laws. As a dedicated Wagnerite he wrote in 1899 a sextet inspired by a poem by Richard Dehmel. *Verklärte Nacht (Transfigured Night)* is the title of the sextet. This is Schoenberg's first composition to survive that is still heard frequently, although *not* as a sextet, but in a transcription for string orchestra made by the composer in 1917.

The Dehmel poem would have appealed to an Impressionist. Under a moonlit sky, a man and woman are walking through a grove. The woman confesses she is bearing the child of another man. The man at her side is initially disturbed, but his love finally inspires forgiveness. The man and woman embrace. Then they resume their walk. The world is transfigured because of the man's compassion.

An Impressionist would have painted the moonlight scene with dark colors and represented the confession and forgiveness in subdued tones. But Schoenberg filled his tone poem with Wagnerian chromatics, sensuous melodies, rich polyphonic textures, and surging climaxes. There are a prologue, two sections blending into each other, and a summary. In the first of the two sections, the walk is described and the woman confesses her guilt; in the second, the man is forgiving, and the world is transfigured. The atmospheric opening, a tonal picture of two people walking through the moonlight, serves as a transition between the two sections and also brings the tone poem to its conclusion.

Next from Schoenberg came a huge work for narrator, five solo voices, three male choruses, and an eight-part mixed chorus, with an orchestra of 145 players: the cantata *Gurre-Lieder*. This work is even more thoroughly Wagnerian than *Verklärte Nacht*. Schoenberg wrote most of the cantata in 1901, then let the manuscript lie idle for about a decade, when he added the final chorus and did the orchestration. Introduced in Vienna in 1913, it made such an enormous impression on the audience that when the final chorus, "Behold the Sun," began, many rose to their feet and remained standing until the end. An ovation followed.

Schoenberg regarded this tribute contemptuously. When he was finally prevailed upon to come to the stage, he bowed gratefully to the performers but refused to recognize the audience. The reason for this is that the Schoenberg of 1913 was no longer the Schoenberg who had written the *Gurre-Lieder,* no longer the arch-disciple of Wagner, no longer a composer who could allow the heart to dictate the kind of music he put down on paper.

Beginning with String Quartet no. 2, op. 10 (1908), Schoenberg anticipated those innovations that would soon carry him to principles and ideals that stood at the opposite pole to Wagner's. The last movement of this string quartet is in an atonal style, the first such piece of music. Then came the first work for orchestra that was atonal from beginning to end: the *Five Pieces,* op. 16 (1909). This was objective music, condensed to essentials, contrived with mathematical exactness, with no recognizable melodies as well as no basic tonality. "I am following an inner compulsion that is stronger than education," he explained, "and am obeying a law that is natural to me, therefore more powerful than any artistic training." His critics and audiences completely failed to understand what he was trying to do. When the *Five Pieces* was first heard (London, in 1912), the audience booed, and the critics were vituperative. About five weeks later, Schoenberg was once again vilified at the premiere in Berlin of a song cycle for "speaking voice" (*Sprechstimme*) and instrucments: *Pierrot Lunaire,* op. 21 (1912). A major Berlin critic wrote, "If this is music then I pray my Creator not to let me hear it again."

No wonder, then, that when the audiences acclaimed Schoenberg for the *Gurre-Lieder* in 1913—for a type of music he now considered outmoded—he refused to show awareness of it. As he explained to a friend, "For years, those people who cheered me tonight refused to recognize me. Why should I thank them for appreciating me now?"

Schoenberg spent the years of World War I in Vienna, where, in 1915, he founded a music school. He did not do much writing during this time of upheaval, but did much theorizing. Looking back at his atonal music, he became convinced that the road of atonality would lead him to anarchy. Art required the discipline of a system to bring order instead of chaos. Schoenberg was sure that the systems of the past were obsolete. A new one was needed to break permanently with all the musical practices of the past and introduce a new age for musical creativity. Influenced by the experiments of an obscure Viennese composer and theorist of that period, Josef Mathias Hauer (1883–1959), who had evolved a new system derived from the twelve tones of the chromatic scale, Schoenberg developed the twelve-tone system. He first tried it out in 1923 in the last of a set of piano pieces and in the fourth movement of the serenade for baritone and seven instruments. In 1924 he used the system throughout a composition for the first time, in a piano suite. From then on, Schoenberg constructed all his music from the twelve-tone technique (sometimes also known as *dodecaphony).* He became the discoverer of a new world into which in time many another pioneer would venture. Schoenberg used the twelve-tone method in great skill and variety, so much so that though he was not officially its inventor, his name has become inextricably identified with it.

The twelve-tone technique or system makes use of the twelve notes of the chromatic scale—that is, all the tones of the white and black keys on a piano from, say, C to the octave above. Before beginning to work on a composition, Schoenberg created a "row": a sequence of these twelve tones in any order he wished, but without repeating a note. This became the material out of which a composition was constructed. There are four different ways this row can be used: in its original form; backwards (last note of the row coming first, followed by the next-to-the-last note, and so on); with its intervals (or the distance between each of the notes) reversed; and backwards with the intervals reversed. These four types of rows can be transposed so that the first note of a row or its variant can begin on any note of the chromatic scale. There are, consequently, forty-eight ways a row can be used. Whether he is fashioning a symphony, a concerto, or a smaller work, the composer fits these forty-eight different rows into a pattern much in the way a jigsaw puzzle is solved. The finished composition becomes the solution of a complex logistical problem rather than the product of human experience; the source of intellectual pleasure for those who can understand the problem and recognize how it has been solved.

For a long time Schoenberg adhered rigidly to the laws of his system, never allowing the human element to intrude, but building his rows into fascinating compositional designs. Through the end of World War II, Schoenberg's music was strident, discordant, harsh. No longer was there even the slightest suspicion of a tune, of euphonious harmony and polyphony, of thematic development or variation. His music offered a series of what, at first hearing, seemed to be a succession of disconnected phrases and rhythmic patterns, together with discordant sounds.

Schoenberg's first orchestral composition in the twelve-tone system was *Variations for Orchestra,* op. 31 (1928). After that came the Violin Concerto, op. 36 (1936); the *Chamber* Symphony, or *Kammersymphonie,* no. 2, op. 38 (1940); the Piano Concerto, op. 42 (1942); and *Theme and Variations,* op. 43b (1943). At the same time he also wrote string quartets; *Ode to Napoleon* for speaking voice, piano, and string orchestra (op. 41b, 1942); the cantata *A Survivor from Warsaw,* for narrator, men's chorus, and orchestra (op. 46, 1947); and an opera, *Moses und Aron* (1931–   , never completed).

The attacks Schoenberg had suffered during his atonal period were multiplied as one after another of his twelve-tone works was introduced to mystified audiences. Few composers before him (with the possible exception of Wagner) were so consistently annihilated in the press and so noisily rejected by audiences. Fortunately Schoenberg lived to see what a cyclonic impact he had made on the music of the twentieth century, as composer after composer began to adopt the twelve-tone system to create some of the most important works of the post–World War II epoch.

Up to 1925 Schoenberg lived in a suburb of Vienna, where he gathered around him his pupils and former pupils, all of them his disciples, unquestioningly following his lead in adopting first atonality and after that the twelve-tone system. His first wife, Mathilde, died in 1923, having borne him two children. A year later Schoenberg married Gertrud Kolisch, with whom he had two sons and a daughter. Between 1925 and 1933 he made his home in Berlin, where he was given a life appointment as professor at the Prussian Academy of Arts. Schoenberg was deposed from this post when the Nazis came to power in 1933. He had been born a Jew and was converted to Christianity in 1921; but in the eyes of the Nazi powers he was still a Jew.

The savage oppressions and excesses of the Nazi regime had a shattering effect on Schoenberg. Sensing that Nazism would continue to grow rather than decline, spread rather than recede, he therefore decided to leave Europe for good, to try to find a new life in the United States. Before coming to America, he stopped off in Paris, in May of 1933, to undergo a ceremony in a Parisian synagogue to be reinstated in the faith in which he had been born.

Schoenberg arrived in the United States on October 31, 1933. He remained there for the rest of his life, becoming a citizen in 1941. In time he acquired a modest home in the Brentwood district of Los Angeles, supporting himself by teaching composition first at the University of Southern California and later at the University of California in Los Angeles. After 1944 he confined his teaching activity to a few carefully chosen private students.

He continued to write music until his life came to an end. But a significant change took place in his approach to his art. The experiences he had undergone in Europe in 1933 led him, for the first time since the early part of the century, to introduce human values into his writing, to try to make his music deliver a political, social, or religious message, or reflect his own reactions to the world outside his art. And so, as a result of his return to Judaism, he began writing music of Jewish interest—*not* Jewish music, but music on Jewish subjects. These included his unfinished opera *Moses und Aron* and his cantata *A Survivor from Warsaw.* He was beginning to be influenced in his music by international politics. His *Ode to Napoleon,* based on a poem by Byron, was a political document in praise of democracy and denouncing fascism. All these compositions were in the twelve-tone system.

Inevitably, Schoenberg's importance as a composer and as a developer of the first completely new musical system in several centuries was recognized. In 1947 the National Institute of Arts and Letters gave him the Special Award of Distinguished Achievement. In 1949 his seventy-fifth birthday was celebrated worldwide, and in several American cities with all-Schoenberg concerts or with individual Schoenberg works. Some of his last compositions inspired ovations instead of catcalls. Just before he died, he was invited to return to Vienna to be the recipient of honors. He wanted very much to go back to his native city—just as, in his last months, he desperately wanted to complete his 1931 opera, *Moses und Aron,* which he now considered his most important work. He did not live to do either. He died at his home in Brentwood on July 13, 1951.

The capacity of the twelve-tone system to produce music of first importance was proved not only by Schoenberg but even more forcefully and convincingly by two of his pupils and disciples: Alban Berg (1885–1935) and Anton Webern (1883–1945). Berg is most famous for his atonal opera *Wozzeck* (1921) and his twelve-tone opera *Lulu* (1935–unfinished). But he also produced several orchestral works. The first was *Five Orchestral Songs,* op. 4 (1912), based on messages (sometimes in verse, sometimes in prose) that a poet, Peter Altenberg, used to send his friends on postcards. This composition, for voice and orchestra, created a scandal when it was introduced in Vienna in 1913.

Three Pieces for Orchestra, op. 6 (1914), honored Schoenberg on his fortieth birthday, carrying Berg still deeper into the atonal world he had begun to explore in the *Five Orchestral Songs*. But not until after he had completed *Wozzeck* did Berg contribute his most important music for orchestra: the *Lyric Suite* and the Concerto for Violin and Orchestra. In both these works Berg proved, before Schoenberg himself did, that it was possible to endow the twelve-tone system with human and personal responses. Both works have melodic and emotional interest. It is for this reason that Berg has come to be known as the "Romanticist of the twelve-tone school."

The *Lyric Suite* (1926) started out as a six-movement composition for string quartet; it is still famous that way. In 1928, Berg orchestrated three of these movements: "Andante amoroso," "Allegro misterioso," and "Adagio appassionato." Using a descriptive word after the tempo marking indicates how consciously Berg was trying to express himself emotionally. The first movement is designated as "lovingly," the second as "mysteriously," and the third, "passionately."

Berg's Violin Concerto is one of the noblest and most touching works of its kind. It was Berg's last completed composition, written in 1935 on a commission from Louis Krasner, who introduced it at the Barcelona Festival in 1936. Entirely in the twelve-tone technique as freely used by Berg, this two-movement work is an elegy in memory of a young girl whom Berg described as "an angel," and who died after a serious illness. She was Manon Gropius, the daughter of Walter Gropius, the world-famous architect, and his wife, Alma, widow of Gustav Mahler. The first movement touches upon the girl's gentle and lovable nature. Where the first movement is basically lyrical, the second is dramatic, for it is here that we encounter the girl's helpless struggle with death. In this final movement Berg quotes a chorale melody from a cantata by Johann Sebastian Bach, first in Bach's own harmonization, then with harmonies derived from Berg's twelve-tone row. This Bach theme is varied before the concerto rises to a climax and ebbs away in a funereal coda.

The Violin Concerto and the unfinished opera *Lulu* were Berg's last works. An insect sting resulted in blood poisoning that brought about his untimely death in Vienna.

While Berg was the Romanticist of the atonal and twelve-tonal school, another of Schoenberg's pupils and disciples, Anton Webern, was its extremist. He went far beyond his teacher and idol Schoenberg in the practice of musical Expressionism. Webern's music is the last word in brevity, compression, condensation, and abstraction. His *Six Pieces for Orchestra,* op. 6 (1910), requires only about ten minutes for performance; its shortest movement lasts just fourteen seconds. There seems to be no set structure to any of these pieces, as unrelated tones follow each other; frequently what might be designated as a theme comprises only a few tones. At times a single instrument is used to present these so-called themes or fragments; a piece, then, consists of brief statements made up of a few notes presented by different solo instruments. This method is pursued further in *Five Pieces for Orchestra,* op. 10 (1913), where the sonority is so limited that with the exception of a single climax, all five pieces are uttered in a whisper, the dynamics ranging from pianissimo to sounds that can hardly be heard.

The full crystallization of Webern's extremist methods can be found in his Symphony, op. 21 (1928). It opened up for the twelve-tone system vistas not even conceived by Schoenberg. In this symphony Webern suggested for the first time ways in which the twelve-tone technique might be applied to elements in music other than pitch, principally tone color. This was the germ of a radical new concept in twelve-tone writing —a concept seized upon after Webern's death by brilliant and influential composers to create the technique known as "serialism," or "total organization." No longer was the twelve-tone method applied exclusively to pitch as had been the case with Schoenberg and Berg. It could now be adapted for rhythm, dynamics, tone color, time values, and so forth. In short, in planning a "serial" composition, the composer not only selected a twelve-tone row for his melodic and harmonic material; he also assembled a row of twelve different note values, twelve different dynamic markings, twelve different instruments (or tone colors), and twelve different rhythmic patterns. From the middle 1950s on, serialism became the most useful tool in the workshop of many avant-garde composers. Thus it was Anton Webern—and not Schoenberg and Berg—who most strongly affected the music of our generation. Since the end of World War II, Webern societies have been founded in eleven countries. Webern festivals have taken place in various cities in America and Europe. All of Webern's works have been recorded.

But Webern did not see these developments take place. During his own time, his music was rarely heard, little known, and—when heard and known—was treated contemptuously. What was it that one New York critic wrote in 1929 when the symphony received its world premiere? "What the audience heard suggested odd sounds in an old house when the wind moans and the floors creak, the shades rustle, and the doors and windows alternately croak and groan." And did not a second New York critic compare the sounds of the symphony to those "uttered at night by the sleeping inhabitants of a zoo"?

But never for a moment had Webern doubted that his was the music of the future. "In fifty years at the most," he once said, "everyone will experience this music as *his* innate music. Yes, even for children it will be accessible. People will sing it."

Webern's end came about through a tragic misunderstanding. During World War II, Webern and his family sought refuge in the Austrian Tyrol mountains, in the town of Mittersill. When, at the end of the war, American troops occupied this town, an American soldier came to arrest Webern's son-in-law as a black-market operator. Webern was strolling outside the house, smoking an after-dinner cigar. Mistaking the composer for the man he had come to arrest, and afraid he might be attacked, the American soldier shot and killed Webern.

Nijinsky in the ballet version of Debussy's The Afternoon of a Faun.

Claude Debussy.

Maurice Ravel.

Arnold Schoenberg teaching a class at UCLA.

Anton Webern.

13

New Sounds for
the Twentieth Century

Igor Stravinsky, Paul Hindemith

Three lives had Stravinsky—that is, three musical lives. Each represented a different movement in twentieth-century music. In the first two lives Stravinsky's contributions proved so monumental that much of what he then produced is now universally accepted as indestructible classics. The creations of Stravinsky's third musical life, compositions of his old age, have not yet won full approbation. But as Stravinsky once pointed out, the public "cannot and will not follow me in the progress of my musical thought. What moves and delights me leaves them indifferent and what still continues to interest them holds no further satisfaction for me." Had not the achievements of his first two musical lives been originally rejected and despised? Stravinsky was certain that time would eventually once again prove him right.

His first musical life began in 1910 and ended about a decade later. This was the time of his "dynamism" or "neoprimitivism": music in which rhythm superseded melody as the prime interest, with considerable stress on percussion instruments; music with ever-changing meters, displaced accents, complicated syncopations, and with different rhythms and meters used simultaneously (polyrhythms and polymeters) in the way a polyphonic composer employed different melodies; music filled with discords and harsh and powerful sonorities and dynamics; music in which melody is displaced by fragmentary themes, repeated over and over again to produce a hypnotic effect. In short, this was music in which the elemental forces of primitive music were combined with sophisticated forms and techniques. For this reason this style was called "new primitivism." This kind of writing was a conscious effort to free music both from the emotional, structural, and symbolic tendencies of Wagner and the post-Romantics, and also from the preciousness, remoteness, and sensitivity of the Impressionists. It was in this neoprimitive style that we encounter the three Stravinsky scores audiences now esteem so highly: the music for the ballets *The Firebird, Petrouchka,* and *The Rite of Spring.*

It might be wise at this point to trace Stravinsky's personal history up to the time he entered upon his first musical life.

The son of a celebrated opera basso, Igor Stravinsky was born in Oranienbaum, a suburb of Saint Petersburg, on June 17, 1882. Though he early revealed an unusual love for music, Stravinsky's parents were convinced he had little talent and directed him toward law after he had finished his preliminary academic schooling. While attending the University of Saint Petersburg, Stravinsky studied harmony with a private teacher, counterpoint from a textbook, and piano by continual experimentation at the keyboard. He also began to compose. In 1902 he played some of his compositions for Rimsky-Korsakov, who was little impressed, but urged Stravinsky to continue with his studies in harmony and counterpoint.

Stravinsky entered the Saint Petersburg Conservatory while still attending the university. Under the eye of Rimsky-Korsakov (whose household he now visited regularly) Stravinsky, in 1904, completed a piano sonata, in 1905–1907 a symphony, and in 1906 a song cycle. The symphony was rejected when first performed in 1908. The cyle, heard the same year, received a warm response.

Meanwhile, in 1905, Stravinsky had completed law study at the university. About a year later he married his cousin, Catherine Gabrielle Nossenko, who encouraged the all-too-willing Stravinsky to forget all about law and concentrate on making music. Now a full-time composer, Stravinsky finished two orchestral works in 1908: *Scherzo fantastique,* op. 3, and *Feu d'artifice (Fireworks),* op. 4. The second was written as a wedding gift for Rimsky-Korsakov's daughter, and both pieces were performed publicly at a concert in Saint Petersburg on February 6, 1909.

In the audience was Sergei Diaghilev, a promoter of the arts then planning the organization of a company—the Ballet Russe—to present to the Western world the finest examples of Russian ballet. One of Diaghilev's skills was to sniff out potential talent. While he recognized that both the *Scherzo fantastique* and *Feu d'artifice* were derivative from Rimsky-Korsakov, he also detected in them a strong individuality trying to assert itself. He engaged Stravinsky to write music for the Ballet Russe. Stravinsky's first major assignment for Diaghilev was a score for a ballet about the Firebird based on an old Russian legend. *The Firebird* (*L'Oiseau de feu*) caused a furore of enthusiasm when introduced in Paris on June 25, 1910. In the legend, Prince Ivan captures the Firebird, then, after releasing it, is given by the bird one of its feathers. With that feather, the prince invades the castle of Kastchei, the evil spirit. Through the feather's magic powers, the prince frees thirteen beautiful maidens held captive and brings death to Kastchei and destruction to his castle. Ivan then marries one of the captive maidens he has liberated.

For this tale, Stravinsky carved the score with which he entered upon his first musical life. It is not music without derivative echoes: echoes of Rimsky-Korsakov in the iridescent orchestration and the occasional Oriental-style melodies; echoes of Russian folk song in the lovely "Berceuse." But page after page has a boldness of imagination, an originality of harmony, a distinctive melodic line, and an irresistible rhythmic cogency that picturesquely evoke the most vivid tonal images. Here for the first time we can hear the voice of the neoprimitive, for example in the section "Kastchei's Infernal Dance."

In 1910 there were many to be outraged by Stravinsky's audacious writing. Pavlova, the great ballerina who had been scheduled to appear in the premiere, hotly rejected any association with such "horrible music." Others described the score as noisy and vulgar. A few, however, recognized greatness. At one of the rehearsals, Diaghilev confided to a friend, "Mark that man, Stravinsky. He is on the eve of celebrity." And after the premiere of the ballet Debussy rushed to the young Stravinsky and embraced him.

Stravinsky drew three suites from his ballet score, the one most often played being the second. It has five sections: "Introduction—the Firebird and Her Dance"; "Dance of the Princesses"; "Kastchei's Infernal Dance"; "Berceuse"; and "Finale."

With his next ballet score, *Petrouchka,* Stravinsky penetrates deeper into the neoprimitive world. For the first time he breaks his stylistic ties to Rimsky-Korsakov, while still remaining unmistakably Russian. Petrouchka is a puppet familiar at Russian fairs. In the ballet story Petrouchka falls in love with a puppet ballerina, but her heart belongs to an Arab, or Moor. Against the colorful but noisy background of a carnival, Petrouchka's sad love unfolds. He discovers his ballerina with the Arab. The Arab pursues and kills Petrouchka—much to the horror of the carnival public until it is reminded by the operator of the show that what has taken place is not an actual-life episode but a drama involving puppets.

In describing the bustle and gaiety of carnival life Stravinsky is brilliantly pictorial, and in his characterizations penetrating. From time to time he spices his music with sardonic or humorous condiments: now with a takeoff on a Russian liturgical melody, now by simulating the hurdy-gurdy sounds of a French popular tune. Though he quotes three Russian folk songs, his voice is basically his own. The neoprimitive takes the limelight. He is more and more daring in using discords, in juxtaposing two melodies in different keys (polytonality), in threading together a continuous succession of epigrammatic statements repeated constantly, in his extraordinary rhythmic virtuosity, and his increased dependence on percussions.

Petrouchka, choreographed by Fokine, was produced by the Ballet Russe in Paris on June 13, 1911. It was a tremendous success as a ballet. As for Stravinsky's music, more than one critic and musician was upset by his unorthodoxy.

At orchestral concerts, *Petrouchka* has long been represented by a suite taken from the ballet score made up of the following parts: Carnival; The Magician; Russian Dance; Petrouchka; The Arab; Dance of the Ballerina; Nurses' Dance; The Bear and the Peasant Playing a Hand Organ; The Merchant and the Gypsies; The Dance of the Coachmen and the Grooms; The Masqueraders; The Quarrel of the Arab and Petrouchka; The Death of Petrouchka. It has, however, become an increasing practice of conductors to present the complete ballet score rather than excerpts. When heard this way, the score is divided into four sections: I. Popular Festival of Carnival Week, The Sleight-of-Hand, and Russian Dance; II. At the Home of Petrouchka; III. At the Home of the Arab, and The Ballerina's Dance; IV. Popular Festival of the Carnival Week, Dance of the Nurses, Dance of the Coachmen and Footmen, and The Disguises.

Perhaps it is not so difficult to understand Stravinsky's later cynicism about critics when we read how complacently *Petrouchka* was being accepted as a masterwork years after it had been so severely denounced. For here is that one American music critic, Richard Aldrich in *The New York Times,* wrote in 1923 when this music was performed in New York: "*Petrouchka* offers an incomprehensive phantasmagoria of tone with only an occasional meaning in and of itself. There are moments of obvious amusement when one instrument after another did funny things. But whether those who laughed dilated with exactly the proper emotion may be doubted." H. E. Krehbiel of the *Herald-Tribune* wrote: "It is but a disjointed series of funny sounds, squeaks and squawks, imitations of wheezy hand organ and hurdy-gurdy grunting, snatches of tunes from a bassoon, clattering of a xylophone, and whirring noises."

Derision, contempt, annihilation in 1923; awe and reverence a half century later. *Petrouchka* was by no means the last of Stravinsky's works to traverse the extremes of public and critical evaluation from A to Z.

In fact, with Stravinsky's very next major ballet score—*Le Sacre du printemps* (*The Rite of Spring*), the gap between the reaction of 1913 and that of today grows even wider. This work is the greatest of Stravinsky's neoprimitive compositions, and one of his towering achievements. But in 1913 it rocked the music world like an atomic blast. The world premiere by the Ballet Russe on May 29, 1913, in Paris caused one of the greatest scandals ever witnessed in a French auditorium—jeering, fistfights, yelling, whistling, angry and insulting exclamations. It was virtually impossible to hear the music. And the critics? "Never was the system and cult of the wrong note practiced with so much industry, zeal, and fury," wrote Pierre Lalo. A critic of *Le Ménéstral* referred to the ballet as "The Massacre of Spring." An English critic reported, "It has no relation to music at all." But sixteen years later, Cecil Gray, the English musicologist, called it "one of the most conspicuous landmarks in the artistic life of our period," an estimate that has since come to be accepted with little questioning. When the fiftieth anniversary of this premiere was celebrated in London on May 29, 1963, a fifteen-minute ovation followed the performance. "In a long experience of London's music," said one London critic, "I do not recall a scene to surpass this one."

The ballet re-creates a pagan rite in old Russia. It does not present a detailed story but rather a series of impressions of primitive man going through the ritual of the adoration of nature; a barbaric dance; a contest in gymnastics and a battle between two groups; the consecration of the earth by a Sage followed by a demoniac dance; the picture of a pagan night; ritual dances; and the final sacrifice where a female dances with ever-mounting frenzy until she dies of exhaustion.

Stravinksy's writing represents the apotheosis of dynamism. The intricate rhythms and meters change all the time, and so do the sonorities and dynamics. Terse phrases are repeated until they become hammer blows on the consciousness. The discords are shattering. The percussion instruments are used unsparingly. Tension is built up until it becomes almost unbearable. And in the final sacrificial dance, the music becomes an orgiastic outburst of sound and rhythm.

Though Stravinsky wrote several more works in this neoprimitive style, he knew he had exhausted its creative potential. Rather than resort to repeating himself, he withdrew from his first musical life to enter a second one. Musically speaking, he was reborn. His style leaped to an opposite extreme: from complexity to simplicity; from power and primitivism to refinement and transparency; from the unconventional and the progressive to reaction; from a Russian identity to a French one. Music had to be freed from the everyday world of human experience, to be rid of extramusical connotations, to be made disinterested in authentic representations. The main concern was with arrangement, design, line, logic. Forms had to be slimmed down and stripped of trimmings. Brevity was to become the soul of wit.

Stravinsky now reverted to the Baroque era, adapting its forms, stylistic aims, and objectivity for twentieth-century use. In this, his second musical life, Stravinsky was transformed from the neoprimitive to the neoclassicist. Several others had preceded Stravinsky in this direction, most notably Ferruccio Busoni (1866–1924) and Max Reger (1873–1916) and, in individual works, Georges Enesco (1881–1955) and Prokofiev. But it was Stravinsky who, above all others, made neoclassicism one of the major new movements in the first half of the twentieth century.

Already a noticeable change was beginning to take place in Stravinksy's music in 1918. The intricacies and dynamism of his earlier works were reduced to simplicity, economy, and understatement in *L'Histoire du soldat* (*A Soldier's Story*), a "narrative ballet" for only three dancers, a narrator, and seven instrumental performers. A year later he took one step further away from neoprimitivism and one step closer to neoclassicism, with a score for the ballet *Pulcinella* where he adapted melodies by Giovanni Battista Pergolesi (1710–1736). Then, in 1923, his neoclassicism was fully crystallized in the *Octet for Winds*.

For the next thirty years Stravinsky remained faithful to neoclassicism. In this vein his major works included various concertos (for orchestra; for piano; for violin); the *Capriccio,* for piano and orchestra (1929); scores for the ballets *Apollon Musagète* (1928) and *Perséphone* (1934); and the *Symphony in Three Movements* (1945). During this period he also wrote several powerful choral compositions, the best of which are the oratorio *Oedipus Rex* (1927), the *Symphony of Psalms* (1930), and the Mass (1947). Stravinsky's last work in the neoclassical style was a work rooted in Mozart: *The Rake's Progress* (1951), his only full-length opera.

While experiencing this radical musical transformation, Stravinsky was also undergoing a change of home and nationality. In 1919 he deserted Russia because he was unsympathetic with the new revolutionary regime. He took up residence in Paris and later became a French citizen. (It took him about forty years to set foot again on Russian soil—revisiting his country to conduct several concerts of his works in September of 1962.) In 1939, for the second time he changed home and country. This time he came to live in Hollywood, California. He had paid a number of visits to the United States as a guest conductor of major orchestras from 1925 on, but after 1939 he came to regard himself as an American. In 1945 he became one officially through citizenship.

In the United States he worked intensively on numerous compositions, made appearances as guest conductor, and in 1939–1940 served as a lecturer at Harvard University. He also became involved in the publication of several volumes of "conversations," the subject matter traversing a wide gamut of music and musicians, in which he expressed some highly individual and at times penetrating opinions—"conversations" that his disciple and assistant Robert Craft had noted down painstakingly. Stravinsky also married a second time (his first wife had died in 1939 after bearing him three children). His second marriage, in 1940, was to an artist, Vera de Bossett, who survived him.

By the time he had become an American, the world of music had long come to realize that the principal results of his neoprimitive period were masterworks. Many critics, and a large segment of his public, however, for a long time felt that his neoclassical music represented creative sterility. It took numerous hearings of these neoclassic works, as well as the passage of time, for the subtlety of Stravinsky's musical thought and logic, the beautiful balance of his structure, and the quiet and subdued beauty of his style to penetrate the consciousness of his listening public.

Once this happened, Stravinsky once again became a powerful influence, a composer who was widely imitated.

Before we desert the subject of neoclassicism, we should bring up for attention the work of another giant composer, a German: Paul Hindemith (1895–1963). As a young man, Hindemith favored both polyphony and the forms of polyphonic music so greatly that he came to be known as "the twentieth-century Bach." Nurtured on Bach's *Brandenburg Concertos,* Hindemith, aged twenty-seven, began in 1922 to write a series of seven compositions designated as *Chamber Music (Kammermusik).* In these, either for chamber orchestra or for solo instrument and chamber orchestra, Hindemith evolved his own style of polyphony. The various melodies, moving simultaneously, were completely independent of any harmonic relationship—a new technique now identified as "linear counterpoint." This makes for dissonant, often atonal, music, Bach recreated in terms of twentieth-century modernism (or "Bach upside down" as one German critic described Hindemith's music). It is not music to make an immediate appeal, being much too cerebral and too unemotional for that. But intimacy with it brings awareness of the skillful, fascinating mental processes involved in the making of these compositions. Once these mental processes are understood, Hindemith's music can be fully admired.

Hindemith was extraordinarily prolific as well as versatile. His output included numerous concertos, both for orchestra alone and for solo instrument and orchestra. One of the more interesting of these has the curious title of *Der Schwanendreher (The Organ-Grinder);* it is a concerto for viola and orchestra written in 1935. This curious title comes from the fact that in the last movement Hindemith quotes an old German folk tune ("Are You Not the Organ-Grinder?"), which receives several variations. Other old German folk tunes appear in other parts of the concerto, too. To explain what this music was about, the composer appended the following explanation to his published score: "A minstrel, joining a merry company, displays what he has brought back from foreign lands: songs serious and gay, and finally a dance piece. Like a true musician, he expands and embellishes the melodies, preluding and improvising according to his fancy and ability. This medieval scene was the inspiration of the composition."

Hindemith also wrote three symphonies. The most famous of them all, and unquestionably his best-known work for orchestra, may be called by its composer a symphony, but it is nothing of the kind. It is a three-movement suite whose music was lifted from an opera. The opera and the symphony are named *Mathis der Maler* (*Mathis the Painter*), the symphony appearing in 1934, the opera not until 1938. To understand the symphony we must know a few things about the opera. Its central character is the sixteenth-century German painter of religious subjects Matthias Grünewald. During the Peasants' War of 1524, Grünewald deserted his art, his job at the cardinal's palace, and his sweetheart, Regina, to become head of a peasant uprising against the tyranny of the church. But when he realized that the revolutionaries were as corrupt and intolerant as those he was attacking, he became disenchanted. He found refuge in solitude, during which he saw the visions that became the subject of panel designs he painted on the Isenheim altar. He now found solace in his art; in the privacy of his studio he dismissed from his life the world outside his windows.

Three salient episodes from the opera become the substance of Hindemith's symphony, each representing one of the pictures on the altar panels. The first movement, "The Concert of the Angels," is the opera's overture, a section that opens and closes with a melody, "Three Angels Sing," heard throughout the stage work. The second movement, "The Entombment," is elegiac music. The third, "Temptation of Saint Anthony," tells of the suffering of the saint while it presents the picture of Matthias taking leave of the world outside his studio. The symphony ends with an exalted "Hallelujah," suggesting that in art and solitude Grünewald had found salvation.

Hindemith's music makes no attempt to be pictorial or programmatic in this symphony, but rather atmospheric. Linear counterpoint predominates. Religious feelings and mysticism are introduced through melodies built upon medieval modes.

Beyond its interest and importance as music, *Mathis der Maler* contributes a dramatic chapter to the early history of Nazi Germany. The Nazis came to power in Germany in 1933, then proceeded to carry out a ruthless program of destroying liberty, expurgating Germany of what they regarded as unwholesome influences (Jews, liberals, and all art and literature opposed to Nazi ideology) and establishing new values for music that opposed modernism.

Though by 1933 Hindemith had already become one of Germany's most famous composers (second in importance only to Richard Strauss), as well as a distinguished violist and a professor of composition at the Berlin High School for Music, he was looked upon by the Nazis with considerable suspicion. Hindemith himself was pure Aryan, but his wife was Jewish; he had Jewish friends; and he had made recordings with Jewish musicians. All this made Hindemith highly unpalatable to the Nazis. So was his music. Hindemith's work, for all its contrapuntal technique and neoclassic tendencies, was decidely modern, and all music with modern tendencies was regarded by the Nazis as "degenerate."

Then in 1934 Hindemith completed *Mathis der Maler,* as a symphony. A work about the revolt of the common man against authoritarian rule was hardly the kind of subject Nazis liked to have circulating. When Germany's foremost conductor, Wilhelm Furtwängler (then music director of both the Berlin State Opera and the Berlin Philharmonic), announced he planned to conduct the opera's world premiere in Berlin, the Nazis let him know they did not regard this venture with favor. Refusing to bow to Nazi dictates, Furtwängler went on with his plans to produce the opera. But first he led the premiere of the symphony, on March 12, 1934. As a symphony, *Mathis der Maler* drew a thunderous ovation, partly because it was important music, mainly because it offered the audience an opportunity to express its resentment of the Nazi regime indirectly without fear of reprisal.

By the end of 1934 Furtwängler had published an open letter in one of Berlin's leading newspapers defending Hindemith and his opera, and urging the Nazi leaders to concentrate on politics and leave musical matters to musicians. This was the last straw. Hitler himself intervened. Furtwängler was forbidden to produce the opera, was forced to resign from his posts, was denied permission to conduct anywhere else in Germany, and had his passport confiscated. (He was subsequently reinstated in his posts.)

Because of this episode, which had violent repercussions throughout Germany, Hindemith was branded as "undesirable." He left Germany and in 1940 established himself in the United States, where he joined the music faculty of Yale University and, in 1946, became an American citizen. Many of his major works, which further enhanced his prestige in twentieth-century music, were written in America. They included numerous significant compositions for orchestra, among which were the *Symphonic Metamorphosis on a Theme by Karl Maria von Weber* (1943), a four-movement composition based on four melodies from little-known Weber music; the Piano Concerto (1945), whose finale uses a fourteenth-century dance tune; the *Symphonia Serena* (1946); two compositions with humorous overtones; the Concerto for Woodwinds, Harp, and Orchestra (1949) and Sinfonietta in E (1950); and another symphony whose music was based upon an opera, *Die Harmonie der Welt* (*The Harmony of the World*) in 1951, in both of which the principal character was the famous astronomer and mathematician Johannes Kepler, and the background the Thirty Years' War. In all these Hindemith remained faithful to the linear style of his earlier music.

In 1948, Hindemith was appointed to the music faculty of Zurich University in Switzerland. He did not resign from Yale, however, nor as yet transfer his permanent residence to Switzerland. Postwar Germany made every effort to get him to come back to his native land, but he refused to consider it. Instead, in 1953, he finally decided to live permanently in Zurich, resigning from Yale, but continuing to make periodic visits to the United States. His last appearance in America was in 1963 during a four-day Hindemith festival in New York.

His final public appearance anywhere took place in Vienna on November 12, 1963, when he conducted the premiere of his Mass for unaccompanied voices. His death came in Frankfort, Germany, before that year was over. With Stravinsky, Hindemith stands as one of the two most important composers of the neoclassic movement.

But let us now return to Stravinksy.

By the time his public and critics were ready to accept the artistic validity of Stravinsky's neoclassic music, Stravinsky (though he was now already seventy) had decided once again to enter upon a new musical life. He had nothing more to say in the neoclassic style; an inner compulsion drove him to a radically different idiom. In 1952 he began experimenting with the twelve-tone technique, and in 1957 his third musical life unfolded fully when he adopted serialism. In this system he wrote major works for chorus on religious subjects, the ballet *Agon,* and the *Variations,* for orchestra (1963–64), the last written in memory of the famous English writer Aldous Huxley. At its world premiere in Chicago in 1965, the *Variations* was played twice at Stravinsky's request to give the audience a better opportunity to follow his serial method, and to allow a fresh outlook on this complex music.

Stravinsky's conversion to serialism shocked the music world, just as it had been shocked when he had adopted neoprimitivism, and when he had deserted neoprimitivism for neoclassicism. For Stravinsky had for a long time expressed his disapproval of Schoenberg's twelve-tone technique. He had so little interest in Schoenberg that although he lived only a few miles from the other composer in Los Angeles he made no effort to contact him. And yet here he was, after Schoenberg's death, proclaiming the importance of both the twelve-tone music and of Schoenberg, and in his own compositions devoting himself exclusively to a system that was the outgrowth of twelve-tonalism! The opposition that arose to Stravinsky's new and last tendency in his art bothered him little. "I can only know what the truth is for me today," he said simply. He knew he had proved right in his earlier artistic decisions, and he knew he was right again.

Until 1970 Stravinsky lived in a small, unpretentious house in Hollywood, with his wife, daughter, cook, gardener, and his dedicated disciple and helper Robert Craft. Stravinsky was always a slave to a routine life, and this persisted into his old age. He adhered to a set schedule, assigning a special time each day for composition, going through his mail, business conferences, relaxation (playing Scrabble or solitaire and watching television), entertaining friends, doing physical exercises and taking his medicines, taking long walks and siestas, and paying daily visits to his doctor. A precise, even fussy, man, he made a fetish of neatness—be it in the way he wrote his manuscripts in calligraphy that looks almost like print, or in the way his working studio was always kept in meticulous order. Being an omniverous reader, he possessed a library comprising in excess of ten thousand volumes. He was also a devotee of art and art objects, of which he had a valuable collection. He was always insatiably curious about developments in art, science, and politics, and he had a philologist's passion for seeking out the derivations or uncovering new meanings of words in several languages.

Convinced that Los Angeles, the city where he had made his home, had consistently failed to pay him the tribute or the number of performances he deserved, Stravinsky, old and sick as he was, insisted on going through the arduous ordeal of moving from California to New York City. Having suffered from circulatory and lung trouble for several years, Stravinsky took a summer cure in Evian, France, in 1970. Upon returning to America, he lived in a hotel while waiting for his new ten-room apartment on Fifth Avenue to be decorated. Between March 18 and 30, 1971, he was confined to a hospital bed because of pulmonary edema. Finally he entered his new home. As his nurse wheeled him around, he said, "How lovely. This belongs to me, it is my home." But sad to say, he was unable to enjoy his luxurious surroundings for long. He died of a heart attack in his apartment only one week after he had left the hospital—on April 6, 1971. He was buried in a cemetery on the island of San Michele in Venice near the grave of Sergei Diaghilev, the first man to realize his genius.

No composer in the twentieth century was more loaded with honors
than Stravinsky had been. In 1954 the Royal Philharmonic Orchestra of
London gave him its highest honor, the Gold Medal. In 1959 Denmark
presented him with its international award, and in 1963 Finland bestowed on him the Sibelius Award, bringing with it $27,000. His eight-
ieth birthday, in 1962, inspired tributes, celebrations, and all-Stravinsky
concerts the world over. President John F. Kennedy invited him to dinner
at the White House and Dean Rusk, Secretary of State, presented him
with a gold medal. Subsequently, the New York Philharmonic offered a
ten-concert Stravinsky festival at Lincoln Center for the Performing Arts
(summer of 1966), and Columbia Records launched a monumental project to record all of Stravinsky's compositions, as many as possible under
Stravinsky's own direction. In June, 1972, the New York City Ballet,
under the direction of George Balanchine, mounted a Stravinsky festival
during which thirty-three of the composers ballets were performed.

"By common consent," commented an editorial in *The New York
Times* on Stravinsky's passing, "Igor Stravinsky was the greatest living
composer. . . . Stravinsky was a seminal figure, and that alone attests
to his strength and assures his immortality. No minor composer in history has ever put his mark on the age. Only the major ones do." Stravinsky was one of the major ones. He had been a legend in his own time
and has become an immortal after his death.

14

Nationalism in the Twentieth Century

Jean Sibelius, Ralph Vaughan Williams,
Manuel de Falla, Béla Bartók

Musical nationalism continued to flourish in the twentieth century. Indeed, the four most famous composers of their respective countries in this century were nationalists: Jean Sibelius in Finland; Ralph Vaughan Williams in England; Béla Bartók in Hungary; and Manuel de Falla in Spain. The common denominator for these four composers is that each developed from mediocrity to greatness only after he had discovered his country's folk music and used it as the source of both inspiration and material.

The struggle of Finland to free itself from Russian domination was the impulse leading Sibelius to become a musical nationalist. Born in Tavastehus, Finland, on December 8, 1865, Sibelius began his studies at the Institute of Music in Helsinki, which he attended until 1889, when a government grant enabled him to complete his musical studies in Berlin and Vienna. His studies there were temporarily interrupted in 1890 to allow him to return to Finland and become engaged to Aino Järnefelt, daughter of a distinguished Finnish composer. Sibelius's permanent return to Finland took place in 1891. On June 10, 1892, he married his betrothed.

In the last decade of the nineteenth century, the Finnish people became increasingly rebellious against the oppressive measures imposed upon them by Russia. Sibelius, too, became preoccupied with his country's fight for freedom. Formerly a composer in the German Romantic style, Sibelius was now concerned with writing music carrying a national message to his people—music whose subjects were taken from Finnish legends and sagas, and whose style absorbed the atmosphere and technique of Finnish folk music. In 1892 he wrote *Kullervo,* for solo voice, chorus, and orchestra (Kullervo being the hero in the *Kalevala,* Finland's national epic). In 1892 he completed the first of his works to gain wide circulation (though in a revision made nine years later): the tone poem *En Saga,* op. 9. In this music the changes of mood from the bucolic to the dramatic that would identify Sibelius's mature works are already noticeable: the bucolic found in a Finnish-style melody for solo clarinet, and the dramatic in the climaxes.

In 1893–95 Sibelius wrote *Four Legends,* for orchestra, op. 22, with subject matter once again taken from the pages of the *Kalevala.* The third of these legends is the now celebrated tone poem *The Swan of Tuonela.* This is the descriptive program note in the published score: "Tuonela, the land of death, the hell of Finnish mythology, is surrounded by a broad river with black waters and rapid currents, on which the swan of Tuonela floats majestically singing." The principal melody pictures the swan as it glides in the waters, a song for English horn. Toward the end of the composition the swan melody is repeated, this time to the accompaniment of noises produced by having the violinists tap the back of their bows on the strings of their instrument to simulate the sound of the flapping of the swan's wings.

More popular still is *Finlandia,* op. 26, the orchestral tone poem that from 1900 on has represented Finland musically to the rest of the world. At first it was the final movement of a suite, *Finland Awakes* (1899), bearing the title of "Suomi" (*Suomi* being the Finnish name for Finland). A year later, Sibelius withdrew the movement from the suite and renamed it *Finlandia.* First heard under its new name (and removed from the other movements of the suite) on July 2, 1900, it caused a sensation, expressing as it did the rebellion against foreign despotism and the aspiration for liberty stirring in all Finnish hearts. All the melodies are so thoroughly Finnish that writers long believed Sibelius was quoting folk songs; but all this material is of his own invention. The most important melody comes after a tumultuous section: a song for the woodwinds that sounds like a plea for freedom. Other themes of a national nature are also prominent, as the music moves with a relentless stride to a thrilling climax. Through its frequent performances *Finlandia* proved more effective propaganda for Finnish freedom than speeches, secret meetings, or pamphlets. Once again it served as eloquent propaganda for Finland's fight for freedom when, early in World War II, the Soviet Union ruthlessly invaded the little country.

Though Sibelius wrote a good deal of orchestral music in the shorter forms, and in a national style, he is most famous for his seven symphonies. The first two—no. 1 in E minor, op. 39 (1899), and no. 2 in D major, op. 43 (1901)—are familiar, though they are not representative of the mature Sibelius. In both these symphonies we find vigor and youthful exuberance—but the voice is not the voice of Sibelius but that of Tchaikovsky, and at times of Brahms. Beginning with the Symphony no. 3 in C major, op. 52 (1907), Sibelius begins to free himself from Tchaikovsky's influence with music that is characteristically Finnish. After that came his greatest symphonies: the no. 4 in A minor, op. 63 (1911), that no. 5 in E-flat major, op. 82 (1915), the no. 6 in D minor, op. 104 (1923), and the one-movement no. 7 in C major, op. 105 (1924).

From the third through the seventh symphonies, Sibelius evolved his own style and structure. He does not use the sonata form, nor is he interested in the process of developing his melodic material. For each of his movements he chose a flexible mold into which he poured sometimes extended melodies but more often terse statements, one following another toward a climactic point that frequently erupts into moments of grandeur. Stylistically, Sibelius favored alternating pastoral moods with turbulent ones, stark themes with windswept melodies. He liked to have his lower strings or plucked strings murmur behind darkly brooding or rustic musings in the woodwinds and horns. He liked subdued instrumental colors, preferring austerity to grandiloquence.

His symphonies have no program, and each has its own character. All, after the third, are predominantly Finnish, with brooding themes suggesting tranquil Finnish landscapes under an overcast sky and further darkened by fringes of grim forests. In his more vigorous pages he seems to recreate the heroic deeds and the passionate love episodes in the *Kalevala*. "He has translated the *Kalevala* into the universal language of music, remarkable for its breadth, large simplicity, and the infusion of a deeply poetic personality." This is what the president of Yale University said when he conferred on Sibelius an honorary doctorate in music in 1914 during the composer's first visit to the United States.

In some orchestral works Sibelius diverged from national interests to

Romantic ones. Such a work is the Concerto in D minor, for violin and orchestra, op. 47 (1903), whose three movements are faithful to the traditional concerto style and whose thematic material has only a passing affinity with Finnish folk music. Less significant is a sentimental little salon piece, *Valse triste,* op. 44 (1903), describing the death of a mother whose son is at her bedside. It was played throughout Europe, sold hundreds of thousands of copies in printed music, and made its composer's name even more famous than it had previously been. Since Sibelius sold this work outright for two hundred dollars, he never profited personally from its fabulous success.

One of Sibelius's best tone poems came late in his career: *Tapiola,* op. 112 (1926). The name "Tapio" refers to the ancient Finnish forest god; the music portrays the Finnish forests Sibelius loved so dearly. In 1904 he had built for himself and his family Villa Ainola, a home in the heart of such a forest, in the little town of Järvenpää, about twenty miles from Helsinki. Here he returned to refresh his spirit and soul whenever he completed a European concert tour conducting his music, and in 1914 following his visit to America to lead a Sibelius concert at the Norfolk Festival in Connecticut. And here he lived in retirement after World War I, when his personal appearances were few and far between.

His last piece of music was a cycle of piano pieces in 1929. Though he lived almost thirty more years, he remained creatively silent: living in quiet inactivity in Villa Ainola, enjoying his family life, and his strolls in the forests, and feasting his eyes on the beautiful vistas from his balcony. Up to World War II he spent a good deal of his time with neighbors, or playing host to the numerous visitors who came to pay their respects. After World War II, however, he went into total seclusion, his main pleasures being to eat good food, smoke cigars, and drink fine brandy.

From the end of World War I he was regarded in Finland as something akin to a national hero. He was the first Finnish composer to have a postage stamp bear his likeness while still alive. A museum, parks, and streets were named after him; so was the music institute he had once attended. An attempt to erect his statue in 1940, however, came to naught because Sibelius refused to allow it. In 1951, the Finnish government inaugurated an annual Sibelius festival in Helsinki. His seventy-fifth, eightieth, and ninetieth birthdays were national holidays.

Death came from a cerebral hemorrhage on September 20, 1957. He was ninety-one years old, nine years short of having lived a century—the greatest century in Finnish music, thanks to his achievements.

Ralph Vaughan Williams was born in Down Ampney, Gloucester-shire, England, on October 12, 1872. Music study began when he was six. From 1890 to 1892 and again from 1895 to 1896 he attended the Royal College of Music in London; in the interim he took a degree in music at Cambridge. The music he wrote while attending the college revealed the effect Wagner and Schubert had had upon him. He returned to Cambridge to take a doctorate in music, which he completed in 1901.

For a while, during his Royal College years, he played the organ at church. Then, after marrying Adeline Fisher in 1897, he resigned from his organist post, temporarily deserted the Royal College of Music, and went to Germany to study composition with Max Bruch. Upon his return to England, he rented an apartment in the Westminster district of London. For about seven years after that he earned his living playing the trombone in orchestras and bands. He was writing music all the time. In 1901 and 1902 several of his orchestral works were performed, over much of which hovered the shadow of Brahms. Vaughan Williams was convinced he was making little progress. Had not one of his professors told him he had no talent whatsoever for composition? "I wondered," he later said, "if I was wasting my time. The years were passing and I was adding nothing to the sum total of my musical invention."

By 1904 the influence of English folk music changed his artistic direction and brought him on new paths to new horizons. The first time he heard an English folk song had been in 1893. It interested him enough for him to discuss it with some of his teachers. Cecil Sharp, an English musicologist, and an indefatigable hunter after and collector of old English songs, introduced Vaughan Williams to other English folk tunes. Now thoroughly fascinated by this field, Vaughan Williams took a trip around England in 1903 to seek out songs native to various regions. He found some good enough to publish in his first edition of English folk songs.

He was now the dedicated folklorist. In 1904 he joined the English Folk Song Society, of which Cecil Sharp was a member. This affiliation impelled him to do intensive research. He traveled to Essex, Norfolk, Sussex, and Yorkshire to seek out neglected national music of the Tudor period (late fifteenth and sixteenth centuries) in libraries and private collections. To his amazement he found a treasure trove. He edited the pieces, provided them with modern harmonizations, and published them in collections. It was mainly through his efforts that a rebirth of interest in English madrigals took place around the world.

The impression of this literature on Vaughan Williams was profound

and indelible. He now said, "Art, like charity, should begin at home.
. . . The greatest artist belongs to his country as much as the humblest
singer in a remote village." His own music became affected by such
thinking. In 1906 he produced three *Norfolk Rhapsodies,* for orchestra,
each quoting some of the folk songs he had discovered in England's
county of Norfolk. The composer later discarded two of these rhapsodies, but the first, in E minor, which uses four Norfolk folk songs, has
survived.

Feeling the need to strengthen his compositional technique, Vaughan
Williams went to Paris in 1909 to study with Maurice Ravel. "It was an
invigorating experience," Vaughan Williams recalled in later years, "to
find all artistic problems looked at from what was to me an entirely new
manner." Back in London, he completed his first (and still most celebrated) masterwork: the *Fantasia on a Theme by Thomas Tallis,* for
string quartet and double orchestra. Tallis was a sixteenth-century
church-music composer who had written eight modal tunes (modes having
preceded major and minor scales). Vaughan Williams took one of those
Tallis tunes and spun it into a sensitive tonal web, as the melody passes
from the string quartet to the string orchestra and back. This was *English* music, acquiring what the great English musicologist Ernest New-
man described as "the vein of mellow mysticism that runs through so
much of our [English] heritage of poetry and prose."

Vaughan Williams's first successful symphony was his second one, *A
London Symphony* (1913), whose four movements capture the sights
and sounds of a great city. The first movement portrays different sections of London at daybreak, as the river Thames flows gently through
the city. A drab region of London, Bloomsbury, is the subject of the second movement, where serenity gives way to gloom. Here Vaughan Williams uses a popular English tune, "Sweet Lavender," as it might be
played by an old musician outside a pub. In the third movement the
composer sits late one Saturday evening by the banks of the Thames
contemplating the sight of the majestic Houses of Parliament on one side
and the slums on the other. The final movement depicts those parts of
the city inhabited by the poor and the unemployed. Big Ben chimes. An
epilogue then offers a general impression of London, closing with the
sounds of the gentle lapping of the Thames in its serene flow.

Vaughan Williams rewrote this symphony several times. The version
today given is the one the composer completed in the 1920s.

After *A London Symphony* Vaughan Williams avoided (with infre-

quent exceptions) quotations of old English music. He preferred using his own melodies but modeled after folk music. The English identity of his writing remained pronounced: the way he often used old modes instead of modern scales; his interest in polyphony; the music's serene atmosphere and at times mysticism.

Vaughan Williams wrote nine symphonies in all. The third is *A Pastoral Symphony* (1921), where a quiet melancholy and introspection prevail through the four movements. In the last we hear a voice singing a wordless chant, almost like a religious hymn to the god of nature. The Symphony no. 4 in F minor (1934) is one of the first in which the composer tried such modern idioms as discords and polytonality. This is a virile, brusque work, the two vigorous themes of the first movement being repeated through the four movements.

The Symphony no. 6 in E minor (1947) is one of the composer's most inspired works. The effect of World War II and its aftermath on Vaughan Williams is felt in a first movement filled with turbulence and at times outright anguish. From these agonized emotions, the composer passes on in the second movement to philosophic contemplation, while in the scherzo he reverts to the disturbances of the first movement. But the most remarkable movement of all is the last, possibly the quietest piece of music in all symphonic literature. It is as if the composer had exhausted himself emotionally and could only speak in a whisper and with subdued resignation. Then the music ebbs away into silence to come to an easy rest on a chord suggesting doubts and questionings. The soul-searching has ended for Vaughan Williams; for him life still remained an insoluble riddle.

Vaughan Williams lived to the ripe old age of eighty-five. It had been a productive life, in aspects beside his creativity. From the end of World War I he taught composition at the Royal College of Music, where he influenced an entire generation of English composers. For eight years, beginning in 1920, he was the conductor of the Bach Choir in London. He paid three visits to the United States: in 1922 to direct programs of his music at the festival in Norfolk, Connecticut (when he presented a performance of his *Pastoral Symphony*); in 1932 to lecture on national music at Bryn Mawr College; and in 1954 to deliver some more lectures at Cornell and Yale universities and to appear as guest conductor with several orchestras.

A patriot as well as a musical nationalist, Vaughan Williams served his country in both world wars. During World War I he enlisted in the army and for three years served as an orderly in army hospitals, after which he saw active service with the Royal Garrison Artillery. He was too old for active duty during World War II, so he had to satisfy himself with driving a salvage truck and performing other nonmilitary functions to help the war effort.

He remained creatively active to the last. His ninth and last symphony, in E minor, he wrote in 1957 and revised a year later. It is the personal document of an old man who, looking back on the past and contemplating the present, is overwhelmed with despair. An important subject in the first movement is repeated with various changes through the rest of the symphony, serving as a kind of leading motive of futility. This futility is forcefully underlined after the final measure, where the composer scribbled in the score the word *Niente* ("nothing"). In the dusk of his life, Vaughan Williams had found no answer to life's meaning.

He had been in despondency since his wife died in 1951. Nevertheless, in 1953, at the age of eighty-one, he remarried, his second wife being his secretary, Ursula Wood. His last appearance before an audience took place on August 5, 1958, when he led a performance of his symphony of futility, the Ninth. Three weeks later, on August 26, he died in London. He was buried in Westminster Abbey, among England's immortals.

Strange to say, composers outside Spain became interested in that picturesque country, and its people, customs, and music even before Spanish composers themselves did. In France, Édouard Lalo (1823–1892) wrote the *Symphonie espagnole* for violin and orchestra in 1874; in 1875 Georges Bizet (1838–1875) completed *Carmen,* an opera with a Spanish setting and characters, and some melodies based on Spanish styles. In 1883 Emmanuel Chabrier (1841–1894) wrote *España.* And in Russia, Glinka's *Jota aragonesa* and *A Summer Night in Madrid* came as early as 1845 and 1848 respectively, and Rimsky-Korsakov's *Capriccio espagnol* in 1887.

But the first significant Spanish composer to become interested in national sources—Isaac Albéniz (1860–1909)—did not begin to write Spanish music until the late 1890s: a Spanish opera, a rhapsody, and pieces for the piano. (He produced nothing of permanent value in orchestral music.) His immediate successor as a Spanish national composer was Enrique Granados (1867–1916), composer of *Goyescas,* which is both a series of piano pieces and an opera; an orchestral intermezzo from the opera is highly popular.

The first composer of authentic Spanish orchestral music, and the first to achieve international renown, was Manuel de Falla. It took Falla

quite a while to seek out Spanish materials for his compositions, but when he finally did he developed into one of the great creative figures of the twentieth century.

Falla was not a prolific composer. A lifetime of creativity produced just a handful of compositions, because he worked slowly and was super-critical of his efforts. But most of his mature works are masterpieces. He rarely quoted Spanish folk songs and dance melodies, but rather absorbed the traits of this music into his own style. He often used the old modes of Spanish church music, melodies with the twisting gyrations, the languor and sensuality of Spanish gypsy songs, rhythms patterned after those of Spanish dances, often imitating the clicking sounds of castanets and the plucking strings of a guitar.

Two Spanish terms help us to characterize Falla's music. One is *cante hondo,* literally "deep song." This is the low-voiced throb of the voice with which Andalusian gypsies perform their songs; *cante hondo* is basic to Falla's melodic writing. The other Spanish term is *evocacíon,* translatable as "evocation." In Falla's music we do not get a realistic picture of Spain: Falla was a musical mystic whose compositions evoke the essence of the soul of Spain.

He was born in southern Spain, in Cádiz, on November 23, 1876. At the Madrid Conservatory he came under the influence of a great scholar, Felipe Pedrell (1841–1922), who had done considerable research into long-forgotten Spanish folk songs, dances, and church music. This research had convinced Pedrell that if Spanish composers were to achieve artistic fruition they must have a national identity. It was Pedrell who had made a Spanish composer out of Albéniz. And it was Pedrell who led Falla to Spanish nationalism. In 1905 Falla completed his first music inspired by native sources, the opera, *La Vida breve,* which captured first prize in a competition conducted by the Madrid Academy of Music. To music lovers of our day this opera is familiar through two Spanish dances, originally for orchestra and now also popular in various transcriptions for solo instruments. *La Vida breve* was introduced in Nice, France, in 1913, and in Paris and Madrid in 1914.

In 1907, Falla established a seven-year period of residence in Paris. He suffered from extreme poverty. But Paris was exciting for its rich and varied musical life so that personal deprivations meant little to him. Falla moved in a circle of distinguished French musicians that included Debussy and Ravel. Their ideas about music and their individual idioms gave Falla a new perspective. He did very little composing, since he was too busy absorbing new influences. This Paris period saw the writing of just four Spanish dances for the piano. Falla made his Paris debut as pianist in 1910 in the first concert ever given in that city devoted exclusively to Spanish music.

Falla returned to Spain in 1914. He now traveled about a good deal in his country to become more intimately acquainted with it and its folk music. As he later explained, he wanted to "really go deep" into his researches, "so as not to make any caricature. . . . You must go to the natural, living sources, study the sounds, the rhythms, use their essence, not their externals."

The essence rather than the externals of Spain can be found in his first masterwork: the ballet *El Amor Brujo* (*Love, the Sorcerer*) in 1915. Its music has since become quite a concert-hall favorite through a twelve-movement suite. The story of this ballet comes from an old Andalusian gypsy tale: the love affair of Candélas and Carmélo with which the ghost of Candélas's dead husband tries to interfere. Carmélo solves the problem by enlisting the services of an enticing gypsy girl to take up the ghost's time and interest.

Falla's music is rich with the style and spirit of Andalusian folk songs and dances. The opening fiery theme becomes a recurring motto. Andalusian gypsy life unfolds in music that is passionate, dynamic, sometimes Oriental. *Cante hondo* melodies are sung by a contralto in three sections ("Scene of Sorrowing Love," "Song of the Will-o'-the-Wisp," and "Dance of the Game of Love"); when the voice is omitted at orchestral concerts, a wind instrument (usually the horn) takes over this music. Exciting, continually changing dance rhythms keep the momentum moving. The most popular dance is "The Ritual Fire," familiar as an orchestral piece, and also in transcriptions, particularly one for solo piano.

El Amor Brujo was succeeded by *Noches en los jardines de España* (*Nights in the Gardens of Spain*), also in 1915. These are three symphonic impressions of Spain, for piano and orchestra: the first of the celebrated Generaliffe gardens near the Alhambra in Granada; the second of a Spanish dance; and the third of the gardens of the Sierra at the city of Córdoba. "The music," the composer explained, "has no pretentions to being descriptive; it is merely expressive." The respective movements are entitled, "In the Gardens of the Generaliffe," "A Dance Is Heard in the Distance," and "In the Gardens of the Sierra de Córdoba."

The ballet *El Sombrero de tres picos* (*The Three-Cornered Hat*), composed in 1919, is best known through a suite of three dances from the score. The second is the most popular: "The Dance of the Miller," in which a decorated Moorish melody is combined with exciting Andalusian rhythms.

The only other important concert work Falla wrote after that was the Concerto for Harpsichord, Flute, Oboe, Clarinet, Violin, and Cello (1926), whose artistic impulse came from the harpsichord sonatas of Domenico Scarlatti (1685–1757).

In 1921, Falla went to live in Granada, not far from the Alhambra. There he became a virtual recluse for the next seventeen years. He rose early to take a walk and attend Mass before going to work on his music. He always took a noonday nap after lunch. In the evenings he did some more composing before retiring early. His home—like his daily life, his dress, and his meals—was the last word in simplicity. For Falla was an ascetic. He preferred solitude to the company of people, even friends. Often he would go off by himself to some little Andalusian village for two weeks, a period during which he remained totally silent. He felt that escape into solitude and silence strengthened his spirit for work.

Since he was a deeply religious man, he regarded the Spanish revolution of 1937 under Generalissimo Franco as a crusade. He became Franco's ardent supporter when the generalissimo assumed power. In gratitude, Franco appointed Falla as President of the Institute of Spain. But Franco's dictatorship soon brought Falla disillusionment. Although frail and ill, he deserted Spain forever. His last five years were spent in Alta Gracia in Argentina, where he lived like a hermit in abject poverty, attended to by his sister. Sick though he was, he worked long and hard on what he hoped would be his greatest work, a "scenic cantata," *L'Atlántida* (*Atlantis*), for solo voice, chorus, and orchestra. He managed to write most of it, but it had to be completed after his death by his pupil, Ernesto Halffter. This is somewhat of an unusual work for Falla, since he departed from the gypsy music of Andalusia to return to the polyphonic methods of old Spanish church music. In his last, unfinished work Falla's religious feelings had displaced his national ones.

He died at Alta Gracia on November 14, 1946. His body was brought back for burial to the city of his birth, Cádiz. The inscription on his tombstone (which Falla himself had written) reads simply, "Honor and glory belong only to God."

"The appropriate use of folk-song material," Béla Bartók once wrote, "is a matter of absorbing the means of musical expression hidden in the treasury of folk tunes." He also maintained that the folk art of Hungary served as "the foundations for a renaissance of Hungarian art." He lived and worked throughout his life ever true to his own credo.

He was twenty-three when he first became aware of the power, originality, and unusual character of authentic Hungarian folk music. He was then vacationing in the interior of Hungary, where he heard a peasant woman singing a haunting melody completely different from anything Bartók had ever known. The peasant woman informed him that it was a folk song from that region. This set Bartók thinking. Was it possible that different parts of Hungary had folk tunes of their own about which the rest of Hungary, let alone the world, was completely unaware? He would travel to different parts of his country to find out, living with peasants, and noting down the melodies they sang. By 1906 he had discovered enough material to publish, along with Zoltán Kodály, *Twenty Hungarian Folk Songs,* half of which were set by each composer. He continued after that to make many expeditions in Hungary, gathering thousands of folk songs and dance tunes, arranging and harmonizing them, then issuing them in publications. Thus he became the prime force in publicizing this wonderful music to the world. These melodies were far different from the sentimental gypsy melodies that Liszt and Brahms had offered in their rhapsodies and dances in the belief that they were authentically Hungarian. Authentic Hungarian folk music was made of sterner stuff. It had a bleak, severe melodic line that was more declamatory than lyrical; it was written in old modes; it was filled with irregular rhythmic patterns; it had an austere, esoteric quality; it created a power all its own.

Once Bartók realized the true nature of Hungarian folk music, his own compositions changed character radically. His melodies began to assume the same kind of declamatory style found in the folk songs, often built from modes, and free in their key relationships. To his music he brought brutal force through frequent use of discords, powerful accentuations, changing rhythms.

In orchestral music, the works most characteristic of Bartók's stark Hungarian style are *The Miraculous Mandarin,* op. 19 (1919), a one-act ballet that the composer adapted into a concert suite; the Concerto no. 2 for Piano and Orchestra (1931); *Music for Strings, Percussion, and Celesta* (1936); and Concerto no. 2 for Violin and Orchestra (1938). This is not easy music to listen to, nor is its remarkable invention readily assimilated at first hearing. But familiarity brings admiration. The more we listen to his pre-World War II music, the more we are captured by it.

Bartók was born in Nagyszentmiklos, a little town in Hungary, on March 25, 1881. He studied from 1899 to 1903 at the Academy of Music in Budapest, where he was a brilliant piano student. His ambition was to become a virtuoso, but after hearing Richard Strauss's tone poem *Thus Spake Zarathustra,* he decided to devote himself to composition.

At that time, a rising tide of nationalism swept over Hungary. Interest in Hungarian culture and history was stimulated. Patriotism, then, became the initial force to drive Bartók to national music, as a result of which he wrote a tone poem, *Kossuth* (modeled after Richard Strauss's *A Hero's Life*), introduced in 1904. His researches into Hungarian folk music, which began at this time, made him a confirmed musical nationalist.

For many years thereafter he lived a quiet and simple life in Budapest with his wife, Márta (one of his piano pupils), whom he married in 1909 and divorced thirteen years later to marry a concert pianist, Ditta Pasztory. He supported his family mostly by teaching at the Royal Academy of Music from 1907 to 1934. All this time he worked hard on composition. His individual style hardly lent itself to popular consumption; for a long time his major works received only scattered performances, and these were not well received. His first real success came with his Second Piano Concerto, introduced in Frankfort, Germany, in 1933, after which it was played throughout Europe.

Those times when he left Budapest, he traveled around Hungary in search of folk music or to make public appearances in Europe and the United States as pianist for his compositions. His American debut took place in New York with the New York Philharmonic Orchestra in 1927.

When he returned to the United States in 1940, Europe was at war. A research grant at Columbia University made it possible for him to live in New York. Those who then met him for the first time were struck by the contradiction between the frail vessel that was the physical man and the indestructible and heroic spirit that represented the inner man, the creative artist. He was small, slight, and fragile. His normal weight of 115 pounds had been reduced to 90. His body was being ravaged by an almost continual fever, which at first defied diagnosis. The pains in his joints were often so acute that walking was difficult. Mental anguish was compounded on physical pain. Though he was now a world figure, he found it difficult to make financial ends meet. The small stipend he had been receiving from his research grant terminated in 1942. Deprived of a regular income, Bartók, his wife, and their son, Peter, were thrown into dire financial straits. Had not the American Society of Composers, Authors, and Publishers (ASCAP) provided the necessary funds, Bartók would not have been able to pay for the hospitalization he badly needed at one time. One other thing caused him endless frustration and despair: his music was rarely played in America.

In spite of the forces combining to destroy him, he remained a man with a fanatical will, with a spirit that would not be defeated. Nothing could tamper with his intellectual curiosity, which kept him *au courant* with politics, science, literature, and philosophy, as well as music. Nothing could smother the creative powers that made this frail little man into a giant. From illness and frustration sprang some of his greatest works: the Concerto for Orchestra (1943), the Concerto no. 3 for Piano and Orchestra (1945), and the Concerto for Viola and Orchestra, which he did not live to complete. In his last works his formerly complex style became somewhat simplified, his cerebral writing became humanized.

Toward the end of his life Bartók expected to return to his native land, World War II having come to an end. But on September 26, 1945, leukemia (for this was the disease from which he suffered) took its toll.

What he had been unable to realize alive—frequent performances in America of his major works—he achieved after his death. Within a few months of his passing, forty-eight major orchestral performances of his compositions took place, twenty-five of them within a two-month period. Several times his music inspired ovations. Since then, Bartók's music has often been played and extensively recorded.

Bartók's best-known orchestral work is the Concerto for Orchestra. Bartók designated it as a concerto because, as he said, it treats "the single instruments or instrument groups in a concertante style or soloist manner." The work is in five uninterrupted movements. Gloom pervades the music of the first movement, whose melancholy first theme is repeated to re-create a funereal atmosphere in the third movement. In two movements—the second and the fourth—there is some relief from despair. In the second movement, to which the composer gave a title ("The Game of Couples"), five pairs of winds present five different themes, each pair of instruments representing a "couple." A choralelike passage of the brass provides a contrast, after which the "pairs" return as trios, quartets, and quintets. The fourth movement is a lyrical intermezzo. The last is in Hungarian style, energetic music that seems to reject defeat and to reaffirm forcefully the composer's faith in life and art.

Though he was deathly sick when this concerto was introduced in 1944 by the Boston Symphony under Serge Koussevitzky (Koussevitzky being the one who had commissioned it), Bartók attended the world premiere. Thus he was a witness to the crowning success of his life, for the response of both the audience and critics was overwhelming. Success of such huge dimension came none too soon. In less than a year Bartók was dead. Like Moses in the Bible, Bartók had been given a glimpse of his own promised land from a distance but was fated never to enter it.

Stravinsky's ballet The Firebird, *with Maria Tallchief and Francisco Moncion.*

Igor Stravinsky at seventy-nine, conducting the BBC Symphony Orchestra.

Sergei Diaghilev, in a sketch by Stravinsky.

Jean Sibelius.

Stravinsky's Petrouchka *in a New York City Center Joffrey Ballet production.*

A study by Pablo Picasso for the stage design of The Three-Cornered Hat.

Manuel de Falla (left) with Léonide Massine, the choreographer of The Three-Cornered Hat, *at the Fountain of Lions in the courtyard of the Alhambra, Granada, 1919.*

Béla Bartók.

15

Proletariats

Serge Prokofiev, Dmitri Shostakovich

In 1917 the czarist regime in Russia was overthrown and annihilated. The proletariat took over the reins of government. A new political ideology came into being glorifying the worker, creating vast social and political and economic reforms, and rigidly controlling every phase of human existence. These were the beginnings of the Soviet Union.

Music was also affected by this revolution. No longer could a composer write as he pleased on whatever subject interested him. Music had become a servant of the state, an instrument of propaganda wherever and whenever possible. The composer was usually motivated to write compositions about the heroes of the Revolution (Lenin and Stalin particularly), or about those heroes in Russian history who had anticipated the Revolution, or about the famous dates and days in the history of the Revolution. Soviet ideology was promoted. Whatever endeavor, national or international, engaged the government became grist for the composer's mill. Music also had to cater to the tastes of the general masses. The Association of Proletarian Musicians formed in Moscow in 1924 made this clear when it issued a manifesto that read in part: "Proletarian music must penetrate into the inmost masses of workmen and peasants and unite the thought and will of the masses and raise them for further struggle and construction, organizing their class consciousness in the direction of the ultimate victory of the proletariat as a builder of communist society."

Composers who were unable to accept the principles of a proletarian society—political, social, or musical—fled from their homeland to adopt a new country. Stravinsky had been one of those. Another was Serge Prokofiev. But whereas Stravinsky remained an expatriate for the rest of his life, Prokofiev eventually returned to the land of his birth to identify himself and his art completely with Soviet ideas and ideals.

Prokofiev was born in Sontzovka (now Dniepropetrovsk Region), in the Ukraine on April 23, 1891. He was such an extraordinary musical prodigy that time and again he was compared to Mozart. When Prokofiev was five he wrote some piano pieces without ever having taken any lessons. He had completed three operas, a symphony (for piano, four hands), and twelve piano pieces by the time he had passed his twelfth birthday. From the time he was thirteen, and for about a decade after that, he attended the Saint Petersburg Conservatory. There, while devoting himself to intensive study of piano and composition, he completed his first piano sonatas, his first orchestral work (a sinfonietta), and several smaller pieces for the piano, one of which (*Suggestion diabolique*) is still played. One of the piano sonatas and some other piano pieces were his first works to be published.

Although he received diplomas in composition and piano playing in 1909, Prokofiev remained in the conservatory another five years to complete his training as pianist and conductor. This period saw him write more piano sonatas, two piano concertos, and an opera. In these works Prokofiev was already beginning to break loose from academic rules by filling his writing with discords, polytonality, and unconventional changes in key. Some of his teachers were shocked by his musical audacities. One celebrated critic, Sabaneyev, referred to the First Piano Concerto as "coarse, primitive cacophony, scarcely deserving the name of music," when it was introduced in Moscow in 1912. The critics were equally severe in criticizing his Second Piano Concerto in 1913; one of them said, "Such music is enough to drive you crazy." And when, in 1914, Prokofiev performed his First Piano Concerto as a graduating exercise, the director of the conservatory—Alexander Glazunov (1865–1936), himself a distinguished composer but in a conservative, Romantic style, "lost his temper," as Prokofiev himself later recalled.

In spite of his revolutionary style, and some of the unfavorable reactions to it, Prokofiev was graduated from the conservatory with highest honors in piano playing and conducting. And in spite of the disfavor with which Glazunov and some professors regarded his works, Prokofiev had enough professors on his side to be able to capture the highly esteemed Rubinstein Prize for piano.

World War I, in which Russia was involved, did not interrupt Prokofiev's creativity. As the only son of a widow he was exempt from military duty and could therefore concentrate on composition. One of the works engaging him was a four-movement composition for orchestra, *Scythian* Suite, op. 20 (1915), first heard in Saint Petersburg on January 29, 1916.

In his Violin Concerto no. 1, op. 19, and his first symphony, the *Classical,* op. 25—both in 1917—Prokofiev perfected those individual compositional mannerisms henceforth individualizing his writing: those tart and saucy melodies with their tendency to leap to unexpected intervals; the conscious practice of going from a naïve subject to a sophisticated one, or superimposing an obviously trite little tune on complex or unusual harmonies; simple chords used in unconventional progressions. These effects injected wit and surprise into the music. Even in his most serious endeavors, Prokofiev seemed to enjoy catching his listener off guard by doing the unexpected.

The First Violin Concerto has received a wide circulation through the years. The same is true of the Concerto no. 3 in C major, for piano and orchestra, op. 26, for which Prokofiev had begun writing some passages as early as 1911, but which he did not complete until a decade later. In each Prokofiev achieves a symphonic texture in which the solo instrument and orchestra share the responsibility for presenting and developing his musical ideas. The violin concerto opens in a reflective mood, but it is not long before the melodies begin to leap, and other Prokofiev idiosyncrasies, together with unusual violin effects, help to create the kind of whimsy and electricity for which the composer is so famous. In the piano concerto the typical Prokofiev melody is encountered most strongly in the main theme of the second movement (which receives five variations) and in the staccato theme that opens the finale.

No less famous is the *Classical* Symphony, where Prokofiev anticipated the neoclassic movement by adapting for the twentieth century the classical symphonic structure of a Haydn or Mozart symphony. The writing is terse, simple, transparent. The structure is classical, with the

substitution of an old-world gavotte for the usual third-movement minuet. But the harmonies and tonalities are decidedly modern.

By 1918, Prokofiev had grown so antagonistic to the new order in Russia that he decided to leave his country. The offer of an extended tour as pianist outside Russia gave him the opportunity to do so. He now made his first American appearance, in New York on November 20, 1918, in a piano recital. His compositions were described as "Russian chaos" and "Bolshevism in art." During this first American tour Prokofiev was comissioned by the Chicago Opera to write a work for its company. Prokofiev complied with *The Love for Three Oranges,* whose premiere was delayed until December 30, 1921. Though this was a delightful fantasy filled with sparkle and wit, the opera was not well liked; it had to wait over a quarter of a century to get another American hearing, at which time it was hailed as a masterpiece. But in the interim orchestral excerpts became repertory numbers, particularly the "March," "Scherzo," and "Infernal Scene." (It was while in Chicago to help in the production of his opera that, in December of 1921, Prokofiev offered the world premiere of his Third Piano Concerto.)

The 1921 tour brought Prokofiev to California, where he married a young Spanish singer, Lina Llubera. Returning to Europe, the Prokofievs made their home in the Bavarian Alps for a brief period and then in 1923 settled in Paris, which Prokofiev left at regular intervals to make extended tours as pianist. From the perspective of distance, the new economic and political society that was slowly emerging in Russia began to acquire interest, then significance, for Prokofiev. This led him in 1925–1926 to write music for a ballet glorifying the development of Soviet industrialization: *Le Pas d'acier* (*The Age of Steel*), op. 41. In this muscular music filled with discords, Prokofiev produced a score described by one Paris critic as "the apotheosis of machinery."

In 1927 Prokofiev paid his first return visit to his native country with appearances as pianist-composer that were successes of the first magnitude. But it was six years more before he finally decided to return to Russia for good. In those years, while still living in Paris, he completed several important compositions, among which were two symphonies (one of which, no. 4 in C major, op. 47, was commissioned by the Boston Symphony in celebration of its fiftieth anniversary in 1930), two piano concertos (the Piano Concerto no. 4 in B-flat major, op. 53, in 1931, being for the left hand alone), and a score for a new ballet, *L'Enfant prodigue* (*The Prodigal Son*), op. 46 (1929).

Then in 1933 Prokofiev transferred his home back to the country of his birth, to live and work there permanently, and to become a part of a society that he now thoroughly endorsed. The Soviet government welcomed him with open arms, to which Prokofiev responded by placing his art at the service of his country. He, too—like the other Soviet composers—would now write much music directed toward the masses: music for the movies and for children, as well as larger and more serious works more readily understood than his earlier works had been. Among the last of these were his Violin Concerto no. 2 in G minor, op. 63 (1935), which was more romantic and melodious than his first had been, and a consistently delightful score for the ballet *Romeo and Juliet,* op. 64 (1935), out of which we get three orchestral suites, the second one being especially popular.

There was no perceptible deterioration in Prokofiev's music even when he was creating functional scores either for the movies or for children. The very first piece of music completed following his return was the score for the motion picture *Lieutenant Kije.* As an orchestral suite (op. 60, 1934) it is one of his most brilliant satirical compositions. The motion picture comedy is a takeoff on military bureaucracy and heroism during the reign of Czar Nicholas I.

Prokofiev made another of his motion picture scores into a major concert work: a powerful cantata for mezzo-soprano, chorus, and orchestra, *Alexander Nevsky,* op. 78 (1939). (Nevsky was the hero in the defense of Novgorod against the invading Knights of the Teutonic Order in 1242.)

Among Prokofiev's many compositions for children, one is a classic. Breathes there a child today who, as part of his musical upbringing, has not been introduced to the joys of *Peter and the Wolf? Peter and the Wolf,* op. 67 (1936), is a symphonic fairy tale for narrator and orchestra with the primary aim of teaching children the sound of the instruments of the orchestra. "Each character in this tale," we are informed by the narrator as the composition opens, "is represented by an instrument in the orchestra: the bird by a flute; the duck by an oboe; the cat by a clarinet in low register; grandpapa by the bassoon; the wolf by three French horns; Peter by the string quartet; and the hunter's rifle shots by the kettledrums and bass drum." The narrator and orchestra then collaborate in unfolding the simple tale of a Russian boy, Peter, who captures a wolf in the meadow, ties it up with a rope, and drags it

off to the zoo. Each theme is so vividly descriptive that it is easy to tell who or what it is describing. All themes are masterfully intertwined into a symphonic texture into which the narrator intrudes from time to time to tell his story.

Prokofiev divorced his wife in 1941, and married again, his second wife being a brilliant linguist, Mira Mendelson. This was the time of World War II. At first the Soviet Union was a neutral, as a consequence of its nonaggression pact with the Nazis. Then in the summer of 1941 the Nazis, in defiance of their pact, invaded the Soviet Union. With his country at war, Prokofiev produced large and small works to help the war effort or that were inspired by it: military marches and anti-Fascist songs on the one hand; on the other, large works including three sonatas for the piano identified as the "war sonatas," a monumental opera, *War and Peace,* based on Tolstoy's novel, and his greatest symphony, no. 5 in B-flat major, op. 100 (1944).

The last of these was Prokofiev's tribute to the unconquerable spirit of the people during the war—a spirit suggested in the majestic and noble music of its first movement. The second movement (allegro marcato), with its motor energy, passes into an expansive third-movement adagio that may be interpreted as an elegy for the men who died defending their homeland. But in the last movement Prokofiev lifts himself from tragedy and grief to sound a resonant hymn to victory and an affirmation of his faith in the future of his land and its people.

During the war years, and for some time thereafter, Prokofiev was esteemed as one of the two greatest composers in the Soviet Union (the other being Shostakovich). The Sonata no. 7, op. 83, for piano (1942), brought him a government award. Nothing could possibly weaken his place in Soviet life and culture—or, at least, so it seemed. But in a dictatorship even those who hold the loftiest government posts sometimes find themselves overnight in disrepute. And this is what happened to Prokofiev at a time when he was at the peak of both his creative ability and fame.

This reversal of fortune, which affected not only Prokofiev but most other leading Soviet composers, came about through a manifesto by the Central Committee of the Communist Party on February 10, 1948. Here was established a new set of values for Soviet music. This manifesto described the works of Soviet composers as "decadent formalism" and accused them of having become infected by Western demoralizing ideals. "Many Soviet composers," the manifesto said in part, "have lost contact with the demands of artistic taste of the Soviet people, have shut themselves off in a narrow circle of specialists and musical gourmands, limiting it to a satisfaction of the distorted tastes of aesthetic individualists."

Henceforth composers in the Soviet Union were required to adopt a completely new orientation to their music by writing simply, melodically, and as often as possible in the style of Russian folk songs. One composer after another now made a public demonstration of confessing his guilt. It was true, each composer announced, that he had been polluted by Western musical thinking, that his music was just a "sermon for atonality, dissonance, and disharmony." Prokofiev, too, joined in this outpouring of self-incrimination.

Prokofiev now made a more studied attempt to win back the favor of the high-ranking Soviet officials. Since the government was accusing the Western world of being "warmongers" he wrote an oratorio, *On Guard for Peace,* as a tribute to the Soviet international peace movement. In another composition, *Winter Holiday* (or *Winter Bonfire*), he tried studiedly to create the kind of music the government demanded. Both compositions were performed in 1950; both accomplished what they set out to do. In 1951, Prokofiev received the Stalin Prize, the first official indication that the government had forgiven him for his past musical "sins." On April 23, 1951, an all-Prokofiev concert honored his sixtieth birthday, still another token of government approval. And on October 11, 1952, his Symphony no. 7 in C-sharp minor, op. 131, received a tumultuous ovation from the audience and singing praises from the critics; this symphony (Prokofiev's last) had to be repeated a few months later by special request of the all-powerful Composers' Union.

Having suffered two strokes, during the period when he had been denounced by his government, Prokofiev was too sick to attend the all-Prokofiev concert in 1951 on his sixtieth birthday. Seriously ill as he was, he managed to complete a beautiful and at times stirring major work for cello and orchestra, the *Symphony-Concerto* in E minor, op. 125 (1952)—a drastic revision and elaboration of his own Concerto no. 1 in E minor, for cello and orchestra, op. 58 (1938)—as well as his Seventh Symphony. He also worked painstakingly on a ballet score, *The Stone Flower,* which he completed. After revising one of its dances, he was stricken by a cerebral hemorrhage on March 5, 1953, which proved fatal that same day. Coincidentally, March 5, 1953, was also the day Stalin died, and the beginning of the end of the ruthless stand of the Central Committee against the major Soviet composers and their modern tendencies. For Stalin's death made possible a more normal, healthier set of musical standards, and a greater latitude for Soviet composers to express their opinions on what had been happening in music since 1948. One of the major Soviet composers who had been condemned— Aram Khachaturian (1903—   ), composer of the ballet *Gayne* from which comes the popular "Saber Dance"—criticized the Central Committee of the Communist Party in 1953 for interfering with Soviet composers. On May 25, 1958, the Central Committee passed a resolution permitting Soviet composers full freedom to select whatever subject matter they desired and to allow them to use whatever idioms and techniques they preferred. How tragic it is that Prokofiev had not lived to see all this come to pass!

Dmitri Shostakovich had also been a victim of government disapproval, not just once but several times. Again and again he was toppled from what seemed to be a permanently high place in Soviet music by government censure. And yet with incredible resiliency he bounced back to reinstate himself in the good graces of the ruling powers, to rise even higher in Soviet esteem than he had been before he fell. The fluctuating fortunes of Shostakovich have had the precipitous rises and falls of a roller coaster.

He had never known anything but a proletarian society. He was born in Leningrad (then still called Saint Petersburg) on September 25, 1906. He was, then, only eleven when the 1917 revolution erupted in Russia. He grew up during his formative years in a revolutionary society and thus was easily able to identify both himself and his music with it. From the beginnings of his career as composer—as a mere boy—he wrote such pieces as the *Hymn to Liberty* and the *Funeral March for the Victims of the Revolution.*

After preliminary music study, in which he easily proved himself to be a prodigy, he entered the Saint Petersburg Conservatory when he was thirteen. At this time he wrote his first orchestral composition, a scherzo, as well as some piano preludes. Glazunov, director of the conservatory, said, "The boy's gifts are phenomenal." In 1926 Shostakovich's first publication appeared, *Three Fantastic Dances,* for piano, op. 5.

The death of Shostakovich's father in 1922 made it necessary for the mother to get a job as a typist in a government agency. For an all too brief period Shostakovich was able to help out with the family finances by playing the piano in a motion picture theater. But he was soon dismissed because he was always too fascinated by the movie to pay attention to his music. He remained at the conservatory during this time, still one of its most brilliant students. In 1923 he was graduated in piano, and in 1925 in composition. He also made some public appearances as pianist in programs including several of his own compositions.

For his graduation exercise in composition at the conservatory in 1925, Shostakovich wrote his Symphony no. 1, op. 10. Its premiere took place on May 12, 1926, when it was received with such tumultuous enthusiasm that performances followed in Moscow, Berlin, and (in 1928) in the United States. Still in his early twenties, Shostakovich had by then acquired an international reputation. He deserved it. This is music with youthful vitality, verve, excitement, electricity—and a good many personal touches. It is still one of Shostakovich's best-known and best-loved works.

In it we can already find some of the stylistic mannerisms that henceforth would identify most of his writing: for example, the way he emphasizes the highest registers of strings and woodwinds and the lowest registers of the brass; the individual manner in which he uses the percussion; the importance he assigns to the piano in the orchestration; his partiality for sharp, rhythmic phrases, scale passages, sudden changes of key and dynamics, and tart and sparkling little melodies and spicy harmonies.

Despite the success of his first symphony, Shostakovich took a year off from composition to clarify his thinking about the kind of music he wanted to write. He produced nothing in 1926. But once he resumed composition in 1927 the flow never stopped. Then, as later, he wrote quickly, easily—sometimes finishing an entire score at first writing without making revisions. He could compose at any time of the day or night, anywhere, and under any conditions. Noises never bothered him. When one work was completed he took a hurried breathing spell, then at once plunged into the writing of a new composition.

During his year of reevaluation, he came to one conclusion: there had been no attempt in his First Symphony to make its music express Soviet ideas or ideals. This, Shostakovich felt, was all wrong. "Good music . . . is no longer an end in itself," he said, "but a vital weapon in the struggle. . . . My aim is to help in every way to enlighten our remarkable country." He also said, "We are revolutionaries and as revolutionaries we have a different concept of music. Lenin himself said that 'music is a means of unifying broad masses of people.' "

And so, in writing his Symphony no. 2, op. 14 (1927), titled *To October,* he used a text by Alexander Bezymensky for its final section; the work as a whole was in commemoration of the tenth anniversary of

the October Revolution. The Symphony no. 3, op. 20 (1929), was called
May Day, after another vital event in the early history of the Revolution. This symphony was dedicated to the working classes. Music with so strong a Soviet slant might be expected to find favor. Yet the premieres of both symphonies were failures from which they fully never recovered. However, these symphonies are occasionally performed and are available on recordings.

Shostakovich's first success following his First Symphony came with the ballet *The Bolt,* op. 27, once again on a proletarian theme. It was decisively acclaimed in 1931. Twenty-four piano preludes, op. 34 (1933), and the Concerto for Piano, Trumpet, and String Orchestra, op. 35 (1933), further helped to raise his prestige. Meanwhile, in 1932, he had married Nina Varzar, a young physicist, whom he had known—and shyly wooed—for five years. In their simple apartment in Leningrad they raised two children, one of whom, Maxim, became a fine pianist and conductor, particularly in performances of his father's music.

The Concerto for Piano, Trumpet, and String Orchestra is still a popular item, with emphasis on wit and satire. It has bouncy tunes, with the trumpet assuming a kind of comedian's role, introducing humorous comments. In the last movement Shostakovich parodies the classical way of writing concertos. Unexpectedly he interpolates a cadenza, toward the end of which he mischievously inserts a quotation from a little-known rondo by Beethoven, *Rage over a Lost Penny!*

Shostakovich's first large-scale opera was *Lady Macbeth of Mzensk,* triumphantly introduced in Leningrad on January 22, 1934. This was at times a satiric and at times a realistic picture of the decay of provincial life and morals during the days of the czar. It involved its heroine in a sordid life that included lust, adultery, murder, and suicide—a helpless victim, the libretto made clear, of an immoral and decadent society in the pre-Revolution years. Shostakovich's music captured the spirit of the libretto felicitously, his style passing resiliently from high-tensioned drama to comedy. The critics hailed the opera as a masterwork. Soon after its world premiere it was produced in many Soviet cities and was called "the first monumental work of Soviet musical culture," by one critic. For the next two years, the opera was frequently heard throughout the Soviet Union; it was also staged in Cleveland and in New York in 1935.

Shostakovich was riding high, but riding for a fall. When Stalin attended a performance of *Lady Macbeth* he was revolted by some of the realistic sex scenes and the music accompanying them. Such a reaction from the mighty Stalin was like a spark to oil: it caused instantaneous combustion. The critics suddenly reversed themselves and now called the opera "crude, primitive, vulgar . . . screaming, neurotic." *Pravda* commented, "The music quacks, grunts, growls, suffocates itself." Though the composer hurriedly apologized for his musical indiscretions, he instantly became persona non grata, and the opera was hastily withdrawn from public view. (It was later revised under the title *Katerina Ismailova,* and under that title it is performed today. It has been recorded and also made into a motion picture.) Fellow musicians who saw Shostakovich in the street avoided him. Friends now kept aloof. The musicians of the orchestra refused to play his Symphony no. 4, op. 43 (1936), and it was dropped from the program after one rehearsal.

But almost as if in challenge to his enemies and critics, Shostakovich went on to write what many critics today look upon as his greatest symphony—no. 5, op. 47 (1937). Through most of the work, Shostakovich abandoned his former tendency toward cuteness, comedy, bouncy tunes, and quixotic effects, substituting for them emotion, power, and majesty. The very opening of the symphony—that powerful sweep as the strings exchange a dramatic utterance canonically—brings forward the serious-minded Shostakovich. The entire first movement is structurally monumental, with its principal themes worked over along spacious lines. The slow movement is one of the composer's most sincerely felt and eloquent utterances.

This symphony was far too good and far too important to be lightly dismissed, even if it came from somebody in disgrace. Probably encouraged by the government, which now stood ready to forgive its wayward son, the critics let out all the stops in their reviews, one of which called it "a work of great depth . . . a milestone in the composer's development."

Shostakovich was back in the favor of the government. Within the next few years his fame and success far exceeded those he had previously enjoyed. In 1940 he received the Stalin Prize for his Piano Quintet in G minor, op. 57. During World War II Shostakovich became a national hero through the writing of a symphony reflecting, to use the composer's own words, "the majestic ideas of the patriotic war." It was the Symphony no. 7, op. 60 (1941), known as the *Leningrad,* because it spoke of the heroic resistance of the Russian people during the Nazi siege of Leningrad. It looked forward to "the victory of light over darkness, wisdom over frenzy, lofty humanism over the monstrous" in the composer's explanation.

Because, in 1941, the Nazis were sweeping across Russia toward Moscow, and were laying siege to Leningrad, the Soviet government moved to Kuibishev. It was there that the Seventh Symphony was introduced on March 1, 1942, before distinguished political leaders, diplomats, and high military officials. It created an overwhelming impression and soon after brought its composer the Stalin Prize for the second time. The symphony was given throughout the Soviet Union, then played in Europe. Leading American conductors competed to be the first to introduce it to the United States, an assignment that finally fell to Arturo Toscanini. After that, practically every major American orchestra performed it, almost as a patriotic gesture in time of war. Wherever it was heard it had a titanic emotional impact.

Shostakovich's Symphony no. 8, op. 65 (1943), was the composer's attempt "to look into the future, into the postwar epoch [in which] the dark and the ignominious will disappear . . . [and] all that is beautiful will triumph," to quote Shostakovich. Even more optimistic in mood is his Symphony no. 9, op. 70 (1945), which the composer referred to as "a merry little piece."

Then, with Shostakovich sharing with Prokofiev the leadership among Soviet composers, there descended on him the hammer blow of the manifesto of the Central Committee of the Communist Party on February 10, 1948 (discussed in the preceding section on Prokofiev). Shostakovich bent with, rather than resisted, the hurricane. He lost no time in confessing how wrong he had been in the style he had favored, and in agreeing with the new standards imposed on composers by the committee. "I shall try again and again," he said, "to create symphonic works close to the spirit of the people."

He was true to his words. He made every effort to write the kind of music the Central Committee wanted. And he emerged victorious. For both his score to the motion picture *The Fall of Berlin* and an oratorio, *The Song of the Forest,* he was for the third time presented with the Stalin Prize. He was also selected to be one of seven to represent the Soviet Union at the Cultural and Scientific Conference for World Peace in New York in 1949 (Shostakovich's first visit to the United States). He revisited America a decade later, touring several major cities in concerts of his music.

With the death of Prokofiev, Shostakovich was acknowledged to be the foremost composer of the Soviet Union and his country fully recognized this. On his fiftieth birthday, in 1956, he was awarded the Order of Lenin. His Symphony no. 11, op. 103 (1957)—commemorating the fiftieth anniversay of the 1905 revolution in Russia—brought him in 1960 the Lenin Prize. (With Stalin now discredited, the prize had had to adopt the name of the founding father of Communist Russia.) High honors also came to Shostakovich from countries outside the Soviet Union: the Sibelius Prize of $22,000 from Finland in 1958, and in 1962 the presentation of all his major works at the Edinburgh Festival in Scotland.

Though the post-Stalin era helped bring about a healthier climate in which composers could work without government interference, Shostakovich once again got into trouble. His Symphony no. 13, op. 113 (1962), honoring Soviet heroes in World War II, set five poems by Yevgeny Yevtushenko, one of them entitled "Babi Yar." Babi Yar is a place near Kiev where hundreds of Soviet Jews were massacred by the Nazis. Yevtushenko used this theme to criticize his government for its anti-Semitism. When Shostakovich's symphony was introduced in Moscow on December 18, 1962, the audience was frigid and the press hostile. Shostakovich, it seemed, was on the brink of a new crisis. He quickly overcame it, however, by prevailing on the poet to rewrite his verses as a tribute to all Soviet victims of the Nazis rather than specifically to Jews. The government (now under the control of Premier Khrushchev) forgave Shostakovich, forgot, and reverted to honoring him. He became the only composer to receive the government's highest award to a citizen, the title of Hero of Socialist Labor. This came as a part of a mammoth celebration of Shostakovich's sixtieth birthday in 1966, when all his major compositions were given at the White Nights festival in Leningrad, together with several new works by other composers written in tribute to him.

In his Symphony No. 14 (1969), Shostakovich once again set verses to music, this time macabre poems by Federico García Lorca, Guillaume Apollinaire and Rainer Maria Rilke. So extensively is the voice here used that this work, in actuality, is more of a song cycle than a symphony. But in his Symphony No. 15 (1971), which was introduced to America in 1972, Shostakovich reverts to a basic symphonic form and once again concentrates exclusively on the orchestra. This is one of the most ingratiating symphonies by Shostakovich since his Symphony No. 9. One of its curious features is the insertion of musical quotations: the famous gallop from Rossini's *William Tell* Overture, used repeatedly; a motif from Wagner's *The Ring of the Nibelungs;* and fragments from his own Piano Concerto No. 1 and Symphony No. 9. Shostakovich provides no clue as to why he used this material. The suspicion is that this

symphony is autobiographical, though it carries no program, and that these quotations had personal implications for him. In reviewing this symphony, Irving Kolodin wrote in the *Saturday Review:* "He is concerned with no ism but humanism, no ideology but the biological urge to survive that unites all who inhabit the same planet. At sixty-six Shostakovich has compounded a commentary on his life's work that should make absorbing listening for years to come."

Away from his music, Shostakovich is a dedicated sports fan (soccer, hockey, and boxing especially). He never misses a soccer match if he can help it; at one time he kept a yearly record of the results of all major soccer events in his country. He is also fond of the circus, reads a good deal, and plays chess expertly. Age has not robbed him of either his boyish appearance or his shyness; in large groups he is painfully self-conscious, behaves awkwardly, and often withdraws into himself. In a heated conversation, his habitual nervousness becomes intensified. His eyes grow increasingly restless behind his hornrimmed glasses, and he either makes continual nervous gestures with his hands or else plays with a second pair of eyeglasses.

Composing is his passion. Nothing seems able to keep him from maintaining a prolific output: not the reversals of fortune he has suffered several times in his career; not a heart attack that temporarily laid him low in 1966; not a broken leg he suffered in 1967; not a siege in a hospital in 1970.

Because he writes so much and so quickly, and because he is so averse to making revisions, there is much in his music that is questionable both as to quality and taste. But when he is good, which is more often the case, he is very good indeed. Shostakovich must be numbered with the greats of twentieth-century music. The permanence of his best orchestral compositions, particularly his finest symphonies, seems assured.

Music Is Reborn
in England

Sir Edward Elgar, Benjamin Britten,

Sir William Walton

For two centuries after the death of Henry Purcell (1659–1695) English music went into a deep slumber. Though English composers who were well schooled and solidly equipped in technique wrote operas and choral and instrumental music between 1695 and 1895, their work was without a clearly defined creative personality. Their names are remembered only by musicologists, and their compositions (with few exceptions) are rarely performed in England, and never elsewhere.

With Sir Edward Elgar, England returned to the world community of great composers. He was the first English composer since Purcell to achieve international renown, the first since Purcell whose works still appear on programs. Elgar wrote no operas but a considerable amount of choral music and some chamber music. But, with the exception of his oratorio *The Dream of Gerontius* (published in 1900), he was most celebrated for his orchestral compositions, or for works for a solo instrument and orchestra.

Elgar was a Romantic to the manner born, a follower of Brahms in favoring classical structures and absolute music, who wrote subjectively and emotionally. He was born in Broadheath on June 2, 1857. He deserted the study of law for music, which had held a strong fascination for him from childhood on. He then held various musical posts in his native city: as bandmaster, violinist, teacher, and organist. His marriage to Caroline Alice Roberts in 1889 was the encouragement and influence he needed to keep him from permanently remaining a humble small-town musician. She convinced him to give up his sundry jobs and settle down to the business of writing music. After establishing residence in Malvern in 1891, where he and his wife remained for thirteen years, Elgar justified his wife's faith in him by writing a number of choral works successfully presented at various festivals.

His first big success came with an orchestral work that is still frequently played: the *Variations on an Original Theme for Orchestra,* op. 36 (1899). Brahms's influence here can hardly be doubted, particularly in the Brahmsian way Elgar uses the variation form, and in the sensuousness and Romanticism that permeate many of its pages.

This work is best known as the *Enigma Variations.* Wherein lies the enigma? Does it consist in the identity of the person being described in each of the variations, since Elgar planned each to be a portrait of somebody close to him? Hardly so—for the person described is identified by initials or a name fixed to each of the variations. The composer himself once hinted that the enigma concerned the theme on which these variations is based. The curious thing about this work is that the theme itself is never presented, yet each variation is dependent on it. Some musicologists maintain that the theme is "hidden," that it serves as a kind of "silent accompaniment." The guesses as to the identity of this hidden theme range from "Auld Lang Syne" to a motive from Wagner's *Parsifal.*

So much for the enigma. As for the music itself, it has such surpassing charm of lyricism and sentiment, and at times such gracious wit, that it never fails to make a direct appeal to listeners everywhere. Here an urbane, cultured Englishman is describing some of his friends in musical terms. The composition opens with an eloquent melody for strings. We are in the presence of a sentimentalist who is unafraid to express his feelings. Fourteen variations (but *not* on the melody we have just heard) follow. The most touching, perhaps, is the first, a portrait of Elgar's wife; the wittiest is the third, which mocks the way an amateur actor uses a falsetto voice to portray old men; the most beautiful is the ninth, a picture of a dear friend of Elgar, a musician with whom he used to discuss at length the genius of Beethoven during long walks (Elgar here introduces a brief quotation from Beethoven's *Sonata pathétique,* for piano);

the most revealing and penetrating is the last, a self-portrait in which the composer pictures his illusions and frustrations and ends up with an avowal of faith in himself and his talent. This episode is followed by hurried reminders of variations one and nine (the two people who had been closest to the composer) to bring the composition to its end.

Other orchestral works by Elgar came during the first decade of the twentieth century. They include a set of five symphonic marches, *Pomp and Circumstance,* op. 39, of which the first in D major (1901) is world-famous. Its main melody has been used for the song "Land of Hope and Glory," and its stately measures have often been used as march music for graduating classes in American schools. *Cockaigne,* op. 40 (published in 1901), is a concert overture describing London. *Introduction and Allegro for Strings,* op. 47 (published in 1905) is somewhat in the structure of the old concerto grosso.

In addition, Elgar wrote two symphonies, a violin concerto, and a cello concerto, all abounding with passages expressing his personal feelings and reveries. These and other compositions placed him in an unrivaled place in twentieth-century English music as long as he lived. In gratitude, Britain conferred a knighthood on him in 1904, gave him the Order of Merit in 1911, appointed him Master of the King's Musick in 1924, and in 1931 paid him an even higher tribute, a baronetcy.

Elgar's last completed major work was the Cello Concerto in 1919. He did little composing after 1920, his creative silence having been brought on by the death of his beloved wife. Toward the end of his life he made an unsuccessful attempt to write a third symphony. But his creative fire had been extinguished. He died at his home, Marl Bank, in Worcester, England, on February 23, 1934.

The imperial position occupied by Elgar in English music was inherited by Ralph Vaughan Williams, Benjamin Britten, and Sir William Walton. Vaughan Williams has already been discussed in an earlier chapter.

The music of Britten and Walton is characterized by a variety of idioms, styles, and moods. Though their language is basically modern in its use of discords, free tonalities, and at times a bleak and stark melodic line, neither Britten nor Walton hesitates to take from other idioms (past or present) that which best serves their immediate needs. In different compositions (and sometimes in one and the same composition) their modernistic tendencies give way to neoclassicism (in their use of counterpoint or their return to such Baroque structures as the partita and the passacaglia), or to Romanticism, or to realism. In brief, both of these men are eclectics—in the dictionary definition of the eclectic as one who selects "according to taste and judgment from different systems or sources." But whatever technique, idiom, or style they choose to adopt, each has revealed a compositional mastery that has made it possible for him to evolve a unified concept from a variety of materials.

Few composers of the twentieth century have been more frequently performed and recorded than Benjamin Britten. A musical prodigy, he was born in Lowestoft, in the Suffolk region of England, on November 22, 1913, the youngest son of a dental surgeon. He was seven when he began taking piano lessons, nine when he started studying the viola, and thirteen when he became a pupil in composition of Frank Bridge, whose immense influence on his development Britten has never hesitated to concede. Composition had always been Britten's first love. In this area he proved so precocious that by his fourteenth year he had written ten piano sonatas, six string quartets, and various other works, including a symphony. Some of the melodies from these early boyhood compositions were later used by Britten in *Simple Symphony* (1925, revised 1934).

After completing his academic education at the Gresham School in Holt in 1930, Britten received a scholarship for the Royal College of Music in London. There, for three years, his principal teachers were John Ireland in composition, and Arthur Benjamin in piano. While still a student at the Royal College, Britten had some of his chamber and choral music and songs performed. His first publication was in the field of orchestral music: a Sinfonietta for chamber orchestra introduced in London in 1933.

Though he was a brilliant student at the Royal College (capturing a prize in composition and an honorary title in piano-playing), Britten could not complete his musical schooling. His father's death forced him to earn a living. For four years, from 1936 to 1939, he wrote music for documentary films for the Government Post Office Film Unit. He also wrote a score for a commercial movie, *Love from a Stranger*. The writing of serious music, however, remained a compulsion. A Suite, for violin and piano, was given in Barcelona, Spain, in 1937 at a concert of the International Society for Contemporary Music. This work was soon followed by Britten's first major work for orchestra and his first composition to achieve something more than limited esteem: *Variations on a Theme by Frank Bridge,* op. 10 (1937), introduced at the Salzburg Festival that year and, a year later, represented at the festival of the International Society for Contemporary Music in London. Soon afterward it was heard about fifty times in Europe and America. *Variations* is still a work to command respect. The ten variations on a melody (taken from the second of Bridge's *Three Idyls*), traverse a wide gamut of moods. Some are poignantly lyrical, some are even touched with drama or pathos, while others are highly satirical. The style passes from modernism to Romanticism and finally with the concluding fugue to classicism.

Already in these *Variations* we are made aware of Britten's gift to write equally well in many different idioms and styles. This gift would henceforth characterize his most important works (including his operas, which have helped make him a world figure in music). This eclecticism is again in evidence in two concertos, one completed in 1938 and the other in 1939, the first for piano, the second for violin. In the piano concerto (which had an impressive success when introduced in London in 1938) Britten named the four movements not with tempo markings but "Toccata," "Waltz," "Impromptu," and "March." To each he assigned that style best suited to it. The violin concerto did use tempo markings for the first three movements, but the fourth was called "Passacaglia." The composer's talent for achieving striking contrasts is prevalent in both concertos.

Britten came to the United States in 1939 to be present at the American premiere of his *Variations on a Theme by Frank Bridge*. He stayed in the United States for three years. War had broken out in Europe in 1939. Britten, a passionate and outspoken pacifist, refused to be a participant even in a life-and-death conflict with the Nazis, whom he despised. His overwhelming emotional response at the sight of Europe being ravaged by war and death filters through the pages of the best orchestral composition to come from him in America. It is the *Sinfonia da Requiem,* op. 20 (1940), ostensibly written in memory of his parents but consciously or subconsciously a lament for war-torn Europe. Another symphonic composition was the *Scottish Ballad,* op. 26, for two pianos and orchestra (1941). For his thematic material Britten went to old Scottish tunes "to evoke," as he explained, "a sequence of ideas and emotions that have been characteristic of the life of the Scottish people during centuries of stormy history."

With Britain subjected to merciless bombing attacks from the Nazi *Luftwaffe,* Britten became conscience-stricken that he was not helping his countrymen when they needed help most. He therefore decided to go home in 1942, settling in the seacoast town of Aldeburgh in Suffolk, which has remained his home ever since. He was still determined never to bear arms. An appellate tribunal in England respected his feelings and recognized his sincerity by exempting him from active military service. Britten now placed his music at the service of his country by giving concerts in hospitals, air-raid shelters, and army camps.

While engaged in war work, Britten labored intensively on an opera that had been commissioned by the Koussevitzky Music Foundation when he was still in America. That opera, produced in London in 1945 with the glaring limelight of international publicity focused on it, was *Peter Grimes*. It is one of the greatest operas of the twentieth century and it immediately brought Britten world renown. With this and subsequent operas, Britten has become universally accepted as one of the world's foremost contemporary composers for the musical stage.

But he continued writing orchestral music, too. *The Young Person's Guide to the Orchestra,* op. 34 (1946), has become a great concert favorite for young and old. Britten did not originally write this music for the concert auditorium, however, but for an educational film describing the instruments of the orchestra. Only afterward did he use this score as a concert work, since its musical appeal was as strong as its educational function.

To illustrate the sound of the different instruments of the orchestra, Britten used the form of theme and variations, each variation presenting one instrument or group of instruments. The theme on which these variations is based came from a little-known composition by Purcell, the incidental music to *Abdelazar* (specifically, the "Rondeau"). This theme is heard in full orchestra in the first eight measures. Four sections follow, which, in turn, introduce the woodwinds, the brasses, the strings, and the percussion, after which the Purcell theme is recalled. Only now do we get the variations. There are thirteen, in which the orchestral instruments appear in the following order: flutes and piccolo; oboes; clarinets; bassoons; strings; violas; cellos; double basses; harp; French horns; trumpets; trombones; tympani and other percussion instruments. The whole package is neatly tied up at the end with a fugue in which the instruments return one by one in the same order in which they had been heard in the variations, climaxed by a rousing presentation of the Purcell melody.

Some of the most important concert music Britten wrote after World War II makes extensive use of solo singers and chorus, and thus belongs within the category of choral music—for example, the *Spring Symphony,* op. 44 (1949), and the mighty *War Requiem,* op. 66 (1962). Of more immediate orchestral interest is the *Symphony for Cello and Orchestra,* op. 68 (1964), written for the distinguished Soviet cellist, Mstislav Rostropovich, who introduced it in Moscow in March of 1964.

Here, once again, variety is the spice of Britten's speech. Irony and gaiety rub elbows with nobility; mystery is a companion to excitement and agitation. In four movements, the symphony rises to eloquent heights in the solemn adagio, in which a persistent drum roll contributes high tension. A cadenza for the solo cello (where the drum is silent) is a transition to the finale, which is a passacaglia, a Baroque structure to which Britten has always been particularly partial.

Britten occupies a red-brick manorial house in Aldeburgh, with a pool, in which, three times a day during the summer, he indulges in his favorite exercise of swimming. A routinized life, which fastidiously allots set hours for his work, allows him ample opportunities to indulge in such diversions as tennis, badminton, taking long walks along the North Sea, and driving his car at breakneck speed through the English countryside. Aldeburgh is not only where he makes his home but also the place where he officiates every June over an important summer festival, which he and some friends founded in 1948, and where many of Britten's important works have received their world premieres.

The honors bestowed on Britten through the years are an indication of how high a station he occupies in today's music. In 1953, Queen Elizabeth bestowed on him the Companionship of Honor. A decade later, in 1964, he received $30,000—the first Aspen (Colorado) Award given to "the individual anywhere in the world judged to have made the greatest contribution to the advancement of Humanities." In 1965, Britain presented him with the Order of Merit.

Sir William Walton is about twelve years older than Britten. Though Walton has written an excellent opera *Troilus and Cressida* (1954), and a powerful oratorio, *Belshazzar's Feast* (1931), his main sphere of activity has been orchestral music.

For the most part his music is characterized by complexity of thought and technique. But his craftmanship is such that, however complicated his harmonic or contrapuntal writing may be, his texture remains transparent, his orchestration brilliant and clearly projected, and his rhythmic power irresistible. His eclecticism reveals itself both in the wide range of his expressiveness and in the variety of his idioms.

Born in Oldham, Lancashire, England, on March 29, 1902, Walton came from a family of musicians. When he was five, William sang in a church choir directed by his father. His father gave him his early musical training, which enabled William, aged ten, to win a scholarship to the Christ Church Cathedral Choir School at Oxford. Six years later he became the youngest student to graduate from that school. Though under age, he was admitted to Christ Church College, Oxford, where his total neglect of academic studies in favor of musical activities led to his expulsion.

But he left no doubts about his talent in music. A string quartet and a piano quartet, written when he was seventeen, achieved recognition when the first was performed at the festival of the International Society for Contemporary Music in Salzburg in 1923, and the second received the Carnegie Trust Award, which provided for its publication, Walton's first.

After being forced to leave Oxford, Walton took up residence in London, where he spent most of his time with the Sitwells—Edith, Osbert, and Sacheverell, all highly talented writers. Edith Sitwell wrote a series of abstract verses whose sounds fell pleasantly on the ear but which made very little sense to the mind. Walton set these amusing verses to music. The result was *Façade,* originally for speaking voice and six musicians playing eight instruments, but later rewritten for speaking voice and full orchestra. Wit, satire, parody, burlesque, and nonsense were some of the ingredients in Walton's spicy music. His score included an American fox-trot, an imitation of a Swiss yodel, parodies of Rossini and Mozart, caricatures of popular songs, waltz music, and the polka. His music was conceived in the spirit of fun, with a little bit of malice to boot. When first heard in public concert—in London in 1923—*Façade* created shock, surprise, and outrage. But a few years later it was finally accepted in the spirit in which it was written. The work became such a favorite that it proved a leading success at the festival of the International Society for Contemporary Music in Siena in 1928, and its music was used for two ballets, one produced by Sadler's Wells in London with choreography by Frederick Ashton. More significantly, as far as twentieth-century orchestral music is concerned, two suites for full orchestra extracted by Walton from his score became his first compositions to gain a wide audience. The first suite (1926) has five numbers (Polka, Valse, Swiss Yodeling Song, Tango-Pasodoble, and Tarantella sevillana), while the second suite (1938) has six (Fanfare, Scotch Rhapsody, Country Dance, Noche española, Popular Song, and the fox-trot "Old Sir Faulk").

Also in a comparatively popular style is a concert overture, *Portsmouth Point,* which came three years after the original version of *Façade.* With a score filled with breezy melodies suggesting chanteys and sailors' dances, Walton here gives us a lively picture of an English waterfront—the British naval arsenal across from the Isle of Wight.

Deserting temporarily the frolicsome levities of *Façade* and the spirited animation of *Portsmouth Point*, Walton soon began to write music more serious and expressive in intent and content. The more sober side of his personality first revealed itself in the Sinfonia concertante for orchestra with piano obbligato (1927), where emotion replaces humor, and religious feeling supplants levity. Now increasingly concerned with emotion that at times borders on passion, and with nobility of thought, Walton completed two works that provided eloquent testimony that here was a composer to reckon with: the Concerto for Viola and Orchestra (1929) and the oratorio *Belshazzar's Feast,* both of which were instantaneously acclaimed upon their premieres in London in 1929 and the Leeds Festival of 1931 respectively.

Just how famous Walton had become by 1935 was revealed by the impatience of the British public to hear his first symphony. Even before the entire work was ready, three of its four movements were heard and acclaimed in 1934. Then when Walton completed the finale, the symphony received its second successful premiere, this time in its entirety, in 1935. The symphony shows an increasing complexity in Walton's technique, a growing interest in elaborate harmonic and contrapuntal schemes and large designs, and his concern with modern idioms. But he remained an eclectic who allowed himself to digress into Romanticism or classicism or Baroque when the spirit so moved him.

This eclectic tendency persisted in such later works as the Violin Concerto (1939), the Cello Concerto (1956), and the Second Symphony (1960). Shorter works supplemented larger ones. In *Scapino* (1940), a comedy overture, he reverts to the boisterous, infectious style of *Portsmouth Point*—Scapino being a character in the old Italian commedia dell'arte. In *Partita* (1958) he combined Baroque style with Walton wit, with a digression into a Romantic episode for oboe and viola solo. In the *Variations on a Theme by Hindemith* (1963) he tapped the same neoclassic vein Hindemith had.

During World War II, Walton wrote music for documentary films as a member of the British armed forces. Then in the years immediately after the war he contributed scores for several memorable commercial films, such as *Major Barbara, Henry V,* and *Hamlet.* In 1947 he received the coveted Gold Medal of the Royal Philharmonic Society of London; in 1951 he was knighted; in 1953 he was commissioned to write a Te Deum for the coronation of Queen Elizabeth II; and in 1967 he was honored with the Order of Merit.

Walton, who had remained a bachelor until his forty-seventh year, married Susana Gil Passo in Buenos Aires in 1948. By now Walton was a wealthy man, thanks largely to a munificent bequest by a friend. He and his wife acquired a beautiful villa on the island of Ischia, off the coast of Italy, which since then has remained their home. There Walton is surrounded by the luxury and elegance to which he is by no means indifferent. He is fond of gourmet food, rare vintage wines, elegantly cut clothes, and expensive cars, and he is a collector of rare books and precious paintings.

At first contact he seems to be cold, austere, and aloof—the typical reserved and dignified Englishman according to the accepted stereotype. But those who know him well find him to be a warm, generous human being who continually brings to his cultured conversation the sparkle of a most engaging, and at times sardonic, wit.

Serge Prokofiev, a drawing by Henri Matisse.

Prokofiev's Romeo and Juliet, *with Natalia Makarova and John Prinz (American Ballet Theatre).*

Sir Edward Elgar.

Dmitri Shostakovich.

Dame Edith Sitwell, whose work Façade *was set to music by Sir William Walton.*

17

American Music Comes into Its Own

Charles Ives, George Gershwin,

Aaron Copland

The history of American music represents a search for a national identity. Once that search ended, American composers could take their rightful place at the side of their most respected colleagues of other nations.

Since the end of the nineteenth century, various American composers have attempted to produce a music that could come from nowhere but the United States. Some did this by simulating or quoting Negro folk songs and the ritual songs and dances of the American Indians. Others preferred to interpolate into serious compositions American popular tunes and national ballads.

The first major American composer favoring the popular rather than the folkloristic approach was also the first great musical nationalist. He was Charles Ives (1874–1954), who both as a man and an artist was in a class all by himself. By profession he was an insurance man who ran a highly profitable firm in New York, where he maintained a town house. He also owned a farm in Connecticut. At that farm, every evening and until the early hours, he devoted himself to composing. He led this dual life with only his wife, stepdaughter, and one or two close friends even aware that this successful businessman was a composer. Ives cherished his privacy. He had no social life to speak of. From 1901, until diabetes and a disturbed nervous system in 1928 made it impossible for him to do any more composing, his private life belonged solely to his music. He wrote exclusively for his own pleasure. He made no effort in all those years to submit his works to publishers, performers, critics, or trained musicians. His music, it almost seemed, was too personal a part of his life for public exhibition. When he finished one work he would put it away, forget about it, and start another. Fame or recognition interested him not at all. He simply had no curiosity in what others thought of his music.

And what music he wrote!—a kind that would have startled his contemporaries out of their senses had they known of its existence. From his very beginnings, Ives was the fully emancipated composer who refused to recognize the validity of past practices and had little respect for most of the music written before his time. He heard new sounds in his mind's ear, and he was determined to get those sounds on paper. He had a fierce belief in the need of an artist to write any way his inspiration dictates—without the prejudices and inhibitions imposed upon him by tradition. He spread his notes over his music paper the way a modernist painter splashes color on a canvas. If the notes clashed (as often they did) to create horrendous discords, what matter? Ives was not concerned with "beautiful" music. "I heard something else," he explained. He wanted to produce new aural and human experiences. He loved the way two different melodies in two different keys sounded when rubbed one against the other. He loved to pile his musical ideas one on top of another, one after another, with a sublime indifference to the fact that nobody was writing music that way at that time.

In his music Ives was a free man, allowing his imagination to soar to regions undreamed of by other composers. He allowed no barriers to him in *his* music within a limited area. And so he freely used different tonalities, rhythmic patterns, and meters simultaneously, and discords. He chopped up his melodic thoughts into fragments. He allowed his music to move freely, unhindered by structural limitations. The wonder of all this is that in all these iconoclastic methods he anticipated idioms with which later modernists would become identified and which would make them famous. Hidden in Ives' drawers and closets and trunks were manuscripts whose techniques and styles were ten, twenty, and at times thirty years ahead of their times!

Nothing, for him, was off limits. His music was not only a mirror to his complete independence but also to his whimsical personality. What others would have considered outlandish, he considered perfectly natural. In one of his orchestral compositions he left several empty measures in the bassoon part—for the purpose of allowing the bassoon, at that point, to play anything it wishes. In a sonata for violin and piano he inexplicably introduced a brief passage for the trumpet. In a string quartet he named the second violin "Rollo"; then, when the second violin was temporarily silent, he wrote over the blank measures, "Too hard to play, so it just can't be good music, Rollo." Ives was, in short, one of a kind. If he was eccentric, however, it was not for eccentricity's sake. It was to liberate music completely.

But his greatest importance lay in the fact that he was the first American composer to succeed in writing *American* music, thoroughly steeped in American experiences, life, backgrounds, geography, history, customs, holidays, cultures, and diversions. He often quoted American national ballads, hymns, and popular songs of the past—not literally, but disfigured and distorted, as he piled the fragments of one tune on another in different keys, or followed one tune with another while interposing some of his own musical ideas. At times he discordantly combined themes by the masters with snatches of popular tunes. "On top of all this," as Leonard Bernstein has written, "there is always that fresh, awkward, endearing primitive style of his, where all of the rules get broken; gauche endings, unfinished phrases, wrong voice-leadings, and inexplicable orchestration. And there are those strange personal jokes of his—burlesques deliberately intended for shock." Ives' music, as Bernstein further notes, is "a sort of personal memoir of Ives' own musical experience. In a way it is music about other music. . . . When you hear 'Turkey in the Straw' . . . you are not supposed to visualize a barn dance; rather to feel the impact of such a tune on this composer's consciousness at a moment in American cultural history when anything that was any good at all *had* to come from Europe. That's what is so touching about all this use of Americana; it comes to us full of Ives' brave resolve to be American, to write American music in the face of a diffident and uninterested public."

The first work where Ives resorted to quotation was his Second Symphony (1897–1901), where, if the ear is alert, it can catch the strains of "Columbia, the Gem of the Ocean" (used as a countersubject to one of Ives's own themes), "De Camptown Races" and "Old Black Joe," both by Stephen Foster, together with country and barn-dance melodies.

"This symphony," Ives once explained, "expresses the musical feelings of the Connecticut country around here [Redding and Danbury] in the 1890s, the music of the country folk. It is full of the tunes they sang and played then, and I thought it would be sort of a bad joke to have some of them in counterpoint with some Bach tunes."

The Third Symphony (1904)—inspired by camp meetings once popular in Connecticut—quotes old American hymns. Its three parts begin with a slow movement, in the middle of which are described the games children used to play outside camp meetings while waiting for their parents.

In the Fourth Symphony (1916) we hear parts of old American hymns in the first movement; in the second movement, "Marching Through Georgia," "Yankee Doodle," "Turkey in the Straw," and "Columbia, the Gem of the Ocean"; hymns again, in the third movement; and in the finale the hymn "Nearer My God to Thee." These themes are not readily recognized (especially when they come in such profusion in the second movement). They are parts of a conglomeration of wild sounds in which tunes and hymns shoot up and die in the air like flaming fireworks.

Besides his symphonies, Ives's important orchestral compositions include a three-movement suite, *Three Places in New England* (1914). This music is deeply rooted in American geography and history, with backward glances to the Revolutionary and Civil wars. The closing movement is a sensitive tonal picture of the Housatonic River in Stockbridge, Massachusetts.

It took between forty and fifty years for both the Second and Fourth symphonies to be heard; thirty-six years for the Third Symphony; twenty years for *Three Places in New England*. It was not until the dusk of his life that Ives's works began to be performed and honored. Success and fame meant nothing to him. He refused to attend performances of his compositions. When he received the Pulitzer Prize in music in 1947 for his Third Symphony, he snarled contemptuously: "Prizes are for boys. I'm grown up." He would not be interviewed or photographed. He preferred to remain completely aloof from society on his farm in West Redding, where he had lived in almost total seclusion following his retirement from business in 1930. Still determined to keep the outside world removed from the peace and security of his isolation, he would not permit either a radio or a phonograph to invade his household, or famous visitors to come to pay him homage. When he played the piano with his stiff and debilitated fingers, it was always his own music that he performed—nobody else's interested him in the least. In old age he remained true to himself. He went around his farm wearing heavy shoes, blue denim trousers, a tieless and faded blue shirt, a tattered sweater, a tweed jacket sadly in need of pressing, and a battered hat. His dress was symbolic of the fact that success could not rob him of his homespun simplicity. When he died in 1954, the world looked upon him not only as the *first* distinguished native American composer, but possibly the greatest. This evaluation would have meant nothing to him. He probably would have commented acidly, "Praise is for children, I'm a man." For him there was just one major consideration: he had written the kind of music he wanted, and the results satisfied him.

The route toward nationalism chosen by George Gershwin was also that of popular American music, though not through quotations, but with materials exclusively his own. George Gershwin was destined to become the first composer of thoroughly American music to gain world recognition, and the first American composer to influence Europeans. He is still the American composer the world reveres most highly and performs most frequently.

Gershwin was just a boy when he was first driven by the ambition to create serious music with popular American idioms (a trend in twentieth-century music sometimes referred to as "popularism"). This was early in the 1910s, when serious musicians looked upon American popular music either with condescenion or with outright contempt. The boy Gershwin, however, felt there were unique qualities to popular music styles (the "blues," ragtime, syncopation) that, if used with serious intent, could result in ambitious compositions with an unmistakable American identity while bringing to serious music new and important techniques. The young Gershwin was convinced of something else too: if a popular composer carried into his writing the advanced methods of serious music, the popular song could become an art form. To accomplish all this in his own music became for Gershwin a mission that lit up the fires of his musical imagination and eventually set it aflame.

Already when he was sixteen, in 1914, he knew where his destiny lay. At that time he was studying the piano with Charles Hambitzer. Hambitzer gave young Gershwin a thorough training in the classics and moderns. Gershwin was an excellent student; his interest in good music was sincere and intense. He was always at the keyboard. He purchased a large gray ledger (the kind used by bookkeepers), into which he pasted the pictures of great composers, programs of concerts he attended, and newspaper and magazine items of musical events or personalities. Though great music and musicians absorbed him, he already had a glimpse of his own promised land. He would lead America's popular music out of the bondage of stereotypes, formulas, and clichés and into the milk-and-honey land of great music. During his lessons, he continually harassed Hambitzer with arguments about how truly American music could be written—if only a composer brought to the writing of symphonies, concertos, and operas the tools provided by American popular music (instead of imitating the European masters, as was usually the case). Hambitzer's reaction to this sixteen-year-old boy was expressed in a letter to his (Hambitzer's) sister. "The boy is a genius without a doubt," wrote Hambitzer. "He's crazy about music and can't wait until it's time to take his lessons. . . . No watching the clock for this boy. I believe I can make something of him. He wants to go in for this modern stuff—jazz, ragtime and what not. But I'm not going to let him for a while."

Gershwin did not abandon the study of serious music; he never did, until the end of his life. But realizing, as he did, that his destiny lay in popular music, he knew he had to learn everything there was to know about it—at its source. Aged sixteen, he found a job in a leading popular music publishing house (Remick) as a piano demonstrator—that is, a pianist who performed the firm's songs for potential clients. His salary was $15 a week. One quiet afternoon, in his piano cubicle at Remick's, a fellow pianist found him practising Bach's *Well-Tempered Clavier,* that monumental volume of preludes and fugues for the piano. "Are you practising to become a great pianist?" the co-worker asked. George's reply with both typical and significant. "No," he answered with the utmost seriousness. "I'm practising to become a great popular composer."

Neither money nor fame nor luxury—all of which came to him from the writing of song hits for the Broadway musical stage—could tempt him to abandon his mission. He kept on studying seriously: theory, composition, orchestration. He hired orchestral players to teach him the elements of playing every instrument so that he might advance his knowledge of orchestration.

He wrote songs for the popular stage and screen, some of which are among the treasures of American song literature, remarkable for their personal, affecting lyricism, spontaneity of expression, and particularly for their agility in using rhythmic devices and meters. And he wrote compositions for the concert hall and opera house, a handful of which

became the most famous and the most widely heard American music ever written. Gershwin, then, succeeded in bringing a boyhood dream to realization. He had made of the popular song a musical art form. He had also contributed a vital repertory of serious compositions in which he used American popular idioms so skillfully and with such originality that major composers in America and Europe were inspired to emulate him. He died too soon, leaving many a masterwork unwritten—but not before he had fulfilled his destiny.

He came from a middle-class and unmusical family, born in Brooklyn, New York, on September 25, 1898. When George was one year old his family moved to the East Side of New York, where he attended public schools. In his first year, music meant little to him. He preferred to play with his friends in the streets, or to roller-skate. Then, beginning in his sixth year, he happened to hear some semiclassical compositions that made such an impression on him that he began taking piano lessons, first with inadequate local teachers, and then with Charles Hambitzer. By the time he was twelve, music had become his all-absorbing interest, and it would remain so from then on.

After working at Remick's, Gershwin devoted himself to the writing of popular songs. His first published song appeared when he was eighteen. A year later he wrote not only the score for his first Broadway musical, which was only a moderate success, but also a song, "Swanee," that sold one million copies of sheet music and two million records. Now a commercial success, Gershwin was contracted to write all the music for one of the leading revues then being mounted annually on Broadway, *George White's Scandals*. Gershwin wrote the music for five editions, between 1920 and 1924 inclusive. A few of his songs already revealed that Gershwin's approach to popular music writing was original; his talent impressed several leading serious musicians and music critics. Thus Gershwin was beginning to realize his first ambition, writing popular songs that had artistic validity. He also made an attempt to realize his second ambition (to create a serious work in popular idioms) by writing the music for a one-act opera, *Blue Monday* (later retitled *135th Street*). It had only a single performance, on the opening night of *George White's Scandals of 1922*. The next morning White, producer of the revue, removed it from the production because he considered it too dull and gloomy for Broadway entertainment.

The man who conducted in the orchestra pit when *Blue Monday* was given was Paul Whiteman, already famous as the conductor of a jazz orchestra. Whiteman was impressed with this opera, but even more so with Gershwin's talent. When, a year later, Whiteman planned a concert of

American popular music in a concert auditorium, he asked Gershwin to write a new serious work in the jazz idiom. Gershwin responded with the *Rhapsody in Blue,* for piano and orchestra, introduced at Aeolian Hall, New York, on February 12, 1924, with Gershwin as soloist and Whiteman conducting. The composition caused a furore. At its premiere it received a thunderous ovation. A few critics called it a masterpiece, "far superior," said one of them, "to Schoenberg, Milhaud and the rest of the futurist fellows." The general public adored it. Paul Whiteman's recording sold a million disks. The rhapsody was performed extensively in all kinds of transcriptions and arrangements. In its original form it was given in stage shows and in movies. The published music became a bestseller. Gershwin was now famous as a serious composer for the first time both in America and Europe (for the rhapsody proved hardly less popular across the Atlantic than it was on its own home ground). He was regarded as "the white hope" of American music.

The *Rhapsody in Blue* has never lost its popularity. It is still being given hundreds of times each year and is continually being released in new recordings. In its rhythmic vitality, exciting use of popular idioms, nervous energy, youthful spirit, and infectious harmonies it is American to the core. It opens with that infectious upward slide of the clarinet toward a bouncy jazz tune that never seems to lose its intoxicating effect on the listener. The momentum now generated is arrested only when the wonderful rhapsodic melody unfolds in the strings, one of the most famous themes to come out of an American composition.

From then on, until he died, Gershwin straddled the two worlds of music—the popular and the serious—making popular music serious and serious music popular. One writer said of him that he was a mighty Colossus bestriding the music world, one foot planted in New York's Carnegie Hall and the other in the Broadway musical theater.

Between periods of fulfilling assignments for Broadway or Hollywood, Gershwin worked hard on his serious music, all of it utilizing and profiting from the vital, indigenous techniques of American popular music. In 1924 Gershwin was commissioned by the New York Symphony Society and its conductor, Walter Damrosch, to write a piano concerto. The Concerto in F was heard in Carnegie Hall on December 3, 1925, with Gershwin as soloist. It has since become second only to the *Rhapsody in Blue* among Gershwin's most favored concert compositions. It opens vigorously with a Charleston motive (the Charleston being a lively social dance favored by young and old in the 1920s). It then proceeds to offer a most delectable assortment of blues melodies, jazz rhythms, and refreshing syncopations and accentuations exchanged between solo piano and orchestra. In the second movement Gershwin allows his lyrical talent to come to the fore with a poetic melody for muted trumpet, and later with a sensual song for strings. This latter song becomes the climax in the finale, after Gershwin has released the fireworks of his rhythmic virtuosity.

In 1928 Gershwin took a year's hiatus from his commitments for Broadway to go to Europe to study with some master and also to write a new symphonic work. When he asked Ravel to become his teacher, Ravel inquired, "Why should you be a second-rate Ravel when you can be a first-rate Gershwin?" Stravinsky also felt there was not much he could teach Gershwin. Gershwin did no studying in Europe, but he was able to attend in Paris the premiere of a ballet inspired by the *Rhapsody in Blue* and the European premiere of his piano concerto. And he was also able to complete most of a new work for orchestra, a tone poem, *An American in Paris,* whose premiere was given by the New York Philharmonic under Damrosch on December 13, 1928, a few months after Gershwin had returned to the United States. This tone poem recreates the sights and sounds of Paris as an American strolls along the famous boulevard, the Champs Elysées. The composition starts with a sprightly tune suggesting the American's brisk walk. Soon we hear actual Parisian taxi horns (imported from France) as the American threads through the traffic while crossing streets. Our American passes a music hall from which come the strains of a jazz tune (in trombone). A brief passage for solo violin suggests that he is stopped by a French girl, but our American is not long deflected from his walk. For a brief spell, he feels homesick (nostalgia for home being projected through a blues melody in muted trumpet, the most important melody in the composition). But the American dismisses thoughts of home and is exhilarated by the delights of Paris as he continues his stroll.

In 1930 Gershwin was called to Hollywood to write an original score for the screen. Together with songs, Gershwin did a six-minute orchestral sequence as background music. Only a minute of it was used when the motion picture, *Delicious,* was released. Gershwin expanded the other five minutes into a full-length symphonic composition to which he finally affixed the title of *Second Rhapsody.* The Boston Symphony under Koussevitzky presented the first performance on January 29, 1932. Though less often played than the *Rhapsody in Blue,* this *Second Rhapsody* has some delectable Gershwin melodies and rhythms, including a rumba theme and an expansive blues song.

During a short holiday in Cuba, in 1932, Gershwin became fascinated with Cuban music and native instruments. This led him to the writing of the *Cuban Overture,* filled with melodies and rhythms inspired by that country and employing a whole battery of Cuban percussion instruments, which assume a prominent role at the end of the work as the background for a colorful rumba melody.

The *Cuban Overture* was introduced at the first all-Gershwin concert given anywhere. This historic event took place at the Lewisohn Stadium, New York, on August 16, 1932, Albert Coates conducting. Since 1932, all-Gershwin concerts have become something of a ritual all over the world, and whenever and wherever given invariably overtax the capacity of the auditorium. Hundreds upon hundreds of such all-Gershwin concerts have been performed in America and Europe. Though their programs comprise the now thrice-familiar Gershwin music, the appeal of these concerts never seems to pall, providing eloquent testimony to both the durability and the universality of Gershwin's concert music.

Gershwin's last orchestral composition was the *Variations on "I Got Rhythm,"* for piano and orchestra. Gershwin wrote it for a one-month American tour he was making, giving Gershwin concerts. With an orchestra and its conductor, he traveled twelve thousand miles and was heard in twenty-eight cities. "I Got Rhythm" was one of Gershwin's most celebrated popular songs. He wrote it in 1930 for the Broadway musical *Girl Crazy,* and it was largely responsible for making Ethel Merman (who introduced it in this her Broadway debut) a musical comedy star of the first magnitude. This song had always been a particular favorite with Gershwin. At private parties he used to entertain friends by improvising variations to this melody. He finally decided to work out these variations formally on paper and develop them into a major concert work. The chorus of "I Got Rhythm" is first suggested in the four notes in the clarinet with which the composition commences. Before long the chorus of the song is given in full by the piano. After that the variations are developed, transforming the melody imaginatively and with great variety of mood. In one of the best of these variations, the melody becomes a throbbing blues version. Gershwin himself was at the piano when this composition received its premiere in Boston, on January 14, 1934, only eight days after Gershwin had put the final touches on his manuscript.

Though the *Variations* was Gershwin's last work for orchestra, it was not his last serious composition. He ended his career as a serious composer triumphantly—with his mighty American Negro folk opera
266 *Porgy and Bess,* undoubtedly his most important work, and just as

assuredly the most extensively performed American opera of all time.

An extrovert, and a highly gregarious individual, Gershwin enjoyed going to parties—or being host to parties, first at his penthouse apartment on Riverside Drive in New York, where he lived from 1928 to 1933, and then at an even more elegant apartment on East 72nd Street. Blessed as he was with charm, personal magnetism, and overbrimming and infectious enthusiasms, he made friends easily. He mingled freely and frequently with the greats of the worlds of music, art, literature, finance, society, and even European royalty. He was a man of many extra-musical interests. Apart from his social life with friends, Gershwin's enthusiasms away from music covered a wide area: tennis, Ping-Pong, photography, horseback riding, backgammon, playing parlor games, fishing, swimming and, toward the end of his life, painting—for which he revealed a remarkable gift. Each time he adopted a new hobby, he reacted to it with the excitement of one who had just made a startling personal discovery. He would master it and then pass on to another one.

Music however—his own music in particular—occupied the dominant place in his life, no matter how much now one diversion and now another fascinated him for a time. One of the most striking, most unforgettable traits about Gershwin was his parental pride in, faith in, and enthusiasm for the music he wrote. He liked nothing better than to play his music to whoever would listen to him. He liked to talk about his music, to divulge his ambitions for the future. Any social evening where Gershwin was at hand was completely overwhelmed by his electrifying personality and even more electrifying music-making. He would be the man in the spotlight, regardless of how famous, successful, or powerful were the other guests in that room. His friends used to say that an evening with Gershwin was a Gershwin evening—by which they meant, of course, that any evening you spent with Gershwin you were given a continual diet of Gershwinia. The famous playwright George S. Kaufman once remarked wryly that he would always bet on Gershwin in a hundred-yard dash to the piano. His mother once scolded him for continually playing his own music at parties. "But, Mother," he replied candidly, "if I don't play my music I get bored." It was at one of these soirées, after Gershwin had monopolized the evening, that his friend Oscar Levant asked him acidly, "If you had to do it all over again, George, would you still fall in love with yourself?"

It was probably this preoccupation with creativity, with artistic goals to be reached, with his destiny still to be fulfilled, that kept him from getting married. He loved many women, and they loved him. But his absorption with his music seemed to make it difficult for him to give himself completely to a woman, even when he loved her. He could be attractive, charming, and entertaining to females—but suddenly, when he was with a girl, he would withdraw into himself and make her feel he was thousands of miles away; the girl with him would be left in utter isolation.

His work always came first. Once, learning that a girl in whom he was then particularly interested, had suddenly married another man, he remarked to his brother, Ira (who wrote the words for George's songs), "I'd be terribly heartbroken if I weren't so damned busy." He never gave himself so completely to a woman that losing her left a vacuum in his life.

In 1936, Gershwin went to Hollywood to work for the screen. Two of his films starred Fred Astaire, and one was a lavish musical produced by Samuel Goldwyn, *The Goldwyn Follies,* for which he wrote what many of his admirers consider two of his greatest ballads ("Love Walked In" and "Love Is Here to Stay")—among the last pieces of music he was destined to write. While working for Hollywood he suffered from excruciating headaches. At one of his concerts his memory deserted him. He was growing increasingly irritable. At one time he was found in his darkened room sitting in a chair, his head bent; he did not know how long he had been sitting there that way.

He was suffering from a tumor of the brain, a fact revealed during an exploratory operation; the tumor could not be operated on. Gershwin died in hospital soon after this operation, on July 11, 1937. But the music he left behind is more alive today than it was on the day he died. His concert works are classics, his name a legend the world over. Now more than yesterday, and yesterday more than in 1937, Gershwin's name and music light up the world's skies. With each passing year their brilliance becomes more incandescent. Over a hundred all-Gershwin concerts are presented annually in different parts of the world. Gershwin festivals have been held in Venice (Italy), Chicago, and Miami. No American composer, probably no twentieth-century composer, is so enthusiastically received in so many different places.

This fact is, of course, of no minor significance. But equally important is the influence he has had on composers since the 1920s. In his book *Makers of the Modern World,* Louis Untermeyer, distinguished American poet and critic, places Gershwin with Wagner, Debussy, and Stravinsky as those most responsible for shaping the music of the first half of the twentieth century. Gershwin's trend—"popularism"—has been a force sending many a distinguished composer to exploit American popular idioms in classical music. Operas, symphonies, tone poems, sonatas, ballets, concertos in a popular American style came down in a veritable downpour in America and Europe during Gershwin's heyday and in the decade following his death. This came about because Gershwin, through his own music, had so convincingly demonstrated that these popular idioms had true artistic importance.

Aaron Copland, who has for many years justifiably been hailed as "the dean of American composers," attracted attention to his talent for the first time in the mid 1920s with two orchestral works in a popular idiom. Having been strongly impressed by the *Rhapsody in Blue,* Copland was impelled to write major symphonic works with jazz materials. He first did so in a suite for chamber orchestra, *Music for the Theater* (1925), which had been commissioned by Serge Koussevitzky, who conducted its premiere in Boston on November 20, 1925. With no specific play in mind, Copland here wrote music of theatrical interest, without being specifically programmatic, in which two of the five movements are particularly notable as examples of American popularism.

Still convinced of the potentialities of American popular idioms for major serious works, Copland next wrote the Concerto for Piano and Orchestra (1926). Its world premiere was given by the Boston Symphony on January 28, 1927, with the composer as soloist, and Koussevitzky conducting. This is a two-movement composition with two principal themes, both of them popular, and the second presented by a soprano saxophone. In elaborating on these musical ideas Copland revealed once again his skill both in writing for the orchestra and in using popular styles. "This is music," reported the New York critic Lawrence Gilman, "of impressive austerity, of true character; music bold in outline and of singular power." When this concerto was revived by the New York Philharmonic in 1964 and 1965, it became evident that the passing of almost forty years had not robbed this vital music of its rhythmic vigor.

Copland was born in Brooklyn, New York, on November 14, 1900. A recital by the great Polish piano virtuoso Ignace Jan Paderewski introduced the fourteen-year-old Copland to the world of music. Copland now aspired to become a concert pianist. He took lessons first with his sister, then with a local piano teacher. While attending high school in Brooklyn he came to the conclusion that he preferred to be a composer. He studied harmony with Rubin Goldmark before becoming the first student accepted by the then recently founded American School of Music in Fontainebleau, France. He left the school to live for three years in Paris, where he studied composition and orchestration with Nadia Boulanger.

His first large-scale work was something Miss Boulanger asked him to write. She was planning to tour America as organist and required a new large work for some of her concerts. Copland wrote for her a Symphony for Organ and Orchestra, a composition in the modern style then so much in favor with avant-garde composers in France. It was performed by Miss Boulanger and the New York Symphony on January 11, 1925, with Damrosch conducting. During a rehearsal, Damrosch—puzzled by the discords in Copland's music—remarked: "If a young man can write a piece like that at the age of twenty-three, in five years he will be ready to commit murder."

Serge Koussevitzky, conductor of the Boston Symphony, liked this Symphony for Organ and Orchestra and performed it in Boston a little over a month after its world premiere. This began an artistic relationship between Copland as composer and Koussevitzky as conductor that helped bring Copland into the limelight, beginning with the two compositions in the jazz style already mentioned. Financial support from a patroness of the arts, supplemented by the money he received in 1925 and 1926 from the Guggenheim Fellowship, gave Copland the financial independence he needed to devote himself entirely to writing music.

After the piano concerto mentioned before, Copland felt he had exploited the possibilities of jazz in serious music as much as he could and abandoned this Gershwinian tendency for good. For a while he adopted a highly complex, esoteric style in the then modern idioms. His *Dance Symphony* received a prize of $5,000 in a contest conducted by RCA Victor Company and was heard in Philadelphia in 1931.

"During these years," Copland recalls, looking back upon this period of modernism, "I began to feel an increasing dissatisfaction with the relations of the music-loving public and the living composer. . . . It seemed to me that we composers were in danger of working in a vacuum. . . . I felt that it was worth the effort to see if I couldn't say what I had to say in the simplest possible terms."

A visit to Mexico in 1932 gave him the idea for his first work in this new simplified style. In Mexico he had become intrigued with the color and atmosphere of a dance hall called Salón México. Then and there he decided to write an orchestral piece depicting Mexico as a tourist sees it. He called his Mexican-inspired composition after the name of the dance hall, making it a skillful collation of popular Mexican tunes, and an adaptation of intriguing Mexican rhythms. This *still* was popularism—

though not of the North American variety. Following its first performance in Mexico City in 1937, *El Salón México* was broadcast over the
NBC network in 1938 and before long was performed by many major
American orchestras. It became Copland's greatest success up to that
time, and it is still extremely popular both in concerts and on records.

Now determined to have his music reach out to an ever-expanding
audience, Copland began writing music for children: a delightful "play-
opera," *The Second Hurricane,* in 1937, and an orchestral work intended for performance by high school orchestras, *An Outdoor Overture,* in 1938; he also wrote music for the movies, the radio, and the
Broadway theater. In his less functional and more serious efforts, he
now decided to exploit American nationalism by deriving subjects for
compositions from American backgrounds and characters, and filling his
music with quotations from American folk and popular songs. In 1938
he wrote music for a ballet, *Billy the Kid,* which touched upon the high
points in the legendary career of the celebrated Western outlaw and ended
with his death at the hands of a posse. Copland here reached into the
storehouse of American cowboy songs by quoting from such folk classics
as "O Bury Me Not on the Lone Prairie," "Old Chisholm Trail," and
"Goodbye, Old Paint" among other numbers. All were neatly inter-
woven in a brilliantly orchestrated fabric. Four years later, Copland
fashioned music for another ballet, this time based on cowboys and their
way of life, *Rodeo,* produced in New York by the Ballet Russe de
Monte Carlo on October 16, 1942. The scenario traces the adventures
of a tomboy cowgirl as she goes to various cowboy haunts and finally becomes feminine enough to win her man at a Saturday night dance at a
ranch house. The music captured "with brilliance, humor and touches of
pathos an episode from life in the hearty, healthy West," reported the dance
critic Walter Terry. Quotations from American folk music and square-
dance tunes added a piquant native flavor to Copland's musical recipe.

From both of these scores Copland drew the most appealing passages for suites capable of performance at symphony concerts. The suite
from *Billy the Kid* comprises six sections, that from *Rodeo,* four. The
"Hoe-Down" from the *Rodeo* suite has met with particular favor.

American nationalism continued to interest Copland for a few years.
A Lincoln Portrait, for narrator and orchestra (1942), is a three-dimen-
sional portrait of the personality of that great American President. For
his text Copland used material from Lincoln's letters and speeches, ending with the final lines of the Gettysburg Address. Copland gave his
music a stronger American profile by using snatches of songs from Lin-

271

coln's time, including Stephen Foster's "Camptown Races" and the folk ballad "Springfield Mountain."

Copland's masterwork in a national style is his score for the ballet *Appalachian Spring,* which is also well known in the form of a suite for orchestra. Copland wrote the ballet music for the dancer Martha Graham, who prepared both the scenario and the choreography and introduced the ballet in Washington, D.C., on October 30, 1944. Miss Graham's scenario presents a housewarming party in the Appalachian mountain region of Pennsylvania in pioneer times. The celebrants are a husbandman and his bride-to-be, a pioneer woman, a revivalist, and four of his followers. "The work has a rare unity and an irresistible winsomeness," said dance critic John Martin. Here Copland's music is less inclined to depend upon quotation than did his earlier ballet scores; only a single folk song is used, a Shaker melody, "Simple Gifts." The rest of the score is of Copland's own invention, but always the folklike character of Appalachian mountain tunes, dances, and religious music is faithfully adhered to.

For his ballet Copland was given the New York Music Critics' Award. For the eight-part symphonic suite, he was awarded the Pulitzer Prize in music. That suite (Copland's best-known orchestral work) was introduced by the New York Philharmonic in 1945.

There is also a strong American spirit and feeling in one of Copland's later works, the opera *The Tender Land* (1954), where his music has folk-song overtones, and quotes an actual American folk tune. But in his orchestral and other instrumental compositions, beginning with the Symphony no. 3 (1946)—once again a recipient of the New York Music Critics' Award—Copland abandons the practice of quoting from American folk sources. In the symphony he prefers to quote material from a few of his own earlier prenationalistic compositions. He was also beginning to favor again modern idioms, a greater complexity of style and structure, and absolute and at times abstract music. Copland's first purely orchestral work after this symphony—*Connotations* (1962), written for the opening of Philharmonic Hall at the Lincoln Center for the Performing Arts—was in the twelve-tone technique. So was the orchestral work *Inscape* in 1967.

This last phase, in which Copland embraced the twelve-tone and serial techniques, has hardly met with the enthusiasm accorded to such earlier Copland works as *El Salón México, Appalachian Spring,* and the Third Symphony. But this did not bring about any decline in Copland's fame. In 1964, President Johnson awarded him the Presidential

Medal of Freedom, the highest honor conferred by the President of the United States for peacetime service. In 1970, Copland's seventieth birthday brought on in the United States and Europe an avalanche of tributes: performances of his principal works, telecasts, articles in newspapers and magazines, honorary degrees, and a supper party tendered him by his publisher. Copland was being honored not only as the foremost living American composer but also as one of the most powerful forces for promoting American composers and American music in half a century. Through those years he had been indefatigable as a lecturer, writer, organizer of American festivals, member of important organizations involved in modern musical activities, and teacher. In whatever musical area he has cultivated he has truly been "the spearpoint of the development of the modern American school," as Olin Downes, the music critic of *The New York Times* once said of him.

Music for Today and Tomorrow

Samuel Barber, John Cage

Two more spheres of creativity should be explored before we conclude our account of orchestral music. They represent opposite extremes in the spectrum of twentieth-century music. One can be labeled as "romantic modernism." This music is a happy marriage of the past and the present in which the discordant, dynamic idioms of the twentieth century are combined with romantic feelings and ingratiating lyricism. This is music that, for all its modern tendencies, respects logically conceived structures and is not reluctant to avail itself of older methods. This music still follows the principle that good music, today as yesterday, must communicate with its audience through the heart rather than the mind. It is yesterday's music dressed up in today's clothes.

The other sphere is the avant-garde movement that has been gaining such momentum since the 1950s. Here music advances beyond atonality, twelve-tonalism, and serialism to make a complete break with the past. All former concepts on how music should sound, the materials it should use, the way it should be produced, performed, and written down, have been discarded. This is a totally new type of musical art, any resemblance to other music being purely coincidental.

Each of these two spheres of music has found a significant voice in an American composer: romantic modernism in Samuel Barber; avant-gardism in John Cage.

Barber's first successful orchestral pieces were highly romantic and lyrical, the work of a traditionalist rather than a modernist. This may very well be because "song" was a powerful influence on Barber's early musical development. As the nephew of one of the greatest opera singers of her time, Louise Homer, Samuel Barber was musically nursed on great arias. Since later on he himself was trained as a singer, he acquired a deep respect for singable melodies. When he began to write music seriously, the creation of spun-out melodies to well-sounding harmonies assumed a position of prime concern for him.

Samuel Barber was born in West Chester, Pennsylvania, on March 9, 1910. When he was six he began to study the piano. One year after that, he wrote a piano composition, and when he was ten he planned the writing of an opera. Music so completely absorbed his time and interests that his parents, eager to have him live as a normal boy, did what they could to get him away from the piano to engage in sports with his friends. Samuel did not take kindly to these efforts. At that time he wrote a note to his mother saying, "I was not meant to be an athlete. I was meant to be a composer, and will be, I'm sure. . . . Don't ask me to try to forget this and go and play football. *Please.*" He then proceeded to delve more deeply in music-making. In his twelfth year he became a church organist for a salary of $100 a month. While attending high school, he organized and led a small orchestra. He also played the piano at club dates.

When Barber was fourteen, a new music school was founded in Philadelphia: the now renowned Curtis Institute. At the advice of the director of the Peabody Conservatory in Baltimore, Barber applied for admission at the Curtis Institute and became a charter student. He remained there eight years (meanwhile graduating from high school in 1928). In 1945 the Curtis Institute awarded him an honorary doctorate in music. While at the institute he studied piano with Isabelle Vengerova, composition with Rosario Scalero, and (since he had a beautiful singing voice) singing with Emilio de Gogorza. By the time he was graduated from Curtis Institute he had written a violin sonata, which won the Bearns Prize of $1,500, and a work for soprano and string quartet, *Dover Beach,* which was introduced in New York by Rose Bampton and the New York String Quartet in 1933.

He did not wait long after leaving Curtis to give serious consideration to orchestral music. A spirited and mirthful little orchestral work, *Overture to the School for Scandal,* op. 5, was heard in Philadelphia in 1933, winning the Bearns Prize for him a second time. In 1933 Barber also wrote *Music for a Scene from Shelley* (inspired by Shelley's *Prometheus Unbound*) which, by contrast, was atmospheric and sensitively poetic; it was well received when given by the New York Philharmonic in 1935.

A Pulitzer Traveling Scholarship (which was renewed for a second year) and the American Prix de Rome, both awarded in 1935, enabled him to make an extended trip to Europe. In Vienna he gave some song recitals. As a winner of the American Prix de Rome he then went to live at the American Academy in the Holy City, where he worked on his first symphony. It enjoyed resounding successes. After being introduced by the Augusteo Orchestra in Rome in 1936, it was played in Cleveland by the Cleveland Orchestra and was heard at the Salzburg Festival, both in 1937 (the first time, incidentally, that the composition of an American was ever programed at the world-famous Austrian summer festival).

In 1942, he revised the Symphony no. 1, the new version being heard in 1944. It is still highly esteemed. Barber here synthesized the four movements of the traditional symphony into a single movement. Three main themes are introduced and developed. Then a transformation of the first theme takes the place of a second-movement scherzo, and an alteration of the second theme becomes the equivalent of a third-movement andante tranquillo. A crescendo leads into what normally should be a finale: a passacaglia based on the first theme but with the other themes adroitly woven into the polyphonic texture.

Upon returning to the United States in 1939, Barber became a member of the faculty at the Curtis Institute, where for several years he taught orchestration and conducting. Two new orchestral works added greatly to his now rapidly growing prestige: the *Adagio for Strings,* op. 11, completed in 1936, and the *Essay No. 1,* op. 12, in 1937. The fact that these became the first American works to be performed by the NBC Symphony under the renowned Arturo Toscanini, over the NBC radio network, was a distinction that added no little luster to the success of this music. The concert on November 5, 1938, presented the world premiere of both of these works.

These two compositions are jewels that continue to shine iridescently in the contemporary orchestral repertory. The *Adagio for Strings* has a single elegiac melody, which is played by the first violins, after which it is taken over by the other instruments. The piece is built up to a high point of dramatic interest through sonority and then allowed to subside. This is such solemn and emotionally moving music that when President John F. Kennedy was assassinated in 1963, the *Adagio* was performed on a coast-to-coast radio broadcast as a touching memorial.

In the *Essay No. 1,* op. 12, Barber ventured upon the unique experiment of trying to adapt for music the form of a literary essay. As in an essay, the composition begins with a single main thought, which is allowed to grow and expand logically and progress to a final conclusion in the same way that any theme is elaborated upon in a piece of prose nonfiction. In 1942 Barber wrote a second *Essay,* op. 17, which is more ambitious in structure and in the working out of the main melodic idea.

Until now Barber seemed to be oblivious, in his music, to the major upheavals that had been taking place in twentieth-century music with such adventurers as Stravinsky and Schoenberg, among others. But in his Symphony no. 2, op. 19 (1944), written while he served in the Army Air Corps during World War II, he began to adopt a more progressive style for the first time. He had done this symphony on a commission from the Air Corps, intending it as a musical tribute to that branch of the service. His subject demanded that he use discords; that he introduce extramusical sounds, such as one simulating the noise made by a radio beam in a message to the pilot (a sound produced electrically by an instrument invented especially for this symphony); that he concentrate on the power generated by rhythm and sonorities and less on romanticism and lyricism. After it was first performed by the Boston Symphony in 1944 (following which it was broadcast around the world by short wave), Barber rewrote it to eliminate any realistic effects and allow it to stand or fall as absolute music. The importance of this symphony in Barber's development is that it represents an important transition from his purely romantic compositions that had preceded it, and the compositions that followed in which modern idioms are used with ever-increasing frequency and ever-mounting effect.

After being separated from the armed forces, Barber acquired a rambling house in Mount Kisco, New York, to which he gave the name of Capricorn and which he shared with the celebrated opera composer Gian Carlo Menotti. They had separate studios in opposite ends of the house where each could work in seclusion, out of hearing distance from each other.

A retiring and withdrawn person, Barber has always been happiest leading the quiet life of a recluse at Capricorn. He has always been at ease only with those he knows well; with all others he gives the impression of being cold and distant. He dislikes large gatherings, formal social functions, parties, and party games. His preference is conversation with one or two stimulating friends, reading, taking solitary walks in the country, traveling, and enjoying art.

His greatest problem in his work as composer is to arrive at melodies he finds suitable; the search is a long, painful process. During that search he becomes more introverted than ever and often lapses into melancholia or bad temper. His mind becomes so preoccupied with his musical problems that he can think of nothing else. But once he arrives at acceptable melodic material, his mood changes magically and a kind of temporary intoxication sets in.

A Guggenheim Fellowship in 1945 helped him to devote himself completely to composition. Following the completion of the Cello Concerto, op. 22 (1945), he worked on a ballet score for the dancer Martha Graham, which had been commissioned by the Oliver Ditson Fund. It became his first successful work in his romantic modern manner. Originally, this ballet was called *The Serpent Heart,* op. 23, and under that name it was introduced in New York in 1946. Later retitled *Cave of the Heart,* ultimately its title was finalized as *Medea.* An orchestral suite from that score was performed by the Philadelphia Orchestra under Eugene Ormandy in 1947, one section of which (revised and reorchestrated) was used in 1955 for a powerful orchestral composition, *Medea's Meditation and Dance of Vengeance,* op. 23a.

In the works that followed, Barber's style was fully developed. His music is often discordant, is free in its tonality (at times with a basic tonality completely avoided), uses polytonal and polyrhythmic combinations, and exploits unusual orchestral timbres. These new techniques, as his biographer Nathan Broder has remarked, are employed "in an attempt to fuse an essentially lyric spirit with an awakened awareness of the restlessness and discordance of our times."

This modern romantic writing characterizes one of his orchestral masterworks, the Piano Concerto, op. 38 (1962), for which Barber received the Pulitzer Prize in music for the second time. (The first time was in 1958 for his first opera, *Vanessa,* introduced at the Metropolitan Opera on January 15 of that year.) The Piano Concerto had been commissioned by the publishing house of G. Schirmer in New York to help celebrate the centennial of its founding. It became one of the more striking events in the week of festivities attending the opening of Philharmonic Hall at the Lincoln Center for the Performing Arts in 1962, performed by John Browning and the Boston Symphony under Erich Leinsdorf. The first and third movements fully tax the virtuoso capabilities of the soloist, for the astringent sounds and the rapid passage work are enormously demanding. But it is not virtuosity that attracts and affects us in this music, but the power of Barber's imagination in building up the most arresting effects and climaxes. But he has not abandoned his love for lyricism. In the second movement, a song first heard in the flute, then repeated by the solo piano, and after that by muted strings, is in Barber's best romantic vein.

Once again Barber was called upon to help celebrate an occasion of the first importance at the Lincoln Center for the Performing Arts—this time the opening of the new auditorium of the Metropolitan Opera. For this auspicious and highly glamorized event, Barber had been commissioned to write a new opera. He complied with *Antony and Cleopatra,* which has proved a failure but whose world premiere on September 16, 1966, was attended by the elite of America's cultural, political, and social life.

However discordant some of Barber's compositions may at times be, he continues the line of development orchestral music has taken for centuries. With John Cage the line is broken. With him, orchestral music begins an altogether untraveled course whose ultimate destination it is still impossible to foresee.

With most twentieth-century modernists, their creative development reached fulfillment with the twelve-tone technique. Cage's evolution as a composer began where others ended. He started out as a twelve-tone composer, and from there he progressed to systems that completely negated everything that up to now music had represented. Cage stands in the vanguard of the avant-garde movement of today. Some may call him eccentric, others a clown, still others a charlatan. Some serious musicians in Europe and America look upon him as a cataclysmic force that has overthrown old, outdated values.

Cage has been responsible for helping to remove at least two of the supports that have sustained the musical art for centuries. Music has always been the organization of pleasant sounds. Cage developed a good many of his compositions from disorganized sounds of a not necessarily

279

pleasant nature—or, in other words, from noises of our everyday world, or those created electronically. "I don't hear noise," he has said. "I hear music."

Serious, or classical, music has always been the result of careful calculation and planning on the part of the composer. On the other hand, Cage has emphasized a process termed "chance" or "aleatory" music, in which a composition is not carefully worked out by the composer so that it will always sound more or less the same when performed. Instead it is produced by various chance methods either by the composer or more often by the performers themselves during a concert. In "chance" music the composer himself does not know how the final product will sound, and no two performances of the same composition are alike.

John Cage is the son of a father who was an inventor and a mother who was an editor of the Los Angeles *Times.* He was born in Los Angeles on September 5, 1912. His music study followed traditional lines. In his boyhood he studied the piano with neighborhood teachers. He continued piano study while attending high school and during the two years he spent at Pomona College in California, completing his piano education in Paris. Then he came to the realization that he did not want to be a concert pianist. The sad truth was that he was bored with the music he was playing, regarding it as old-fashioned, even obsolete. Some deep inner compulsion made him dream of writing a far different kind of music, a kind in tune with the mechanized, industrialized world of the twentieth century. And so, when he undertook to study composition, he chose teachers who were ultramodernists. Some, including Schoenberg himself, introduced him to the twelve-tone technique, which Cage adopted for his early compositions.

But another teacher had an even greater impact on his development and thinking than Schoenberg: a French-born naturalized American composer, Edgard Varèse (1883–1965). Varèse was a pioneer in trying to use outlandish sounds and noises as serious music. Between 1923 and 1934 he wrote a number of compositions, including *Intégrales* and *Ionization,* the latter scored for forty-one percussion instruments and two sirens, all played by thirteen players. Varèse's compositions had no melody, harmony, or counterpoint. They were highly percussive and extensively rhythmic, consisting of the most unusual sonorities, dynamics, timbres, and sound effects. When he used instruments he had them arrive at new tonal effects by exploring the extremes of sonorities and

range or combining them in the most unusual ways. Sometimes he had them imitate the voices of birds or insects. Frequently he introduced into his percussion family instruments of his own invention capable of creating new qualities of sounds. The critics laughed at him (disregarding that he was not only a thoroughly trained musician but also a scholar), refusing to take his efforts seriously. "A catastrophe in a boiler factory," is the way one famous New York critic described his music, while another called it "a ribald outbreak of noise." Varèse lived to see himself hailed as a prophet even among many who a few decades earlier had treated him with derision.

Varèse was still the much-rejected, much-abused composer when Cage became his pupil and was completely won over to Varèse's unique type of music-making. The need to seek new sounds became a compulsion with Cage. While teaching formal music at the Cornish School of Music in Seattle, Washington, Cage began attaching all kinds of objects (screws, bolts, leather, wood, spoons, clothespins) between strings of the piano at set degrees and distances from the dampened point to get the piano to produce strange new tone qualities and pitches. The process of stuffing materials between strings he called "preparing," and, beginning in 1938, for his "prepared piano" Cage invented various pieces whose similarity to any piano music previously devised was remote, to say the least.

He also began writing for percussion instruments, and before long introduced such nonmusical items capable of percussive effects as tin cans, a metal wastebasket, cow bells, and rattles. In 1940 he wrote *Living Room,* in which the percussions reproduced everyday noises encountered in a room, such as closing of windows, banging of doors, the moving about of furniture. The conviction that there is music in noise became a fixation with him. In 1939 in *Imaginary Landscape No. 4* his ensemble comprised twelve radios operated by twenty-four players. Each radio required the service of two performers, one to turn the dial, the other to adjust the volume. In his score Cage indicated the wave lengths for each radio, time values, and the dynamics. A veritable cacophony ensued as the various radios released sounds of music, static, and talk all at once with varied volumes of sounds. In *Water Music* (1952) sounds were produced by pouring water from a full container to an empty one, (with a stopwatch to regulate the time for this procedure), by riffling a deck of cards, by using static from a radio, and with whistles.

Cage has also taken advantage of electronics in devising new sound textures. He recorded on magnetic tape the sounds made by the wind, *281* sounds on the streets, and other noises. For his material for *Williams Mix* (1952) he made six hundred recordings on tape, from which he extracted the material he found most interesting.

He was not the first to use magnetic tape for this purpose. This method originated in Paris in the late 1940s with a radio engineer who manipulated tapes for esoteric, weird sound production. Sounds, musical or otherwise, were put on tape, then distorted by slowing down or quickening the rotation, or combining a number of different tapes. This method came to be known as "concrete music," indicating that the music begins from already existing sounds, rather than as an idea in a composer's mind. Pierre Schaeffer wrote a composition called *Symphony for a Single Man* for magnetic tape, capturing the sounds heard by a solitary man during a single day, arranged in rhythmic patterns.

Cage used concrete music not only in *Williams Mix* but even in larger works, such as the *Concert for Piano and Orchestra* (1958). Here electronically produced sounds on tapes are combined with noises produced by a pianist who thumps on the underside of a piano with his fists, by having a trombone player blow through the mouthpiece of his instrument, and by calling on a wind player to play two tubas at once. In *Atlas Eclipticalis* (1961), for orchestra and electronic instuments, Cage abandons magnetic tape for "live" electronic music by using electronic circuits (microphones, amplifiers, speakers).

Chance methods are as important an element of Cage's creativity as the production of new sounds. One of his earliest such experiments was to write a composition on individual sheets of manuscript paper. The performer scatters these pages at random on the floor. He then picks up one sheet at a time, plays it, picks up another, plays that, and continues the process until the last sheet has been played. Every performance, then, is different, since the disorganized arrangement of the sheets on the floor varies each time the composition is thrown about haphazardly. Not even Cage himself knows how his composition is supposed to sound until he hears it performed each time.

This scrambling of manuscript paper on the floor is a primitive form of "chance music," which Cage went on to develop in more complex ways. In some compositions he resorted to use of a dice game taken from the Chinese book *I Ching* (*Book of Changes*). Having devised a formula whereby various numbers produced by the throws of the dice are related to elements in music (time values, rhythm, pitch) Cage then creates a composition by putting down on paper those musical values which each throw of the dice has dictated.

Cage has also combined chance with electronics. In *Reunion* (1968) he uses an electrified chessboard upon which a real game is played. The sounds of the movement of the chess pieces are magnified by being passed through an electronic filter.

Chance enters into the *Concert for Piano and Orchestra,* which has already been mentioned. The piano part is made up of eighty-four different compositions, which the performer can play in their entirety and in the order the composer has put down on paper, or in part, or in any sequence; he can also pick out any two compositions, at any point, and play them contrapuntally. At each presentation, the performer adopts a new procedure, usually arrived at spontaneously. Chance plays an even more significant role in *Variations I* and *Variations II* (1958, 1961), where the performers, during a concert, are allowed to introduce whatever sounds, noises, or improvisations they favor. Novel sound effects are also extensively explored in these compositions, produced by the dropping of ashes in a tray, writing a letter, putting on or removing eyeglasses, all amplified electronically. Some of the performers have microphones attached to their throats to amplify the sounds of swallowing, coughing, grunting, clearing of the throat, smoking a cigarette. Horrendous noises are created by scraping microphones over sheets of glass, with the amplification increased to maximum capacity.

It is quite true that in his experiments Cage has often gone to extremes. But it would be a mistake to dismiss his innovations lightly. Vital contributions have already been made by other composers in the use of "chance" music, particularly within the context of written-down music ("controlled chance"), among whom will be found Pierre Boulez (1925–   ), Karlheinz Stockhausen (1928–   ), and the brilliant Germanborn, naturalized American composer-conductor, Lukas Foss (1922–   ). Foss, once a composer of highly romantic tendencies, has, since 1957, been won over, to the importance of "chance" methods, especially when they are controlled. His most important composition in this medium is *Time-Cycle* (1960). Leonard Bernstein thought so much of it that when he introduced it with the New York Philharmonic and soloists, he played it twice so that the audience might better be able to understand and appreciate it. The music critics of New York also gave their official stamp of approval by selecting it as the best new work of the 1960–1961 season.

Time-Cycle is a group of four songs for soprano, four solo instruments (piano, clarinet, cello, and percussion), and orchestra to texts by W. H. Auden, A. E. Housman, Kafka, and Nietzsche. The written-down

283

music is the songs presented by the soprano accompanied by orchestra. Between each song, the four solo instruments enter with a commentary on the music just played through an improvisation invented at the time of the performance. Thus with each performance of *Time-Cycle* these improvisations are different, contributing an exciting form of aural adventure and surprise both to the audience and to the performers every time this work is given.

Nonmusical sounds (whether produced electronically or with nonmusical implements) are increasingly penetrating the worlds of both orchestral music and opera. Boulez, Stockhausen, and South America's foremost living composer, Alberto Ginastera (1916–   ) are among those who have proved that dramatic and emotional intensities can be realized through these means, far beyond the capabilities of traditional instruments.

If there are those who laugh at Cage's indiscretions, then there are many others who are convinced of their musical value. In 1949 Cage received a Guggenheim Fellowship, and in that same year the National Academy of Arts and Letters gave him an award for extending "the boundaries of music." Cage was appointed composer-in-residence at the University of Cincinnati in 1967–1968, and in 1968 he was elected a member of the National Institute of Arts.

He is particularly revered by the younger generation of avant-garde composers in Europe, having been wildly acclaimed at the Darmstadt Festival in Germany in 1961, and chosen the outstanding personality at the Zagreb Music Bienale in Yugoslavia in 1962. To these younger composers, Cage has been both a guide and an inspiration. Ezra Laderman made this clear when he wrote in *The New York Times Magazine* in 1966, "We do not have a single composer with a European reputation, with the exception of George Gershwin and John Cage. . . . Cage is the first American composer, excepting Gershwin, truly to change the thinking of a tremendous number of European composers from Poland to Greece."

Whither music? Will it continue to pursue the radical innovations of John Cage and other avant-gardists toward regions of sound yet undreamed of? Or will the music of tomorrow reject the new discoveries to return to old, long-established values? History offers us a third possibility: the marriage of the best of the past with what is most valuable in the

revolutionary practices of the present.

George Gershwin.

Charles Ives and his wife Harmony.

The American Ballet Theatre production of Copland's Billy the Kid.

Aaron Copland.

Martha Graham, an American dancer who has had a major influence on contemporary music, in particular by asking composers to write music for dances she has already choreographed.

The Merce Cunningham company dancing in Variations *to the accompaniment of the sound of their own body movements— a musical concept devised by John Cage.*

Samuel Barber.

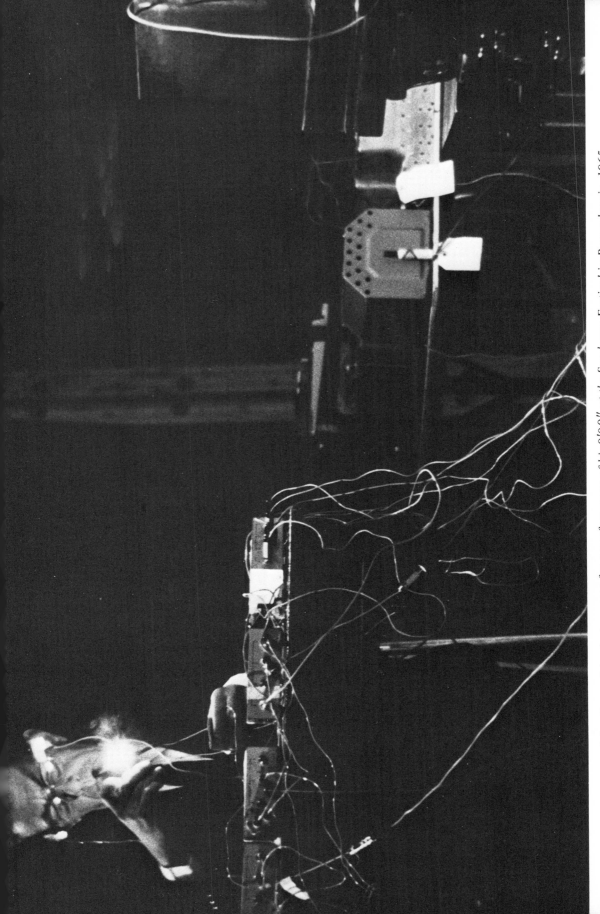

John Cage wiring instruments for a performance of his 0'00" at the Sundance Festival in Pennsylvania, 1965.

Glossary

Absolute Music   Music with no literary, pictorial, or programmatic interpretation, deriving its interest exclusively from musical content and structure, as opposed to program music.

Accelerando   Quickening of tempo.

Accent   Stressing one tone over others.

Accidental   An altered note, foreign in pitch to the key of the composition; also the symbol of a sharp, flat, or natural to raise or lower a tone.

Adagietto   Diminutive of adagio, indicating a somewhat faster tempo than adagio.

Adagio   Very slow, faster than largo, slower than andante.

Agitato   Agitated.

Aleatory Music   *See* Chance Music.

Allegretto   Light and fast, slower than allegro.

Allegro   Fast and lively, faster than andante, slower than presto.

Allemande   Dance in two-part form usually in moderate 4/4 time, probably of German origin. It is sometimes found as the first movement of the Baroque suite.

Andante Slow, but faster than adagio.

Animato Spirited.

Appassionata (or Appassionato) Passionately.

Appoggiatura A grace note, embellishment, or ornament.

Arpeggio Consecutive playing of ascending or descending notes of chord.

Assai Very, as in allegro assai.

Assonance Agreement of sounds.

Atonality Absence of key center, music without basic tonality. For explanation, see Chapter 12.

Bar (or Measure) Section of music marked off by bar lines.

Baroque An era in music between the late sixteenth and early eighteenth centuries. For discussion see Chapter 1.

Bassoon A woodwind instrument. For explanation, see Introduction.

Baton Stick used by conductor to beat time in directing an orchestra.

Batterie The percussion instruments of the orchestra.

Binary Form A two-part form, as a movement in a symphony, consisting of two principal sections or two contrasting themes.

Bitonality Simultaneous use of two different keys.

Bourrée Dance form of French origin, in two parts (each repeated) and usually in 2/4 or 4/4 time. It is sometimes found as a movement of the Baroque suite.

Bow A wooden implement strung with horsehair used in the right hand by string players to create vibration on strings. Originally it was shaped like the bow used in archery, hence its name.

Bowing Way in which bow is applied to strings, or manner in which a passage is to be played.

Brass Instruments Instruments in the orchestra of the horn, trumpet, and trombone families. For description see Introduction.

Bridge Passage Transitional section from one main theme to another or from one movement to another.

Broken Chords Arpeggios.

Cacophony Discordant combination of tones.

Cadence Ending of phrase, section, or movement.

Cadenza Virtuoso passage for solo instrument near end of a movement of a concerto, generally unaccompanied by orchestra. The musical ideas are taken from main themes of the movement.

Canon Style in contrapuntal music in which the melodic theme is given by one instrument, then taken over in strict imitation by one or more other instruments.

Cantabile To be played in a singing style.

Capriccio Caprice. A composition consisting of a medley of popular melodies; also used for short piano pieces of a light character.

Capriccioso Free, playful style.

Cassation A Baroque form of light instrumental music in several movements, similar to divertimento and serenade.

Celesta A percussion instrument. For explanation see Introduction.

Cello Contraction for *violoncello*.

Chance Music (or Aleatory Music) Music produced not through calculation but spontaneously through chance methods. *See* Chapter 18.

Chord Combination of three or more tones.

Chromatic Tones foreign by a semitone to key or chord.

Chromatic Scale A scale made up of twelve half tones in the octave.

Clarinet A woodwind instrument. For explanation see Introduction.

Classical Period An epoch beginning in about the middle of the eighteenth century and ending in the first decade of the nineteenth. For discussion see Chapter 1.

Clef Sign preceding each staff to indicate pitch.

Coda Concluding part of a passage or movement.

Codetta A short coda; also the closing passage at the end of an interior section of a movement.

Col Legno With the wood of a bow.

Common Time Popular term for 4/4 time.

Con Amore Tenderly.

Con Brio With spirit and vigor.

Con Moto With motion or movement.

Concert A performance of orchestral or choral music in a public auditorium.

Concert Overture *See* Overture.

Concertante A term for one or more solo instruments performing brilliant parts; also an eighteenth-century symphony for two or more instruments and orchestra.

Concertino In the concerto grosso, the solo instrument or instruments in contrast to the orchestra (*ripieno*); also a small concerto, usually in a single movement.

Concertmaster Leader of the first violin section of orchestra. For explanation see Introduction.

Concerto A major work for one or more solo instruments and orchestra. For explanation see Introduction and Chapter 3.

Concerto Grosso Predecessor of concerto. A composition in several movements for solo instrument or instruments (*concertino*) and orchestra (*ripieno*). For discussion see Chapter 1.

Concitato Agitated.

Concrete Music Musical and other sounds recorded on tape, sometimes including distortions or changes of already recorded sounds. The electric manipulation of these sounds forms the composition of concrete music. *See* Chapter 18.

Conductor Director of a group of musical performers.

Consonance Pleasing combination of sounds.

Contrabass *See* Double Bass.

Contrabassoon A large bassoon, a woodwind instrument. For explanation, see Introduction.

Cor Anglais English horn. For explanation see Introduction.

Counterpoint Simultaneous combination of two or more independent melodic lines.

Courante Old French dance (originally Italian) in two sections and usually in triple time, sometimes found as a movement in Baroque suite.

Crescendo Gradual increase of volume.

Cyclic Form A style in large compositions in which thematic materials from earlier movements are repeated in later ones to achieve unity. Used as a principle of composition by César Franck, among others. See discussion in Chapter 6.

Cymbals Percussion instrument. For explanation see Introduction.

Da Capo Indication that a section is to be repeated from beginning.

Decrescendo Gradual decrease of volume, also called diminuendo.

Development Working out of thematic material. The term for the second principal section of the sonata form.

Diatonic Scale Scale made up of the consecutive tones of any key without foreign sharps, flats, or naturals. The diatonic are the standard major and minor scales.

Dissonance (or Discord)   Dissonant combination of tones, harmonically
unresolved.

Divertimento   A Baroque form of light instrumental music in several movements, similar to cassation or serenade.

Dodecaphony   *See* Twelve-Tone System.

Dolce   Sweetly.

Doloroso   Sadly.

Double Bass   Largest and lowest in pitch of the stringed instruments. For explanation see Introduction.

Double Bassoon   *See* Contrabassoon.

Double Concerto   Concerto for two solo instruments and orchestra.

Downbeat   Downward movement of conductor's baton that designates first beat of measure.

Drum   Percussion instrument. For explanation see Introduction.

Dynamics   Gradations of volume from loud to soft and vice versa.

Elegiac   In the style of an elegy.

Elegy   A musical composition in a melancholy or pensive mood, or a song expressing sorrow, especially for a person who has died.

Encore   Call from audience for repetition of a work or for a further work. Also the performance in response to such a demand.

English Horn   Woodwind instrument of oboe family. For explanation see Introduction.

Ensemble   Group of performers or combination of instruments.

Exposition   First principal section in the sonata form, in which thematic material is presented.

Expression   Nuances of dynamics, phrasing, and other elements left to judgment of conductor or performers, too subtle to be indicated in the music.

Expressionism   A twentieth-century art idiom. For discussion see Chapter 12.

Extemporization   *See* Improvisation.

False Cadence   Cadence that is either imperfect or interrupted.

Fanfare   A flourish for brass, usually for trumpets.

Fantasia   Instrumental composition free in form and in the way thematic material is presented and developed.

Fermata   Symbol indicating holding of note or rest.

Finale   Concluding movement of a composition.   *295*

Fine   The end.

Flat   Symbol indicating the lowering of a note by half a step.

Flute   A woodwind instrument. For explanation see Introduction.

Forte   Loud, louder than mezzo forte.

Fortissimo   Very loud.

Fugato   Passage in fugal style.

Fughetta   Little fugue.

Fugue   A complex contrapuntal form generally for three, four, or five parts, called "voices." The subject theme is presented by each voice in turn. Stated in the first voice, the subject is repeated a fifth higher or a fourth lower by the second voice, while the first voice continues with that subject; the third voice enters an octave higher or lower than the first voice, as do subsequent voices. A free development follows.

Gamut   Range of instrument; a scale.

Gavotte   A two-part dance of French origin, each part being repeated. It is in 4/4 time, beginning on the third beat. It is often found as a movement of the Baroque suite; Prokofiev used it as the third movement of his *Classical* Symphony.

Gebrauchsmusik   Functional music, a term coined by Hindemith for music for movies, radio, theater, and amateur performances, and for use with children. The term gained prominence in Germany in the late 1920s.

Gigue   A lively dance of British origin in two parts and in 3/8, 6/8, or 6/4 time. It is often found as a movement of the Baroque suite.

Giocoso   Joyful.

Giusto   Exact.

Glockenspiel   A percussion instrument. For explanation see Introduction.

Grace Note   An ornament.

Grave   Slow and grave.

Habanera   Slow dance in 2/4 time originating in Havana but which became popular in Spain.

Harmony   The science of combining notes into chords and chords into progressions.

Homophony   Style emphasizing single melody and its harmony.

Idée Fixe   A recurring theme, a term devised by Berlioz. For explanation see Chapter 6.

296   **Imitation**   Polyphonic technique wherein a phrase or theme is repeated

by another "voice," usually in a lower or higher pitch, while original voice continues with the theme.

Impressionism   A style of composition made famous by Debussy. For discussion see Chapter 11.

Improvisation   A spontaneously conceived performance.

Interlude   Short section connecting two movements.

Interval   Distance in pitch between two notes.

Intonation   Correctness of pitch.

Introduction   Preface to a movement of a symphony.

Kapellmeister   Current German term for conductor; formerly meant director of a musical establishment.

Kettledrums (or Tympani)   Main section of percussion group. For explanation see Introduction.

Key   The first, principal, or tonic note of a scale.

Key Signature   Written grouping of sharps or flats placed immediately after clef at beginning of staff to indicate key of section or composition.

Largo   Slow and stately, slower than adagio.

Legato   Smooth connection from one note to next without pause.

Lento   Slow, a tempo between largo and adagio.

Linear Counterpoint   Contrapuntal music in which lines move independently of harmonic relationships, a twentieth-century idiom. For discussion see Chapter 13.

Maestro   Italian term of respect for a distinguished musician.

Maestro Di Capella   Italian equivalent of Kapellmeister.

Major Scale   Scale whose half steps occur between the third and fourth and the seventh and eighth degrees of octave.

Malagueña   Spanish dance originating in Málaga whose main melody has the character of an improvisation.

Marcato   Accented.

Measure   *See* Bar.

Melody   Succession of single tones in a logical and pleasing pattern.

Meter   Recurrent series of pulses with which music is measured.

Mezzo   Half.

Mezzo Forte   Moderately loud.

Mezzo Piano   Moderately soft.

Minuet   Graceful dance of French origin popular in eighteenth century. It has three sections, the third repeating the first, and the middle one called a "trio," being another minuet itself. It was sometimes used in the Baroque suite, and in the Classical symphony the third movement was usually a minuet.

Mode   A type of scale—major or minor. Preceding the time when major-minor tonality was evolved, music was constructed from a medieval system of scales known as church modes.

Moderato   Moderate speed.

Molto   Very.

Monothematic   The use of a single theme.

Mordent   An ornament made by a quick alternation of a note with the note below it.

Motif   Short musical subject.

Movement   A significant, self-sufficient part of a larger composition, such as a symphony.

Mute   Device for muffling sound of an instrument.

Nationalism   Attempt of a composition to express national feelings or backgrounds in music. For discussion see Chapters 8 and 14.

Natural   Symbol nullifying sharp or flat.

Neoclassicism   Movement in the twentieth century reviving classical styles and forms of the eighteenth century. For discussion see Chapter 13.

Neoromanticism   An extension of the Romanticism of the nineteenth century following Brahms and Wagner, usually music with philosophic or ideological implications. For discussion see Chapter 10.

Notation   System of writing down or printing notes of music.

Note   Symbol representing a tone.

Octave   Consecutive series of eight diatonic notes, beginning and ending on a note with the same key name.

Oboe   Woodwind instrument. For description see Introduction.

Opus   The term, meaning "work," used with a number to indicate the order of composition and publication of a composer's work.

Orchestra   Ensemble comprising varied musical instruments. For explanation see Introduction.

Orchestration   The aspect of composition concerned with combining various instruments of the orchestra.

Ornament   An embellishment, such as grace note, trill, or mordent.

Overture   An orchestral introduction to an opera, oratorio, or play

(sometimes also called prelude). It was sometimes used as the first movement of the Baroque suite. An overture written for concert performance is known as a concert overture.

Percussion Family of instruments whose sound is produced by the process of striking. For explanation see Introduction.

Phrase Smallest division of a melody.

Phrasing Marking off phrases of a composition, either as indicated in the music or as interpreted by the performer.

Piacevole Graceful, without excessive expression.

Pianissimo Very soft, softer than piano.

Piano Soft.

Piccolo A small flute, highest register of woodwinds. For explanation see Introduction.

Pitch Relationship of one tone to another in sound.

Pizzicato Plucked, instead of bowed, strings.

Polymeter Two or more different meters sounded simultaneously.

Polyphony Two or more different melodies sounded simultaneously.

Polyrhythm Two or more rhythms sounded simultaneously.

Prepared Piano An innovation by John Cage in which dampers of rubber, felt, metal, and other objects are stuffed between strings of the piano in carefully prepared positions to produce new timbres, pitches, and percussive effects. *See* Chapter 18.

Presto Very fast, faster than allegro, slower than prestissimo.

Prestissimo *See* under Presto.

Primitivism Adaptation of rhythmic, dynamic, and melodic elements of primitive music for sophisticated musical forms. For discussion see Chapter 13.

Program Music Music depending on a literary program, or describing a specific scene or mood—in short, music with extramusical interest, as opposed to absolute music.

Program Notes Descriptive and historical analysis appearing in the printed program of the music being played on that occasion.

Progression Advance of melody from one tone to another, or of harmony from one chord to another.

Proletarian Music Music reflecting ideology and social and political interests of the working classes, most usually of the Soviet Union. For explanation see Chapter 15.

Quarter Note Half of a half note.

Quaver   An eighth note.

Range   Compass between lowest and highest note of an instrument or voice.

Realism   Reproduction of realistic effects or sounds in music.

Recapitulation   The third section of the sonata form, in which the exposition of themes is repeated with modifications.

Register   The range of a musical instrument, or of a human voice.

Reprise   Repeat.

Resolution   Passing from dissonance to consonance.

Rest   Symbol indicating silence while tempo is maintained.

Ripieno   In the concerto grosso, the full orchestra in contrast to the solo instrument or instruments (*concertino*).

Ritardando   Gradual slowing down of tempo.

Rococo   Delicate, refined, graceful style favored in last half of the eighteenth century. *See* Style Galant.

Romantic Period   Period in music history beginning approximately with Beethoven's later works and continuing through the nineteenth century. For discussion see Chapter 5.

Rondo   Form in which main subject is repeated several times, with new subjects appearing before each repetition. It is often found as the last movement of a concerto.

Rubato   Stolen time; giving some of the time value of longer notes to shorter ones without change of overall rhythm.

Sarabande   Slow and stately dance probably of Spanish origin. It is in triple time and is frequently found as a movement of the Baroque suite.

Scale   Formal succession of notes within an octave, such as diatonic and chromatic scales.

Scherzando   Playfully.

Scherzo   Music in quick time and in a light style. The scherzo is usually in 3/4 time and in three-part form. It succeeded the minuet as the third movement of compositions beginning with some of Beethoven's piano sonatas and symphonies.

Score   The complete arrangement of the instrumental and vocal parts of a composition.

Secular Music   Music other than that for the church.

Segue   Follows.

Semiquaver   Sixteenth note.

300   **Semitone**   Half a tone.

Sequence   A frequently repeated melodic or rhythmic phrase.

Serialism   Application of the twelve-tone technique to elements other than pitch, such as dynamics, rhythm, tempo, timbre. For explanation see Chapters 12 and 13.

Sforzando   Sudden emphasis on a note or group of notes.

Sharp   Sign raising a note half a step.

Signature   *See* Key Signature.

Sinfonia   In the seventeenth century, an instrumental composition; overtures were then often called sinfonias. In the eighteenth century it was a synonym for *symphony*. For explanation see Chapter 1.

Sinfonietta   Little symphony.

Snare Drum   Percussion instrument. For explanation see Introduction.

Sonata Form   An important form encountered in orchestral and instrumental literature in the concerto, symphony, sonata, and sometimes concert overtures. The sonata form comprises an exposition, a development, and a recapitulation. For discussion see Chapters 1 and 2.

Song Form   Form made up of two or three parts. When in two parts, it consists of subject and countersubject; in three parts, the third part repeats the first.

Sonority   Richness of sound.

Sostenuto   Sustained.

Staff (or Stave)   The five parallel lines on which music is written.

Style Galant   A profusely ornamented style of musical composition favored in the mid-eighteenth century.

Subject   A musical theme or motive.

Suite   A composition comprising several movements, which in the seventeenth and eighteenth centuries were mostly in dance forms. For explanation see Chapter 1. In Romantic music, the suite comprises pieces representing different facets of one subject.

Tempo   Time, rate of speed.

Tempo Giusto   Exact time.

Ternary Form   A form consisting of three principal sections.

Theme   Melodic subject of a section, movement, or composition.

Theory   Science of composition.

Timbre   Tone color of a particular instrument or voice.

Time   Rate of speed.

Tonality   The organization of tones and chords in relation to a tonic.

Tone   Musical sound.

Tonic   Principle note of scale, key or chord; the tonal center to which other notes are related.

Transcription   Adaptation of a musical piece for instrument or instruments different from that or those for which it had originally been written.

Treble   The high register.

Tremolo   Quick repetition of a single note on string instrument while pitch remains steady.

Triad   Chord with three notes.

Triangle   A percussion instrument. For explanation see Introduction.

Trill   Rapid alternation of a note with its auxiliary note (major or minor second) to produce quivering effect.

Trombone   A brass instrument. For explanation see Introduction.

Trumpet   Highest register of brass instruments. For explanation see Introduction.

Tuba   Lowest register of brass instruments. For explanation see Introduction.

Tutti   Entrance of entire orchestra after solo passage.

Twelve-Tone System (or Row, or Technique)   Construction of a composition from an established row of twelve tones of the chromatic scale according to a set plan. For explanation see Chapter 12.

Tympani   *See* Kettledrums.

Unison   Playing or singing the same melody together.

Upbeat   Raising of hand or baton for unaccented part of measure; note or notes that are unaccented and begin a phrase before the first bar line.

Veloce   Swift.

Virtuosity   Display of brilliant technique.

Vivace   Lively, faster than allegro, slower than presto.

Voice (or Voice Part)   As used in instrumental music, the musical line of the individual instrument or groups of instruments.

Whole-Tone Scale   A scale consisting entirely of whole tones. For explanation see Chapter 11.

Index

304